THE MISSING CLASS

The Missing Class

Portraits of the Near Poor in America

**Katherine S. Newman
and Victor Tan Chen**

BEACON PRESS
BOSTON

Beacon Press
25 Beacon Street
Boston, Massachusetts 02108-2892
www.beacon.org

Beacon Press books
are published under the auspices of
the Unitarian Universalist Association of Congregations.

10 09 08 07 8 7 6 5 4 3 2 1

This book is printed on acid-free paper that meets the uncoated paper
ANSI/NISO specifications for permanence as revised in 1992.

Text design and composition by Wilsted & Taylor Publishing Services

Library of Congress Cataloging-in-Publication Data

Newman, Katherine S.
  The missing class : portraits of the near poor in America /
Katherine S. Newman and Victor Tan Chen.
     p. cm.
  Includes bibliographical references.
  ISBN-13: 978-0-8070-4139-0
  1. Working class—United States. 2. Poor—United States. 3. Poverty—
United States. 4. United States—Economic conditions. I. Chen, Victor Tan,
1976– II. Title.
  HD8072.5.N487 2007
  305.5'60973—dc22   2007013553

For Phillip Selznick,
mentor, teacher, and friend
K.S.N.

To my parents,
for their sacrifice,
and to Emi, for her love
V.T.C.

CONTENTS

Foreword by Senator John Edwards ix

ONE: The Missing Class 1

TWO: Whose Neighborhood Is This Anyway? 11

THREE: The American Dream,
in Monthly Installments 47

FOUR: The Sacrificed Generation 83

FIVE: In Sickness and in Health 119

SIX: Romance without Finance Is a Nuisance 149

SEVEN: On the Edge: Plunging Out
of the Missing Class 177

EIGHT: Missing Class Mobility 203

Acknowledgments and
a Note on Methods 227

Notes 231

Index 253

Throughout our country's history, books have held the power to capture the American imagination and spark historic social and political change. A half century ago, for example, Michael Harrington published *The Other America* and introduced readers to millions of people living in poverty in inner-city housing projects, Appalachia, and rural America. In the 1960s and 1970s, our nation launched a war on poverty that helped move millions of Americans out of poverty and into the middle class. But today, thirty-seven million Americans still live in poverty. While we were able to make some important progress, much more work remains.

In the pages that follow, Katherine Newman and Victor Tan Chen give us insight into another—and much larger—forgotten group of people they call the near poor or Missing Class. Fifty-seven million near-poor Americans—including one in five children—live in households earning incomes between $20,000 and $40,000 for a family of four. They live at 100 percent to 200 percent above the poverty line but just one pink slip, divorce, or health crisis away from the edge. They are less likely to have a savings account or own a home or other assets that soften the blow of a financial crisis in middle-class families.

Ask them about a tax cut for the rich, and they will shrug and get back to work. A total of 1.6 million Americans fell into personal bankruptcy in 2004. In fact, more people file for bankruptcy than graduate from college each year. Plenty more fear they will be next.

Through meticulous research over a seven-year period, Katherine and Victor tell the personal stories of nine families in four New York City neighborhoods. You'll find yourself, as I did, rooting for each and every one of them. Their grit and determination are extraordinary. In sharing their lives and struggles, these families have done more to educate the nation than any set of statistics or government report ever could. Policymakers, journalists, think tanks, and people of good conscience everywhere must take notice and begin the challenge of building an America that works for all of us.

When we set about fixing welfare in the 1990s, we said we were going to encourage work. Near-poor Americans do work, usually in jobs that the rest of us do not want—jobs with stagnant wages, no retirement funds, and inadequate health insurance, if they have it at all. While their wages stay the same, the cost of everything else—energy, housing, transportation, tuition—goes up.

As you'll see in the stories that fill this book, the near poor work hard to provide for their children and to take care of their elderly parents. In fact, they are the backbone of our economy. They work in transit, construction, nursing-assistance, cooking, trades, retail, and even teaching jobs. If they belong to a union, they are more likely to have benefits.

Yet, Missing Class families are far from stable or secure. If they have a setback—a layoff, an illness, an unanticipated expense or loss—they risk joining their cousins and neighbors living in poverty. The near poor are susceptible to predatory lenders, credit-card debt, and oppressive mortgages with unfair interest rates. They struggle to find money for a child's tuition or simply to get time off work to get a checkup that they will have to pay for in cash. They need a helping hand to start to put money away or to recover from the lost income of a spouse sent overseas in the National Guard or Army Reserve. Their dreams are simple—to find affordable housing near decent schools, to hold a steady job, and to give their children opportunities they didn't have.

For generations, America has been the land of opportunity—the place where if you worked hard and played by the rules, you could get ahead. Unfortunately, millions of Americans are working just as hard or harder but still struggling to make ends meet.

In recent years, the nation's leaders have abandoned working families. By focusing on those who need help the least, leaders in Washington, D.C., have made things worse for everybody else. When President George W. Bush talked about an "ownership society," he meant that the more you own, the more you get. For most Americans, his approach has meant that the more you work, the more you pay and the less you make.

This book is about more than nine families. It's about the millions of people who hold down two or three jobs, put in long hours, and struggle to find time to read to their kids and help with their homework. It's about the people who have made it out of poverty, but for how long? We have a responsibility to apply what we learn about their struggles and begin to create an economy that works for all Americans, not just the privileged few.

I cannot think of any more significant test of leadership than the challenge of improving the circumstances of Americans living in poverty and the Missing Class living at the edge of poverty. Katherine and Victor identify solutions, such as stimulating home ownership and other forms of asset building, creating better employment opportunity in underserved communities, and improving the benefits that go along with those better jobs. They focus correctly on starting education earlier, making it more thorough, and increasing college enrollment and the chances for graduation. As Americans, we all must do our part. The first step is educating ourselves. In writing *The Missing Class: Portraits of the Near Poor in America*, Katherine and Victor have done America a tremendous service by bringing these issues to light.

I hope that people across the country read *The Missing Class* and take it for exactly what it is—a call to action to change America. If we care about our national community, we must accept this great challenge. We know that no one succeeds on their own. We know that when one person is down, it drags us all down. This is not something we do for them. This is something we do for us—for all of us.

Like other books that transformed our nation, *The Missing Class* will inspire us to work for an America that doesn't ignore those in need and lifts up those who wish to succeed. It will move us to hold our government accountable for ignoring the suffering of so many for far too long. It will stir us to build the America that we have dreamed of—where the bright light of opportunity shines on every person—an America where the family you were born into or the color of your skin never controls your destiny.

Senator John Edwards
Chapel Hill, North Carolina
2007

ONE

The Missing Class

Valerie Rushing starts her shift at midnight. A train pulls into the station, and she hops on it, mop in hand. The thirty-three-year-old mother of one is an employee for the Long Island Rail Road, the busiest commuter railroad in North America, which every morning carries an army of groggy suburbanites to their Manhattan offices, and every night shuttles them back home. When their day ends, hers begins. Most nights she'll mop twenty cars. Tonight it's twice that because she's working a double shift—midnight to 8 A.M., and 8 A.M. to 4 P.M.

Toilet duty, of course, is the worst. Long Islanders are a more slovenly sort than the city's notorious subway riders, Valerie grouses. "You figure that they would have some consideration for the next person that is going to use the bathroom, but they don't. They'll throw their whatevers there in the garbage, in the toilet.... And they are the most alcoholic people that I know." Every night, an eclectic assortment of paper-sheathed beer cans and bottles awaits her.

But don't feel sorry for Valerie Rushing. With a union card in her pocket, she makes $13.68 an hour, plus full benefits.[1] Her earlier life at the minimum wage—as a child-care worker, shoe-store employee, and fast-food cashier—is a distant memory.

Two years with the Long Island Rail Road have broadened Valerie's outlook. Before, she hardly ventured into the other boroughs; now she feels comfortable traversing the city and doesn't think twice about heading out to Manhattan to shop. Yes, it's janitorial work, but Valerie doesn't complain. "If it's sweeping, it's sweeping," she says. The point is, it pays the bills.

And Valerie has a lot of bills. She has sole responsibility for her daughter and has custody of her niece's six-year-old son because his own grandmother, Valerie's crack-addled sister, can't be bothered. Valerie sets aside part of every paycheck for the children's clothes, toys, and excursions. She puts aside another part to pay for her $700-a-month Brooklyn apartment, and she stashes away what she can toward that suburban house she hopes to buy someday soon.[2]

Valerie is not poor, but she is not middle class. Instead, she occupies an obscure place between rungs of the nation's social ladder—somewhere between working hard and succeeding, between dreaming big and living in the shadow of her ambitions. People like Valerie don't make the headlines. They aren't invited to focus groups. Blue-ribbon commissions on poverty do not include them. They are a forgotten labor force—too prosperous to be the "working poor," too insecure to be "middle income."

They are America's Missing Class.

They are people like Tomás Linares. A year shy of fifty, he is still clocking in seven days a week at two jobs in centers for people with developmental disabilities, where Tomás spends his days patiently demonstrating to his charges how to brush their teeth, reprimanding them for stealing and scratching, and occasionally wrestling an unruly resident to the floor. For his efforts, he makes a little less than $20,000 a year.

Tomás is not poor, but a look at his rundown Brooklyn apartment might suggest otherwise. He lives in an urban borderland sandwiched between two extremes: the concentrated poverty of rampant drug dealing, sporadic gang violence, and shuttered factories that Tomás has known since his youth and the collateral prosperity that middle-class newcomers and mounting real estate prices bring to Brooklyn these days. Divorced and lacking a college education, Tomás has few prospects for rising much higher in life and no illusion that he'll ever leave his seedy corner.

Gloria Hall is part of the Missing Class as well, but perhaps for not much longer. An employee of the city's health department, she stopped working after falling seriously ill. She has insurance, but her policy won't cover the specialized treatment recommended for her rare form of cancer. So Gloria is a frequent visitor to the local teaching hospital, a drab health-care assembly line where patients like her are nonchalantly wheeled from room to room, waiting interminably for their release. For Gloria, living in near poverty means walking a tightrope over this frayed safety net, unsure of what each new step in her treatment will bring.

It also means worrying about what her deteriorating health will mean for her two adolescent sons, who suffer from the affliction of a deadbeat dad. What will happen to them if she dies? Who will care for them when she's not there? She knows that the odds are stacked against children like hers, those who are unlucky enough to be born black and male and statistically at risk—as crime victims and perpetrators, developmentally disabled and dropouts. Her two boys are unluckier still: they live in a household that is not poor but near poor. "I know some parents that are in worse situations than I am, financially," Gloria says. "And they get everything. Every year their kids go away to summer camp.

"You either got to be on the bottom, or you've got to be on the top."

Thirty-seven million Americans live below the poverty line. We know a lot about them because journalists, politicians, think tanks, and social scientists track their lives in great detail. Every time the poverty rate goes up or down, political parties take credit or blame for this important bellwether.

Yet there is a much larger population of Americans that virtually no one pays attention to: the near poor. Fifty-seven million Americans—including 21 percent of the nation's children—live in this nether region above the poverty line but well below a secure station.[3] This "Missing Class" is composed of households earning roughly between $20,000 and $40,000 for a family of four.[4]

The hard-won wages of Missing Class families place them beyond the reach of most policies that speak to the conditions of life among the poor. Yet they are decidedly *not* middle-class Americans. In decades past we might have called them working class, but even that label fails to satisfy, now that many Missing Class workers toil in traditionally white-collar domains like health clinics and schools, even as their incomes, households, and neighborhoods lack the solidity of an earlier generation's blue-collar, union-sheltered way of life. Missing Class families earn less money, have few savings to cushion themselves, and send their kids to schools that are underfunded and crowded. The near poor live

in inner-ring suburbs and city centers where many of the social problems that plague the truly poor constrain their lives as well. Crime,
drugs, and delinquency are less of a problem in near-poor neighborhoods than they are in blighted ghettos, but they are down the block,
within earshot, and close enough to threaten their kids.

Sending Missing Class teens to college, the single most important
fault line in determining their long-range prospects, is difficult for the
near poor. Many are unaware of the financial aid that might await their
children. Parents who have never navigated the shoals of college admission are poorly prepared to offer advice, and the schools that might take
over this stewardship are overwhelmed with the task of getting kids to
graduate in the first place. Near-poor kids are the ones who work many
hours while still in high school, who hardly ever see their guidance
counselor, and who struggle to complete homework assignments that
no one nearby can help them with.

Yet, because their earnings place them above the poverty line, the
Missing Class is rarely on the national radar screen. We just don't think
about them. This needs to change. The fate of Missing Class families is
a test for this country of what it can offer to those citizens—immigrants
and native-born alike—who have pulled themselves off the floor that
poverty represents. If they can move up, they clear the way for those
coming behind them. If they can at least stay where they are, their
example will matter to others. But if their children fail to advance—if
they fall back into the hole that the parents labored so hard to escape
from—we will have defaulted on the promise of this wealthy nation.
We will have seen a temporary respite in a single generation from the
problems of poverty, only to see it emerge again in the children of the
Missing Class. The danger is real—and growing with every new crack
in our increasingly open and vulnerable economy.

Ironically, some of their problems stem from what most would
agree is an entirely positive aspect of Missing Class life. Near-poor parents are firmly attached to the world of work. While many arrived in
the Missing Class as graduates from the ranks of the welfare dependent,
they are now lodged in jobs as transit workers, day-care providers, hospital attendants, teachers' aides, and clerical assistants. They pay their
taxes and struggle to keep afloat on wages that are better than the min-

imum—if not by a huge margin. Yet even as these men and women dutifully turn the wheels of the national economy, their devotion to work takes a toll on their family life, especially on their children, who spend long hours in substandard day care or raise themselves in their teen years.

Of necessity, Missing Class families live fairly close to the margins. They have a hard time saving to buffer themselves from downturns in the economy because a large portion of their income disappears into the pockets of landlords and cash registers of grocery stores every month. As long as the adults—and many of the teens—stay on the job, they can manage. But the slightest push can send them hurtling down the income ladder again. In fact, even in the prosperous years of 1996–2002, about 16 percent of the nation's near-poor families lost a tenth or more of their income. It is important to recognize that the majority actually went in the other direction: they gained income in excess of 30 percent. These upwardly mobile families are headed out of the Missing Class for something much better. Nonetheless, the group that slides is not insignificant, and its ranks have probably grown, now that the economy has cooled.[5]

Missing Class Americans live in safer communities than the truly poor. Indeed, many look out upon their neighborhoods in amazement because they are barely recognizable from the destitute and crime-ridden days of yore. As gentrification has taken root in overheated real estate markets, once-affordable enclaves are now almost beyond the reach of the Missing Class. The arrival of affluent new neighbors brings with it more attention from city officials and the police, more investment in the aesthetics of the community, and something closer to a rainbow of complexions on the streets. For the African Americans, Dominicans, and Puerto Ricans who used to "own" these neighborhoods, this is mainly a blessing. Still, some wonder whether they still belong—whether they are still welcome on their own turf.

Sixty-eight percent of Americans are now the proud owners of their own homes. The near poor must struggle to join their ranks. Many of them missed out on the great run-up in housing prices that created so much wealth in the 1990s and the first five years of this decade. Trapped in a renter's limbo, the Missing Class cannot feather its nest for retirement or borrow against houses to pay for children's college educations. What's more, the children won't enjoy anything approaching the inheritance—in property, cash, or other assets—that their middle-class counterparts will surely reap. These wealth differences are crucial: savings are the safety net that catches you when you falter, but Missing Class families have no such bulwark.[6] As a result, they experience an odd fusion of optimism and insecurity: the former from their upward mobility, the latter from the nagging concern that it could all disappear if just one thing goes wrong. One uninsured child sick enough to pull a parent off the job; one marriage spiraling into divorce; one layoff that shuts off the money spigot.

Like most American consumers, the Missing Class is impatient for just rewards. No one wants to sit on a couch with holes in it, but for the near poor, a new couch is beyond their means. The answer, too often, is debt. Missing Class families are generally uneducated in the ways of credit, and credit card companies are all too happy to indulge them. They deluge the mailboxes of Missing Class families with offers; they avert their eyes as Missing Class households rack up outrageous bills. (In 2005 Congress passed bankruptcy laws that prevent consumers from shielding their assets from creditors, making this kind of debt even more lethal.)[7] What's more, Missing Class families live in neighborhoods that are chronically underserved by financial institutions and scrupulously avoided by grocery chains and other major retail outlets. Denied even the most basic infrastructure for savings or loans at reasonable rates and forced to pay a premium on virtually everything they buy, these harried workers turn to check-cashing stores that exact a cut before handing over their wages. They purchase their food, household goods, and furniture at corner bodegas and other small shops with high margins.

At the same time that the pull of rising wages and the push of welfare reform have drawn millions of low-income parents deeper into the labor market, new policies governing the lives of their children have emerged that clash with the demands of the adult work world. The No Child Left Behind Act has thrust the burly arm of the state into third-grade classrooms, where kids used to the demands of finger paints and Autoharps are now sweating high-stakes tests every year. Eight-year-olds wake up with stomachaches because they are afraid of being held back in school if they cannot pass these exams. Missing Class kids do not fret needlessly; the failure rates on statewide tests are high in their neighborhoods.

School district officials have their own problems to contend with. If their charges do not show significant improvement every year, they find their schools on watch lists, threatened with the loss of funds. How do they exact these improvements? Not by themselves. School systems see parents as an auxiliary teaching force. Notes come home every day explaining to parents that they must take their children to the library, read to them, and drill them on their arithmetic. For those who have the time and the skills to tutor their kids, this is not an onerous task. For the immigrant factory worker who leaves home at 7 A.M., commutes ninety minutes each way to a bottle-packing plant, and works a back-breaking eight-hour shift on an assembly line, the additional burden of helping her son with his reading every day is simply too much. All this "neglect" adds up in the end and yields dismal outcomes on high-stakes tests. For teenagers, it also means a license to misbehave. When Mom and Dad are working every hour they can find, no one is around to make sure that Johnny is doing his homework, and now that he's fourteen, there is no longer an after-school program to occupy him. Johnny may live in a safer, higher-income community than his poorer cousins, but chances are his neighborhood abuts rougher enclaves.[8] This sets up temptations and risks that snare many a Missing Class teen.

The kinds of jobs that sustain the near poor may not come with health insurance or retirement benefits attached. For the more fortunate whose employers do bestow these perks, the versions they enjoy are likely to be of lower quality than the middle-class kind. Medical insurance often comes with very high deductibles, amounting to something closer to catastrophic coverage.[9] It's a big step beyond no insurance at all, but it often exposes the Missing Class to medicine of middling quality, not to mention a host of bureaucratic complications not unlike what the uninsured face, including delayed care and expensive emergency-room treatment. And yet Missing Class families, more so than their wealthier counterparts, *need* first-rate health care. They live in apartments laden with lead paint and plagued by roaches.

Asthma is epidemic in low-income neighborhoods in part because the housing there is in shambles and situated near highways belching out exhaust fumes.[10] When it comes to health, the near poor and the real poor can be hard to tell apart.

Every family has its own way of making decisions about finances and responsibilities, but among the fragile households of the Missing Class the negotiations are especially contentious and complex.[11] Figuring out who does what and for whom is no easy matter where "recombinant families"—made up of stepparents and children by different fathers—are concerned. What is a stepfather's financial responsibility for his wife's child from an earlier relationship? Is he supposed to buy him new Nikes? Or is that the responsibility of the boy's "real" father? What is a mother to do if her new man doesn't feel like paying for a school uniform? Should she take some of the money that he gives her for the phone bill to cover the cost? And how, exactly, should a mother feel when her tight household budget has to stretch even further because her husband has obligations to the children he had with his first wife?

Millions of divorced Americans cope with these sticky questions, albeit with difficulty. But many Missing Class families have only enough to get by, even when two parents are working. The stress of their dicey finances never bodes well for their marriages. Secrecy is rife. Husbands don't tell their wives what they make; they just dole out money for approved purposes. Working wives keep their earnings to themselves as well. Single mothers lean on boyfriends for help and may make their continued affection contingent on some form of support. Men who live alone make regular cash donations to their girlfriends. Thrusting monetary considerations into relationships of intimacy can lead to mutual wariness, even distrust. It is one of the many ways that life in the Missing Class is so delicately held together, even if it is clearly more comfortable than living below the poverty line.

With all these complexities and uncertainties, one might imagine that being near poor is a bleak existence. Not so. Missing Class families know far too many people who are genuinely mired in hardship to think that they deserve pity. In general, they see a good deal of promise in their lives. Comparisons with others who are in distress are always at hand because the near poor live cheek by jowl with the real poor. Chances are good that the less well-off members of their own extended family are among the truly disadvantaged.[12] The Missing Class sees itself as a success story from this vantage point—albeit one hanging on by its fingernails.

To understand what inspires members of the Missing Class to work long hours every day, what drives them to seek a better life for the next generation, and how precarious their good fortune truly is, we dwell here on nine families in four New York City neighborhoods. For seven years—roughly 1995 to 2002—our research team followed their lives from home to work and from parent to child.[13] We interviewed the community leaders and service providers who tend to the Puerto Rican families of Sunset Park, the Dominicans of Washington Heights, and the African Americans in Fort Greene and Clinton Hill. We got to know the teachers who instruct their children, the police officers who patrol their streets, and the managers who supervise them at work. Most of all, we came to know the nine families themselves.

In many respects, they represent hopeful evidence of upward mobility. As this book shows clearly, the problems of the near poor are not the same as those who live below the poverty line. They are not living in socially isolated neighborhoods, working jobs that have no future, or standing on the welfare lines. They are as likely to stroll past the gleaming new espresso bar on the corner as they are to be frequenting the seamy check-cashing storefront on the other side of the street. Indeed, these are the families for whom the nation's promise of opportunity has actually worked. But did it work well enough? Have they graduated from poverty for good? The question for the Missing Class is not whether they are doing better than their counterparts in the income bracket below them. The question is whether the gains they have made will endure, or disappear in the maelstrom of an increasingly uncertain economy.

TWO

Whose Neighborhood Is This Anyway?

Like many of his neighbors in Bedford-Stuyvesant,
Charles O'Connor has grown accustomed . . . to frequent
and unwanted visits from strangers interested in buying the
home he has owned for 35 years. One day, though, the banging
on his front door was like an alarm. Mr. O'Connor opened it
to find a man hammering up a "For Sale" sign, even though he
had already told the man's real estate company that he did not
wish to sell. "I said, 'What are you doing? This is my house,'"
Mr. O'Connor recalled. "The man said, 'Are you sure?'"
                              —*New York Times*, July 19, 1999

THE FLOYD FAMILY

John Floyd points out his home with a stab of his finger, a taut expression of pain flickering across his face. The large beige house, recently refurbished, sits serenely in the middle of a well-maintained street. Gazing at it makes him sick.

At fifty-one, John is not prone to bouts of self-pity. He is, in fact, rather cheerful and outgoing: invariably polite, incessantly generous, and always ready with a wide smile and energetic wave of his hand. It may be one of the ways John keeps his sanity, saddled as he is with the responsibility of seven rowdy grandchildren at home, whom he and his wife, Sondra, took in when the parents—Sondra's children—begged them to. A chef by training, John cooks for his family, watches over the grandkids, and tries to keep his cool until the little ones fall asleep, when he can finally uncork a day's worth of tension by picking up his favorite reading material: a cookbook. Flipping through pages of recipes relaxes him.

But when John steps onto that familiar block in his Clinton Hill neighborhood, all his hard-won amiability unravels. This was his house. This *was* his house. Now it's just a symbol of his failure: the loss of his family's one financial asset.

About a year ago, a contractor contacted the Floyds with an enticing proposal. If they would sign a few papers, the company would do some much-needed work on the place, which had fallen into disrepair in the years since Sondra's mother bought it. The company insisted the Floyds would be able to pay the loan back over time. John and Sondra happily inked their signatures. Months of shoddy work later, the company claimed the Floyds owed $92,000 for the renovations—almost twice what the work was supposed to cost. A lien was levied against their house, and bitter court proceedings followed. By the time the legal wrangling ended, the Floyds had lost their home.[1]

His was not an isolated case, John explains to a companion standing on the sidewalk. The company, Home Builder,[2] has been in the headlines frequently in recent weeks after the attorney general launched an investigation into its predatory lending practices, accusing the firm of deceiving home owners by concealing its exorbitant interest rates—and much, much worse. "They forged documents, and they also gave false statements to the court and to the bank," John says, beginning a litany of the company's sins. "It's been on Channel 7 news," he adds—not his case, which he lost, but the attorney general's investigation. Stripped of their home, John and his family now rent an apartment just a block away.

This kind of fraud could have happened anywhere in America, but it is telling that it happened in Clinton Hill, a small patchwork of streets located just below the old Navy Yard in north-central Brooklyn. Once in decline, the neighborhood is now on the upswing. Walking down the street, John points out the various factories that have shut their doors, the affordable housing that has disappeared, and the upscale apartments that have sprouted, all in the last several years. Down the block, a renovated apartment with seven rooms and two baths, priced way out of reach. On the other side, three houses torn down, their occupants forced to move. An empty storefront, the business relocated because of high rents. A horse stable built in the 1940s that was converted into a factory a few decades later, where John worked until it too shut down. A For Sale sign is pasted on the front door. "I don't know what they're gonna turn it into now," John says. "They're gonna turn it into something." In fact, the only business remaining on the block is a church, whose food pantry is doing a brisk trade twice a week.

In this awakening corner of Brooklyn, developers and speculators are on the prowl. With them has come gentrification, and voracious greed—the kind that lights up the eyes of unscrupulous lenders seeking to swindle longtime residents of their savings and homes. The Floyds were sucked into this racket and paid for it dearly. Now John fears for his community. He worries about what the influx of newcomers—affluent white Yuppies among them—will mean for the neighborhood's identity. "I know everybody on this block. Everybody," John declares proudly. His neighbors have lived here for at least twenty years. What happens when they disappear? Will it still be his community? Better yet, will it still be a *black* community?

Clinton Hill stands at a historical crossroads, wedged between the Mecca and Medina of Brooklyn's African American cultural heritage. To the west is Fort Greene, where in 1870 more than half of the borough's black population lived, home of Brooklyn's first school for African Americans and a waypoint for abolitionists and runaway slaves following the Underground Railroad to freedom.[3] To the east is Bedford-Stuyvesant, the Harlem of Brooklyn, a destination for black southern sharecroppers following the Great Migration to opportunity —or at least the promise of it.

Some of black America's most gifted artists emerged from this corner of Brooklyn. Richard Wright penned *Native Son* while living on Carlton Avenue in Fort Greene. A Bedford-Stuyvesant teen by the name of Christopher Wallace sold drugs out of a garbage can on Fulton Street before rocketing to international fame as the large-and-in-charge rapper Notorious B.I.G. Spike Lee, another homegrown talent, set up his production company—40 Acres & a Mule Filmworks—on DeKalb Avenue in Fort Greene.[4]

It was Lee, in fact, who in 1989 crafted one of the neighborhood's most enduring images. The backdrop to his racially charged drama *Do the Right Thing* was Bed-Stuy—a Bed-Stuy barren of well-paying jobs and fractured by ethnic animosity but peopled by colorful, larger-than-life characters like Radio Raheem, the laconic black tough who walked the streets bearing a screeching boom box and the words "love" and "hate" on four-fingered brass knuckles. Radio Raheem was either a madman or a martyr, but in Bed-Stuy he was undeniably in his element.

Perhaps no longer. The outsiders have arrived, in fierce and bewildering numbers—in Fort Greene, in Clinton Hill, even in Bedford-Stuyvesant. Yet even John admits that gentrification has brought good things to his neighborhood. The restoration and renovation of derelict housing stock by outside investors has nudged up real estate values everywhere and improved the overall quality of life for those willing and able to stay. John remembers a time not long ago when nearby Bedford Avenue was drug central. "People used to stand on line out there . . . like they're going to the cash register." Around the time that the developers started building, though, the dealers went underground and the streets became safe to walk again. More investment in the community has meant a greater police presence, less crime, and more shopping. The politicians in City Hall lavish attention and dollars on the neighborhood's newcomers—and some of those benefits have trickled down, John concedes. "You don't have to worry about getting attacked," he says. "You don't hear no shooting now, compared to what it used to be."

Just down the block from his old house, John stops at the home of an old friend. Renee Burgher is another longtime resident, a community activist in her sixties who serves as the president of the block association. She, better than most, understands the changes that are happening in this part of Brooklyn. Her late husband's people were among the first African American families to settle down in Clinton Hill; Renee herself has lived here for two decades and taught elementary school in another Brooklyn neighborhood. She's well versed in the local history. "I know there's a lot of gentrification going on. And, you know, that's part of living in an urban area." The instability has always been there, she says. When she was growing up, the neighborhood was Irish, German, and Italian. Once the black families moved in—around the time of World War II—the whites "scattered," she says.[5]

Much to Renee's amazement, they're back. One group of white residents just moved into the co-op on the corner. What draws them is the easy transportation into Manhattan and Queens; there are subway and bus lines galore, and even a bus route that goes straight to Manhattan's City Hall. Affordable rent—affordable, that is, for "white folks"—is another attraction. In the eyes of old-timers like Renee and John, real estate prices are soaring upward at an alarming pace, but for newcomers used to Manhattan's bloated rents, Clinton Hill is a bargain-basement paradise. Here they can get something for $700 to $800 a month, Renee notes; across the river, even in bohemian Greenwich Village, it's $1,400 and climbing.[6] "There's not a week that goes by," she says, "that we don't get mail from some realtor wanting to know if we want to sell the house." Some play dirty. "They know what the market price is, you know. And they feel that you will settle for anything, say, $150,000 and under. That's what they think." Real estate agents may not appreciate what her husband's parents put into their house, but Renee does; forty years ago the $8,000 price of the house was their reward for years of backbreaking labor.

Most of the area's black home owners are not going to sell, she insists. Their family roots are in the South, where property carries with it both tradition and responsibility. "This is something in our culture . . . ownership of your land and your house." That said, some of the younger generations have lost that pride in ownership. People don't care enough, Renee explains, or they are ignorant of what's going on. She, too, fears for the future of the black community.

These Brooklyn neighborhoods have followed an ever-twisting demographic path familiar to much of urban America over the last several decades. In the 1940s they were racially integrated—across white ethnic lines, to be sure, but also with a smattering of blacks and Latinos. In the fifties and sixties, whites left, along with the manufacturing jobs, and communities of color—African Americans in Clinton Hill—took over the abandoned apartments and houses.[7] John Floyd remembers what the neighborhood was like back then. The Brooklyn home where he grew up was surrounded by a close-knit community, the kind that sociologists have long eulogized. The adults John knew were civic-minded. Their neighborhood possessed an ample supply of "social capital," the bonds that connect individuals and sustain communities.

"Everyone was close," John recalls. "Everybody knew everybody else's kids, and all the kids knew everybody else's parents. As simple as that. You couldn't get away with anything because there was always a parent around somewhere. It was very together."

It was also very segregated. With the opening of the great white way out to the suburbs, John's neighborhood became predominantly black, with little mixing racially, but some across class lines. If segregation meant more-affluent black families were limited in their choices of where to live, it also meant poor African American youth grew up surrounded by examples of middle-class stability and success. "Back in those days," John says, "you didn't single out one person to say that he was a role model or something like that.... All the parents were a role model."

Over the next two decades, neighborhoods like these became mired in crime and drug addiction, whose manifold afflictions devastated once-proud and cohesive communities. Around that time, too, the spoils of the civil rights struggles were beginning to materialize, to a chorus of hallelujahs from a besieged middle class. National legislation banning housing discrimination offered an escape valve to those whose options were once hemmed in by segregation. Pushed out by crime and pulled away by the draw of newly opened neighborhoods, middle-class African Americans and Latinos relocated en masse, solidifying and concentrating the poverty that remained.[8]

In Brooklyn those families who could not afford to move were left to deal with the scourge of crack cocaine, which was blazing a bloody trail of fatal overdoses and gangland killings through the heart of the borough. The shootings took place out in the open, in daylight hours. Once, John recalls, a bullet went through the window of a nearby day-care center. It didn't even matter that the police department's Eighty-eighth Precinct was right across the street from Lafayette Gardens, a housing project where much of the dealing and shooting was taking place; no place was safe.

The infestation eventually wound its way into the Floyds' own home. Sondra's oldest son, Yul, grew up to be a boy full of rage. "He just wanted to fight everything and everybody," Sondra says. She took him to see psychiatrists, but her son never learned to stifle the fire inside of him. When Yul started "messing" with crack and robbing people for drug money, his parents knew an explosion was bound to happen. It came in 1988, when Yul was twenty-two. "He hadn't been on the street long," Sondra muses. "They get out there and think they know everything." Yul's violent temper eventually exasperated his gun-toting peer group. "A boy just got tired and shot him."

The "boy" put four bullets into her son. Right on Lexington Avenue. "Our neighborhoods," Sondra says, "are poison."

There didn't seem to be much hope for crime-plagued ghettoes like this one. But then the boom years of the late 1990s arrived. For a crucial span of time, jobs trickled back into the neighborhood. Wages rose. Missing Class families across the country—the Floyds among them—suddenly woke up to find themselves in a completely changed world. With soaring profits and bolstered incomes came renewed investment, and Americans poured their extra cash into real estate. The boom in prices fed ever-more investment, persuading middle-class and affluent buyers to go farther and farther afield—and eventually into these troubled borderlands. Legions of prospective home buyers and renters, buoyed by a resurgent economy and reassured by falling crime rates, sought out the cheap real estate to be had. Developers uprooted and refurbished neglected properties, spurring increases in rents and housing prices and putting pressure on longtime residents—sometimes poor, sometimes not so poor—to pack up and leave.[9]

Old-timers acknowledge the irony. It was white flight, after all, that brought about the urban blight that neighborhoods like these have known for decades: a rot of stultifying segregation, bare tax coffers, and epidemic crime. Now the flip side of white flight—integration by gentrification—is swiftly bleaching the black core of Brooklyn. According to the Floyds, raising the rent has only one purpose: moving whites in and pushing blacks out. "They take a low-income house . . . refurbish it and then rent it at a price that's not affordable by the people that used to live there," John declares. "That's a way of just forcing them out." The unending incursions upon his neighborhood by rent-raising developers leave his family feeling helpless. "What are you going to do? How can you stop it?"

The high real estate prices also mean that neighborhood stores that longtime residents have relied upon for years are quickly closing shop. "They can't really afford the prices," Sondra says of the store owners. "They're being forced out, and the whites are just coming in and taking over." It's unclear whether the shops opening in place of the ones that have closed are going to cater to Missing Class needs and preferences. The Floyds' favorite pharmacy, for instance, shut down because the owner couldn't afford to pay the rent as well as his three employees. Now the Floyds have to walk farther to fill their prescriptions. They miss their old pharmacist, who used to sell them smaller portions whenever they couldn't afford an entire prescription's worth of drugs. Business may be thriving on the nearby commercial strips, but these aren't the sort of businesses that care much for a clientele like the Floyds.

What they faced before gentrification was concentrated ghetto poverty. What they face today is relative deprivation. It is a little-discussed problem in studies of urban America but well known by millions of Americans—anyone, that is, who can turn on the TV and gape at the lavish comforts and extravagant whims of the rich. Nowadays, what old-timers like John once saw only on a silver screen stares back at them from the polished counter of their local Starbucks. Ensconced in their cleaner, safer, richer, and whiter neighborhoods, members of the Missing Class are coming to the realization that they're doing better than they ever have, and yet worse in comparison with those now around them. This conspicuous divide between the have-mores and the have-*much*-mores is at work in urban America.[10]

"If you're white, you're here," John points out, but if you're any other race, "you are an alien." The Floyds are, once again, strangers in their own house.

THE STYLIST-SOCIOLOGIST

Anna Walker, a tall, sturdily built woman in her late forties, runs her own beauty salon with the help of one assistant. She has been styling hair here for a quarter century. A no-frills operation with a retro seventies feel, the salon is housed in rented space along the notoriously crime-plagued strip of Myrtle Avenue, on the upper edge of Fort Greene and Clinton Hill.

For years a tangible boundary line has walled off the area north of Myrtle Avenue—once called Murder Avenue, thanks to its narcotics-laden housing projects, shootings, and robberies—from the more hospitable blocks to the south. On the northern end of the avenue, right across from verdant Fort Greene Park, lie the troubled Walt Whitman Houses, which have long been associated with desperate poverty; as far back as 1959, *Newsweek* called them a testament to the failure of public housing—another "million-dollar barracks" with shattered windows, elevators used as toilets, and utterly no sense of belonging or responsibility.[11] The reputation stuck. One young black floor manager at a nearby grocery store, who was born in the Walt Whitman projects and still lives there, says he no longer bothers hiring any of his neighbors; they inevitably steal groceries or take money from the cash register. The people living south of Myrtle, on the other hand, are more "high class" and motivated. Another local points out that neighborhood residents like to distinguish between the "great side of the park and the not-so-great side." On the "great side," you can find a house selling for half a million dollars. On the not-so-great side? "That's Myrtle Avenue," she explains.

Yet Anna remembers its virtues from long ago, during the years when she grew up on Myrtle Avenue. In the 1960s, back when the neighborhood was mostly white, her mother owned a corner candy store—the first black candy store in the area. People strolled down Myrtle Avenue late into the night. When she was young she regularly picked up a local newspaper called the *Night Owl* to plot her evening excursions. There was even a merchants' association that beautified the boulevard by planting trees and installing benches.

People helped each other, too. The owner of the local meat market, a friendly white man named Frank, gave Anna's family credit and took a liking to her. When Anna told him about her dream of becoming a stylist, Frank promised her that when he retired, she could take over his space. She didn't take him too seriously then, but after Anna finished college and Frank retired, he renewed the pledge. If Anna would convert the meat market into a salon, Frank said, he would give her six months of free rent. She eventually took him up on his offer. Plus, Frank knew "the man at ConEd," so with his help Anna was able to skip the deposit on her electricity bill. "My first dollar, he gave me," Anna remembers. Another kindly man at the beauty supply shop ("he was white, too") allowed her to furnish and supply her salon on credit. When she opened shop, the only thing Anna had to pay for was the telephone.

Frank passed away soon after she started the business. With him went her good luck. Frank's daughter didn't like Anna and refused to sell the building to her. Even after the place changed hands, she couldn't buy it. That was the biggest mistake she's ever made, says Anna, whose business has struggled since then with ever-soaring rents.

Back then, though, it didn't seem as if there was much of a future for the neighborhood. Gangs sprouted up in Fort Greene in the late sixties. Break-ins and rampant drug use spoiled the community's once-affable and open atmosphere. The merchants' association took away the trees and benches because of all the loitering, drinking, and public urination. By the early eighties, Anna's mother had had enough. Tired of the frequent burglaries, she closed the candy store. Many of the suspects the police caught were from the projects around Fort Greene Park. The young people who lived there generally were law-abiding students, whose parents were working in factories, hospitals, and stores. But the miscreants got the attention and dragged the neighborhood down as they became more brazen.

In the last few years, the crime and drug problems have subsided, and newcomers have moved in. Anna's customers, who are mostly on the older side, now include whites and Hispanics as well as African Americans. She notices many Orthodox Jews and Chinese in the neighborhood buying property, especially warehouses, on a strip one block away. A whole new crop of hair stylists have set up shop on Myrtle Avenue. Meanwhile, the costs of doing business have gone way up. "I don't know how long I will be here, because of the rent," she says. The monthly payments to lease her storefront have gone from $400 when she started to $1,800 today, which has forced her to raise prices. She used to be able to get ten-year leases but counts herself lucky now to secure one for five. If only she had bought the property, she chides herself. Unfortunately, black business owners in general haven't been able to follow this simple advice; on the several blocks of the Myrtle Avenue commercial strip that she's familiar with, there is only one black-owned building.

Nevertheless, Anna is hopeful that Myrtle Avenue is regaining some of its long-departed luster. People she knows who left the neighborhood years ago now want to return. Maybe they realize how easy the commute is from here to Manhattan, compared with Long Island or New Jersey or even Queens. "If you don't have any money...you just walk across the bridge."

THE LINARES FAMILY

> Sunset Park has never staked out a single, coherent identity because it has never had the luxury. It has always been a place where poor workers chased subsistence. When there were jobs, they moved in. When better work could be had elsewhere, they moved on. In terms of ethnicity, Sunset Park is rented by the generation.
>
> —*City Limits Monthly*, January 1999

Brooklyn's Fifth Avenue is bustling. Street vendors flood the concrete, hawking several warehouses' worth of cheap merchandise: belts and body lotions, CDs and snow cones, perfumes and cookware. On this Thursday evening, a United Nations assembly seems to have spilled out onto the sidewalk. A Peruvian woman dressed in colorful indigenous garb sells handmade jewelry. An Arab fruit seller uses hand signals to explain the price of bananas to a Chinese customer. Four fingers on one hand, one finger on the other—the Chinese man hands over a dollar for a bunch of four. Mexican bakeries sit alongside Ecuadorian restaurants next door to Chinese mini-marts. A truck bearing a Child Health Plus logo is parked on the corner, with a city representative inside fielding questions from residents applying for New York State's health insurance plan for children in poor families.

This is Sunset Park, a multiethnic, working-class enclave in southwestern Brooklyn nestled around the green hillock that gives the community its name. The neighborhood spans a broad swath of blocks, from Ninth Avenue all the way to Brooklyn's waterfront, sliced unceremoniously in half by the fume-spewing Gowanus Expressway. In times past, Sunset Park was home to many of the city's Irish, Polish, and

Scandinavian families, who manned the bayside piers for the Brooklyn Army Terminal. After World War II, the terminal shut down and the waterfront industries headed across the river to New Jersey. Cut off from their livelihoods, many of the workers and their families followed. By then, the Puerto Ricans had started to move in, seeking out the neighborhood's much-desired brownstones as homes for their young families; by the 1980s the community district was more than half Hispanic. What came next was a wave of Mexican immigration that washed over the neighborhood, followed by smaller ripples of Dominicans, Ecuadorians, and other sojourners from southern lands.[12]

Today, head into a Sunset Park bakery in early November and you'll find cookie sheets overflowing with white sugar skulls—a holiday treat given out during Día de los Muertos (Day of the Dead). Walk down Fifth Avenue, and you'll bump into women sporting wickedly long nails painted in the colors of the Puerto Rican flag. Stop by the CD store, and you'll see *música mexicana* from floor to ceiling; stroll past the brownstones, and you'll spot Puerto Rican tricolors flying alongside American stars and stripes.

Yet Sunset Park is no longer monolithically Puerto Rican, Mexican, or even Latino. Starting from Eighth Avenue, and sprinkled throughout the surrounding streets, Hasidic temples and Pakistani delis have sprouted up, adding a mélange of new signage to the storefront mix. The growing Chinese presence—in part, the overflow from the hemmed-in confines of Manhattan's Chinatown—is especially evident, from the frenetic commercial strip on Eighth Avenue to the quieter residential streets alongside, where the front doors of some homes display, in gold characters on red paper, the twin Chinese characters for happiness. At the basketball courts that crown the neighborhood's hilltop park, new and newer groups jostle for space: Asian immigrant children shooting hoops at one end, Latino ballplayers on the other. Not far from there, Hasidic men in black hats, accompanied by women in long drab dresses, usher their children to school buses marked with Hebrew lettering, while Hispanic teenagers saunter down the same sidewalk, effortlessly slinging down the N-word and other choice expressions drawn from the hip-hop vernacular.

Tomás Linares has witnessed the transformation of Sunset Park over four decades. A tall, thin man with short-cropped hair and a broad mustache, Tomás moved here from Puerto Rico as a teenager, in 1965, and has been in Sunset Park ever since.

The fortunes of the neighborhood have followed his own. When Tomás was first getting acquainted with Sunset Park, he was a bewildered island boy who was terrified of big-city life and couldn't understand a word of English. Even setting foot in school was nerve-racking for him, but his mother pushed him to study, and at first he did. But it was the "hippie time," as Tomás puts it, and the neighborhood's smoke-drenched park was a regular hangout for people doing acid and lighting reefers. His mom tried to keep him out of trouble, but after a while Tomás started smoking, too. For fun he'd while away the night at a bar or head out to Sunset Park's piers, where the older men would drink and fish. Sometimes he hung out under the Gowanus Expressway playing dominoes.

By the 1980s no one bothered to fish on the pier anymore, and only a fool would set foot near the expressway, unless he wanted to see the inside of a paddy wagon. By then, Sunset Park had become a war zone, with criminals and police vying for every block. Tomás learned quickly how hazardous the neighborhood had become. Once, while he was walking down the street, a bullet ricocheted off the ground and grazed him ("It was not something grave, thank God."); another time, his car battery was stolen; twice he was held up. "It used to be bad," Tomás recalls. "Every once in a while I heard that somebody was killed, that two or three were killed." Tomás barely escaped the violence; he did not outrun the drugs and drinking, which he claims ruined his marriage. "I started drinking and smoking when I was nineteen years old," he says. "You experiment with drugs, too. It's the environment you live in. If everyone does it, that's what you learn." He cruised around town with the guys; he neglected his wife and two young daughters. "I was young and ignorant," he says. "And where I was living, [there were] low-class people with drugs." The corner of Forty-sixth Street and Third Avenue was his hangout. "I used to know everybody there." Eventually, he found himself divorced, unemployed, and on public assistance.

Things could only go up for Tomás, and in 1990 they did. On a tip from his mom, Tomás found a job in Coney Island tending to patients

at a center for people with mental and physical disabilities. He was going to work every day, paying his own bills, and finally being a dad to
his two daughters. Over the next few years, he started noticing some
positive changes in his neighborhood, too. The police became a more
familiar presence on the streets. "Before, there used to be many groups
on the street, smoking, drinking beer," Tomás noted in 1998. "And the
police has stopped that. They have been [handing] out tickets to everybody that they find with a beer." The streets, once littered with trash,
were finally swept clean. Local artists rejuvenated the graffiti-marred
walls, replacing the drug wars with mural wars, as each ethnic group
staked out its presence in the neighborhood with a distinct artistic
style.

Nowadays, the divisions are more or less clear. The local labor market scoops each group up and pours them into niches of their own. The
Mexicans work mainly in factories; the Dominicans manage the local
car services and bodegas; and the Chinese own shops and factories.
Over the last few years, as the Mexican community has grown, the
Puerto Rican old-timers have started complaining louder. Some have
made it known they won't rent to Mexicans, who have a reputation for
cramming many people into one apartment. Others have gone further,
calling the Mexicans uneducated and prone to crime. (Tomás doesn't
agree—"The Mexicans, in my opinion, are hardworking people"—but
his mother admits to being terrified of them.) For their part, the
Mexicans have made it clear they intend to stay; their restaurants, bars,
and groceries now line many of Sunset Park's commercial strips.

Over the last several decades, Sunset Park has traced the same
trajectory that we have seen in Clinton Hill and Fort Greene: a neighborhood once mixed, then segregated, and now vibrantly (and con-
tentiously) diverse once more. The difference in Sunset Park is one of
degree. Located farther afield from Manhattan, Sunset Park has drawn
fewer Yuppie transplants than its northern neighbors. It has instead become a beacon for working-class immigrants, from newcomers fresh off
the plane to already established communities seeking space to spread
their wings. Here, integration by immigration has created a cacophony
of tongues rather than a chorus. Communities sit side by side, bleeding
at the edges but largely maintaining their distinct forms and loyalties.

Meanwhile, the rent has jumped. Tomás is one of many who are feeling the financial toll of living in a desirable location. That said, the quality of the housing stock is also better, now that landlords have fewer excuses to scrimp on repairs. Tomás has seen the improvements first-hand. For the last three decades he has lived in a nondescript building with dented aluminum siding on Fourth Avenue. When we first met him, in 1996, the building was in a perilous state of disrepair, with hall-way floors variously covered with linoleum, riddled with holes, or patched with flimsy wood paneling—halfheartedly, it seemed, since some of the nails were still sticking out. Tomás—then forty-six—was sleeping on a lonely mattress plopped down onto the living room floor; one of his daughters was staying temporarily in the alcove, a makeshift bedroom separated by a sheet tacked to the door frame. Between a sip of his beer and a drag of his cigarette, Tomás would occasionally stop to squash a cockroach wandering across the living room floor. The next time we saw him, in 1999, Tomás was living alone and had upgraded to a sectional sofa, a coffee table, and a television set on a cart. The walls were still cracked, the linoleum floors torn. His plastic kitchen table was surrounded by shoddy Kmart chairs intended for a backyard patio. He complained of yet another leak that had sprung in his ceiling after a torrential downpour.

Years later, the place that Tomás calls home is unrecognizable—as if it, too, has made the leap from poverty. The eighty-year-old building is, at long last, under renovation. The drab hallway walls? Repainted. The gloomy stairwell? New lights installed. The broken entrance door? Fixed—well, at least until the "crackhead" in apartment 6 broke it again ("she's in jail right now"). The city, which owns the building, has come to the belated conclusion that the apartments themselves might be due for some remodeling, too. At one time Tomás's place had gaping holes in its ceiling—a portion of which collapsed, thankfully when Tomás wasn't under it—but after a steady enfilade of complaints followed by persistent dabs of plaster, the building's administrator finally paid to have the entire ceiling replaced.

No one would call Tomás's home luxurious, but it's clear that his once-dilapidated dwelling—and the once-destitute neighborhood that surrounds it—has ridden the arc of neighborhood development toward a plateau of respectability and relative comfort. Today Sunset Park is much safer and more livable. "Those who were holding up people are, if not dead, in prison," Tomás says. "Police now show up more, not [like] before."

As for his neighborhood's changing complexion, Tomás doesn't pay it much mind. He lives in a world of these differences, having grown up amid their shifting patterns. He bumps into them every time he walks out of his apartment door. He acknowledges them, trades pleasantries with them, and closes his door on them every night.

> This use to be an Italian area. Then the Puerto Ricans arrived and fell in love with the Italian girls. Sometimes they liked us. Other times they didn't and we'd fight. Little by little the Italians left and this became a Hispanic area, but there are still Italians around.
>
> There have always been Dominicans. But I've seen more Dominicans and Mexicans, too. Seems like Mexico is very poor, 'cause there are lots of Mexicans here.
>
> But they are calm. The owner of the place next door is Mexican. He bought the building with the money he made selling *tortas* [Mexican sandwiches]. People like them. They call him Don Paco. He's even been featured in the newspaper. . . .
>
> The ones next door are Indians. I talk to the husband, but I think he's in India 'cause I haven't seen him in about six months. He works in construction. I see his son. He [works for a] car service. He comes in and out; I guess he's the one paying the rent. His mother is always there 'cause she has to take care of her young son. Downstairs there's another Indian family. The wife works, the husband works. They probably split the rent. They have two daughters. They're young, like twenty years old; maybe they also work and help out.
>
> Next to them lives the crackhead. She lives there with her mother, who has Parkinson['s] disease. She's like a prostitute; she always around Third Avenue. She takes men into her apartment, they take drugs and all that, and break the door, and she fights with the super.
>
> On the second floor there's a Puerto Rican who's been here longer than I have. She's been here about twenty-eight years. She's

on Social Security. I guess that's how she pays her rent. Then next to her is the super; she doesn't pay rent because she the one that cleans. I don't know how she gets by. . . . In the first-floor rear apartment lives the building administrator's sister with her husband. I haven't seen her husband, but I see the worker who fix my ceiling; he lives there. I've also seen a Chinese couple there.

Sometimes the woman on the second floor brings me food. . . . She knocks on my door. That's only for Christmas or Thanksgiving. She doesn't talk to anyone; she stays inside her home. She says, "Hi, how are you?" The super does, too. "Hi, how are you? How's everything?" Same thing with the woman in the first-floor front [apartment]. She's Dominican. She says, "Hey, how are you?" And that's it.

THE CORONADO FAMILY

In Manhattan, home of the city's priciest housing, you've got to go uptown for good rent deals—way uptown. It isn't enough to head for Harlem—it's got to be the north end of Harlem or beyond, into Washington Heights and Inwood.

—*New York Daily News*, November 7, 2005

Julia Coronado is changing diapers in the living room of her Manhattan apartment. Ten days ago, she gave birth to a baby boy. Miguel is her second son, the first with her new husband, César, whom she married earlier in the year. The delivery was rough, ending in a Cesarean section for the twenty-eight-year-old mother. But Julia and the baby are finally home, resting under the care of her mother, Sandra, who recently came from the homeland, the Dominican Republic, to help out. César is working another long day at a New Jersey shipping company.

In many ways, Julia's family is much like any middle-class family in America: two parents, one working and the other temporarily at home with the kids, saving for the future and blessed with a network of family to help ease the burden of child care and illness. Even if Julia complains from time to time about life in New York, she knows she has much to be grateful for. She remembers growing up poor in the Dominican Republic, her family abandoned by a womanizing father who left Sandra and the children "without a coin." Julia, her mother, and her four siblings lived in a humble house that might politely be called "rustic" when it came to plumbing and sewage. Julia left that home at the age of fifteen and started out on her own, working odd jobs to survive. When she moved to America, following her first husband, she kept working—at factories, as a housekeeper, anywhere she could— for hourly wages as low as $3.35.

Things are better now. Back on the island of Santo Domingo, Julia didn't have the opportunity to go to college. Now she's a student at a community college. Before, she didn't have a place to live or anyone to live with. Now she has her own apartment. Two of her siblings—her half-brother Alejandro and her sister Carola—have also made it to New York, and the siblings see each other regularly. "I don't live like a rich person, but I have what I need," Julia says.

But does she? At other moments, the worries abound. Julia may not be poor, but she does not enjoy the security and opportunity that come with wealth. She and her sons live in relative comfort thanks to the steady paycheck of her husband, César, but what if he abandons the family, as her father did? Her family has found a new home in Manhattan, the most modern of metropolises, yet they live on its outskirts—its very northern outskirts, in fact—where the going is tougher and the complexions browner. Julia looks at her newborn child and knows he deserves to grow up in a place with better schools and safer streets. Will that ever happen?

The doorbell rings, interrupting the delicate work of dislodging a soiled diaper. Julia, still recovering from her Cesarean, hobbles over to the apartment door. "Who is it?" she calls out.

"City investigator," the voice behind the door answers.

Something tells Julia not to open the door. She hesitates, then unlocks it.

A man walks into the living room and peers around the apartment. "Is your husband home?" the man asks.

"No, he's working," Julia replies, too quickly to catch herself.

On cue, three men barge into the apartment. They grab Sandra and Julia and shove them into the bathroom. While one of them watches over the cowering mother and daughter, the others begin to ransack the place.

Julia wails for her baby, who is still lying in the living room, naked and diaperless. The man watching them shows some remorse for the pleading mother and calls out to his comrades. One of them brings over Miguel, wrapped in a towel.

After a few moments the men have found the $2,000 that Julia has tucked away—savings that her brother Alejandro had given her to hold. They storm out of the apartment.

After the footsteps have receded, when they're sure the men are gone, Julia and Sandra creep out of the bathroom.

This is the neighborhood that Julia Coronado calls home: Washington Heights, the heart of New York's Dominican community, an assortment of skinny blocks set alongside angular avenues on the knuckle of Manhattan's long finger—farther north than even Harlem, the barrier separating most white New Yorkers from their known world. Julia lives at the far end of Washington Heights, on a patch of city streets surrounded by parklands that overlook the Hudson River, not far from the Cloisters, the reconstructed castle that houses the Metropolitan Museum of Art's medieval tapestries and manuscripts.

Washington Heights has seen many waves of immigration over the years, but nowadays the most dominant group—by far—is the Dominicans, who over the last three decades have made their presence known on this strip. English and Spanish take turns on many of the signs along Broadway, declaring *"cambiamos cheques"* and "checks cashed" in one breath, *"compramos oro y plato"* and "we buy gold and silver" in another. Storefronts advertising international calls and overseas money transfers sit comfortably alongside pizzerias and fast-food chains. Even in an all-American franchise like McDonald's, lively Dominican merengue music is piped through the speakers. Meanwhile, the local streets have become fertile ground for street vendors selling *frío-frío* (shaved ice doused in syrup) and a wide range of other Dominican treats. Americanized teenagers in baggy jeans and sports jerseys may congregate on these corners, as on any other city block, but just a few feet away are older immigrant men huddled around folding tables, slapping dominoes down with Old World gusto.

In the mid-eighties, Julia's neighborhood was overrun by narcotics.

With its six bridges and three major highways, Washington Heights is a quick drive from New Jersey, Westchester County, and Connecticut, an ideal staging ground for a drug-distribution network. Gangs of recent Dominican immigrants fought turf wars in the streets and served as middlemen for Colombian cocaine suppliers. The killings crested in 1991, when Washington Heights and the adjacent neighborhood of Inwood led the city with 119 murders. By the time Julia's younger son, Miguel, was born, though, the worst had passed. Crime statistics fell by an order of magnitude. By 2001 only fifteen murders were reported.[13] As Julia saw it, the police had finally gone after the drug dealers, and as they left the streets so did the crime. "The corners have been cleared," she said in 1998, two years after the break-in and robbery at her home. "The police are doing their job....I am not afraid to go out at any hour. I am not afraid to stand outside with my children."

As in Clinton Hill, as in Sunset Park, order has returned to the streets of Washington Heights. With it has come—here, as elsewhere —a new crop of outsiders, seekers of affordable rents and discount housing. Julia has only recently discovered an "immense" population of whites living nearby, seemingly coming from nowhere. "I haven't noticed because, truthfully, in the last three years all I've done is get up early every day and go to work," she says. The sudden appearance of these newcomers is a surprise. When she first moved into her apartment, in 1990, there were many white tenants in the building. But they all moved out, save one couple ("They're homosexuals and they live upstairs"). Now the whites are moving back, in search of rent in the realm of the $750 that Julia pays monthly for a two-bedroom apartment. The neighborhood, too, has been buoyed by the growth of Columbia University Medical Center, a major employer, which also houses medical students on the blocks near 168th Street. A number of restaurants and other businesses catering to professionals have mushroomed in the hospital's shade, some open only for lunch and selling salad-bar fare by the pound for a time-pressed business crowd.

With falling crime rates, burgeoning businesses, and cut-rate rents drawing affluent families, the fortunes of Washington Heights are clearly improving. The transformation has its share of detractors—one local politician speaks scornfully of how the big chains abandoned the neighborhood for two decades but now are happy to shove out the mom-and-pop stores that labored during that dangerous interval to build a customer base—but Julia doesn't seem to mind. What's more, there are noticeably fewer homeless people on the streets. "When you stop seeing them," she notes matter-of-factly, "it's because they've died."

Washington Heights' rising quality of life has moved in tandem with Julia's own professional ascent from welfare recipient to urban professional. After years of working in factories and motels, and then more years of collecting from the government dole, Julia has managed to land an administrative job at a health clinic downtown. In her case, the years in which welfare subsidized her college education paid off: her salary started at $21,000 a year and within months moved up by several grand, as Julia proved time after time that she was an indispensable gear in the clinic's administrative machine.

It is perhaps no coincidence that Julia's upward ascent has occurred at the same time as Washington Heights' own; for all her drive and smarts, Julia is also a creature of her habitat, and she has clearly benefited from the rising profile of her neighborhood, which has meant no more robberies at home, jobs aplenty for her friends and relations, and fewer worries about her young sons. All the same, Julia's climb up the occupational ladder has been so quick that she already has the feeling she's outgrown her neighborhood. It's true that Washington Heights is much safer than it was only a few years ago—the crack cocaine on the corner has given way to double-shot espressos at the coffee shop—but this isn't good enough for her. She worries, in particular, about raising her children here. Next year Eduardo will start attending the local middle school, Intermediate School (I.S.) 99, which recently made the headlines when an eleven-year-old boy killed another boy. "That's a jungle," Julia says of the school. "I hope to God that my son won't have to go to [I.S.] 99." If she can save the money, she'll enroll Eduardo in a private academy so that he never has to set foot in that pit of vipers. Plan B is to move out of Washington Heights altogether. Westchester County, that bucolic suburb upstate, sounds quite appealing. The education there is superior, the population more professional.

"You can't compare [Westchester] with people who live on public assistance, who only think about gossiping," Julia says, referring to the high numbers of welfare recipients in her current neighborhood. "That's the same thing the children learn.... I get up at seven and by eight I'm taking the train. I don't know what happens all day... [unlike] a person who spends all day at home talking on the phone with the neighbor, in the front of the house."

Gentrification is in the eye of the beholder. What seems a whitewashing of a proudly black Brooklyn for John Floyd is a much-needed —in fact, much-overdue—upgrading for Julia Coronado. How you judge a neighborhood depends on where you stand in relation to your neighbors, and in Julia's case, her rapid improvement in wages is outpacing even Washington Heights' recent revival. John lacks the income to even contemplate moving and must make do with what he has, and so the loss of his neighborhood to Yuppie colonists grates on him. Julia makes enough money to think of other possibilities. For her, gentrification cannot happen soon enough.

DISCREET ON THE STREET

Discretion is the key to solid police work. Officer Hector Serrano, a seven-year veteran of the New York City Police Department (NYPD), insists on it. Yes, there's the police procedure they teach you in the books and in expensive, worthless college classes, but in this line of business you learn from experience. After years of living and working in tough neighborhoods, the thirty-two-year-old Bronx native has learned a lesson: if you take care of people, people look out for you. There's no other way to survive on these streets.

Tonight's assignment is the Adams Sector, a three-street-wide zone from one of Manhattan's rivers to the other, one of four patrol areas in Washington Heights' Thirty-third Precinct. Serrano gets behind the wheel while his partner, Officer Eddie More, rides shotgun. Four to six of the precinct's cars should be on the street right now, Serrano says. That doesn't include undercover units.

The first stop is a restaurant on St. Nicholas. The officers sit at the counter nursing their cups of coffee when a middle-aged Dominican man parks himself a few stools away. Two ugly red scrapes crisscross his nose. He glares at More and Serrano. "You got something to say?" Serrano asks the man in Spanish.

"The innocent are always guilty, so why bother saying anything," the man growls back.

It was the drunk they picked up just the day before, Serrano explains. In a fit of rage he took a swing at the superintendent of his apartment building, who proceeded to rough him up. "He's the nicest person when he's not drunk," Serrano notes, shaking his head.

The two officers drive off, down 163rd Street. Serrano, who served in the U.S. Army, likens this part of the neighborhood to Vietnam. The drug dealers used to own these blocks, he recalls. It was even worse here than in the South Bronx, that hardscrabble part of the city where Serrano was born and raised. But then the police changed their tactics. One Hundred Sixty-third Street between Amsterdam Avenue and Broadway was the first target of the city's so-called model-block strategy. In 1997 the department applied the full force of its manpower, conducting drug sweeps, setting up police barriers, and covering up graffiti. Officers were on the street twenty-four hours a day, stopping passersby to check their IDs and working with residents to organize tenant groups and a block association.

The barricades in Washington Heights and elsewhere came down after several months, but the police department credited them for the sharp drops in crime. In the years since, drug dealing has diminished, homicides are down, and muggings are less frequent. Though chastened, the dealers have adapted, moving indoors and out of sight, Serrano says.[14] Like any good investor, the dealers have learned ways to distribute their risk. One person brings in the customer, another steers him to the location, yet another takes the money, and a fourth hands over the drugs. The network as a whole is protected even if one person gets nabbed. All the same, the dealers these days have to hide more than they used to, and that's a good thing.

The other major problem in Washington Heights is the resurgence of gangs. The Bloods, the Latin Kings, and other shady outfits have moved into town, including a few Dominican start-ups. The Mexican gangs are the worst, Serrano says. He calls them *brutos*—thugs who like to slash and thrash other teens in the neighborhood. Their numbers are rising, especially in East Harlem.

The police cruiser heads uptown on Broadway and drives by the aftermath of a drug bust. Undercover police officers have just stopped a car with four Latino men in it. Two of the men are standing behind the car with their hands on the trunk; one is handcuffed. The men, young and clean-cut, are dressed like college students—khakis and striped shirts—and watch with horrified expressions as a police car with wailing sirens pulls up beside their car. One of the plainclothes cops carries a yellow envelope. It's for contraband: the man in handcuffs has just been arrested for possession of narcotics.

The next stop is the African American section of the neighborhood: 158th and 159th Streets. Relations with the police are at a low point here. In 1999, Serrano explains, this community flatly refused the police department's offer to set up a "model block." Especially since the Amadou Diallo shooting, residents have made it known they don't want the police around. Notice all the boarded-up buildings? See all the people hanging out on the streets, up to no good? Serrano insists that these blocks are more derelict than others because it's a no-man's-land for police. (Tonight, though, the men on the streets are mostly Latinos.)

Serrano and More spot another patrol car cruising by and stop to stay hello. One of the officers updates Serrano on a local girl named Alma. A while back, Alma's mother had come to the precinct, desperate because her adolescent daughter was veering into a life of delinquency. At the mother's request, Serrano had a long talk with Alma, reminding her of the consequences of messing up at her age. Before long he got a call that Alma had hit her mother. This time Serrano arrested the girl and sent her to a juvenile home in upstate New York.

Washington Heights parents with troubled teens often approach the police, asking them to intervene in their children's lives before it's too late.[15] Only a few—Serrano among them—are prepared to moonlight as counselors for at-risk youth. And even when they try to help, there is often little they can do, as the officer is reminded tonight. Fourteen-year-old Alma is back in town—and pregnant. "She just wants to hang out and date men who are much older than her," Serrano says wearily as he heads back into traffic.

Driving past a corner, Serrano notices four Latino men leaning against the wall. He pulls the car up beside them, opens his window, and smacks his hands together twice. Encounters like these appear to be routine, because the men don't bother to speak a word of protest; one of them merely claps his hand and says, "Let's go," and they walk off. "Those men were not playing dominoes," Serrano notes with a smirk. Every night he runs into little social gatherings like this one, and the rule should be clear to them now: two or more men standing on a corner is not acceptable, at least in this neighborhood.

It is the trade-off that occurs on every street block where drug dealers and thieves ply their trade: you can have heavy-handed cops who hunt down the crooks but also catch law-abiding citizens in their nets, or you can have laissez-faire police who leave the residents, and the criminals, alone. That's the way veterans like Serrano see it, and many residents of the communities they patrol agree. The Missing Class in this part of town wants no-nonsense, Rambo-tough cops like Serrano, a former soldier who has already been involved in three shooting incidents—three more than his laid-back partner. They also want more respect from the police and find it troubling that they cannot achieve a balance: responsive officers who are there when they are needed, and cops who don't lord it over the decent people who are in the majority here, as they are everywhere.[16]

When Serrano and More roll out again, it's getting late. A call comes in for a domestic disturbance on 174th Street. It's out of their assigned sector, but they race over to the address, a well-maintained building with spacious apartments just west of Broadway. A middle-aged Colombian woman answers the door. In rapid-fire Spanish she demands that the police serve a court order of protection against her daughter's boyfriend, who won't leave the apartment. The daughter, twenty-year-old Nelyn, is feeding her baby and barely speaks to the police. When pressed, Nelyn finally hands over two court orders of protection—one for herself, one for the baby—neither of which has been served. Nelyn says she's changed her mind and doesn't want the order of protection anymore. Her mother is furious. Serrano points out that by law he has to enforce the court orders.

Carlos, the boyfriend, appears and hands the police officers his own set of papers. One of them is a court order that apparently grants custody of the child to Carlos. Which court order should be enforced? By now, four other police officers, including the sergeant, have shown up at the apartment. All of them are standing in the hallway, eyeing the court orders like tea leaves. The mother rails against Carlos to anyone who will listen. He has a criminal record, she says. Her daughter is gullible, and Carlos threatened her into signing the court documents giving custody of the baby. Carlos wants custody only so that he can apply for welfare, the mother alleges. "Have you ever heard of such an absurd situation?" she fumes. Carlos, meanwhile, maintains that he and Nelyn are going to court the next day to rescind the orders of protection.

Serrano, the after-hours guidance counselor, takes Nelyn into the bathroom and talks to her. He asks her why she signed the custody paper. Nelyn admits to being depressed at the time.

Domestic calls like this one bring the police into more uncertain terrain: the household domain, with its intricately twisted relations between husband and wife, boyfriend and girlfriend, mother and daughter. For Missing Class households unlucky enough to fall into their purview, the police become a social support of last resort. They are sometimes the only ones who can offer first aid to families drifting, no longer quietly, into despair.

But whether they're trained to provide this kind of care is a different matter. While the sergeant vacillates between siding with the smug boyfriend and favoring the irate mother, Serrano and More make their exit. By now, the officers in charge of this sector have arrived, so the case is no longer in their hands. An hour later, Serrano and More hear another call come in over the radio—for the same address. "This time someone is going to be arrested," Serrano observes wryly.

Dispatch barks out new orders: the partners are sent to check out a report of a shattered apartment window. Calls like these may seem like a waste of time, but a focus on this kind of neighborhood blight was the foundation of the wildly popular "broken window" theory of policing, which held that suppressing petty infractions of the law could prevent an atmosphere of more heinous crime from materializing. This theory inspired the kind of "quality of life"–obsessed campaign against crime pioneered in New York during the 1990s. Since then, police officers have come to see their role in the community as not just jailing crooks but policing the very boundaries of what is acceptable. By rooting out the drugs, breaking up the packs of men huddled on the corners, and taking notice of every literal or symbolic broken window, officers like Serrano and More have become de facto instruments of gentrification: changing, block by block, the character of the neighborhoods they patrol.

Tonight they won't find their broken window. Instead, they'll stop an erratic driver, respond to a false call of a downed officer, and toss a raucous homeless man out of a McDonald's. Then the two partners will head over to their favorite bodega, where dinner awaits them, the neighborhood perhaps a little quieter in their passing.

THE FLOYD FAMILY

"Rasheea, is there something wrong?"

Rasheea Fletcher, the granddaughter of John and Sondra Floyd, meets her teacher's gaze, puzzled. Ms. Keeler has a concerned look in her eyes. She just finished reprimanding the class for not bothering to look up an assigned vocabulary word for last night's homework. Now her star pupil, Rasheea, seems to be observing the class from another plane of existence. "You normally participate more in class," she tells Rasheea. "Why are you not raising your hand to respond to some of these questions?"

Rasheea shrugs her shoulders but doesn't say a word. Ms. Keeler calls on another student to continue reading aloud.

This is Ms. Keeler's sixth-grade class in Public School (P.S.) 444, an elementary school just a few blocks from the Floyds' apartment in Clinton Hill. There are twenty-six students, all African American save for two. They sit at desks arranged in small circles, five to a cluster. Ms. Keeler guides the class through the day's reading lesson with a firm hand, at one point abruptly stopping the class to chasten a student for an outburst. Hers is not a talented and gifted class, but Ms. Keeler is well known for her high expectations, salted with heaping portions of discipline. It's no surprise that her class outperforms all the others on standardized tests.

Rasheea is one of her stars, scoring nationally in the ninety-second percentile for reading and in the eighty-sixth for math. Mr. Vihan, her teacher last year, said flatly that a student of this caliber didn't belong at P.S. 444; she needed more of a challenge. Rasheea, her grandfather says proudly, has a "thirst for learning" and is bored when not at school. Both John and Sondra dote on the girl, whose many school certificates and awards are pasted to the walls of their apartment.

It's not clear what exactly is occupying Rasheea's mind as she sits mute in Ms. Keeler's class this Wednesday morning, but there's a good chance it has to do with her mother. Hannah is a crack addict. She has been for years. Hannah foisted Rasheea onto the Floyds right after she gave birth, declaring that she couldn't take care of the child. The same thing happened to Chinyere, Rasheea's two-year-old sister, who contracted her mother's HIV infection. Hannah, who is Sondra's daughter from a previous relationship, has since given up all claims to being a mother, but she still manages to hover around the margins of Rasheea's life, like an unwelcome apparition.

Simply ignoring Hannah will no longer work, however. A few months ago she drifted into the household once again, thanks to the unwanted interference of the city. Hannah went on welfare, and her caseworker came up with the brilliant idea that she should move back in with her parents. Now that she's moved in, Hannah is not always at home—she'll disappear now and then for a fix or occasionally stay with her husband, a seventy-two-year-old man whom Hannah married, the Floyds allege, just so that she'd have a family member to sign off on her early release from a mandatory drug treatment program. Rasheea is learning to deal with her mom being around again, but it's an awkward and painful situation.

Her deadbeat mother is not the only threat to Rasheea's promising trajectory. There are also the dangers posed by the Floyds' neighborhood, Clinton Hill, with its population of children tempted so young by crime, drugs, and thrills.[17] Rasheea already knows kids who are on probation, though they aren't yet thirteen. Gang members hang out in the streets, demanding respect. When some people refuse to join up, Rasheea explains, they get their faces sliced up. "Sometimes that frightens me," she says. "Sometimes I think about it—God forbid—that somebody come to ask me that, and I say no, and I wind up getting my-self hurt." Many of the kids who do "bad things," Rasheea says, live in the housing projects at the other end of the neighborhood, across the dividing line of Myrtle Avenue. They tease other kids mercilessly. Rasheea has been teased herself, but that hasn't stopped her from get-ting elected president of her class last year. It doesn't stop her friends from the projects from doing well in school, too. She and her friends are leaders, not followers, Rasheea declares.

Back in Ms. Keeler's classroom, a police officer has shown up to give a presentation on this very topic for D.A.R.E., the antidrug education program. Officer Roberts goes to the front of the room and writes the word "self-esteem" on the blackboard. Parents often give nice compli-ments to their children, Roberts tells the kids. Can anyone tell her why they do this?

"The parents want their children to feel good about themselves," one student answers.

"You should really think about talking to Royce about this," the police officer says, waving the sheet of paper.

Sondra says nothing, but a look of cold fury is fixed upon her face. How could her grandson skip school? How could he get caught by po-lice on the streets, with gang material on him? Hadn't she told him—*all* of her grandchildren, multiple times—that if any one of them got arrested, she'd dropkick them? Fifteen-year-old Royce, his two sisters, and his mother all live in the Floyds' home; as a member of their house-hold, he's supposed to follow *their* rules, not some harebrained honor code put together by a couple of boys with too much time and testos-terone for their own good.

When the officer leaves, Sondra and Royce's mother, Kirsten, get to work. Wordlessly, they drag Royce into the far room. Then the scream-ing begins. John shakes his head. Rasheea, Royce's cousin, sits in the corner, anxiously twisting her braids between her fingers.

John's nephew D.J. is also seated in the living room, his visit to the Floyds interrupted by the unexpected apprehension of a family mem-ber. As Sondra's fire-and-brimstone version of justice proceeds—quite audibly—in the background, D.J. finally pipes up. Children these days are so out of control, he says. When he was growing up, he could never disrespect his mother the way kids do now.

He's interrupted by another outburst from the back room. "You want to be in a gang, I'll show you exactly what it is to be in a gang!" Sondra screeches. "You'll be in a gang all right!"

It may be too late for Royce, John admits. He has been hanging out with an eighteen-year-old named Toothpick, a crack dealer who shot another boy and put him in a wheelchair. Royce has a record of his own, too. A little while back, he was spotted with a group who had threatened a boy with a knife, and by association he got placed on probation.

"It's peer pressure, but you don't have to be with them, you understand me?" John grouses. "It's your decision not to be with them."

Having finished with their ministrations in the back room, Kirsten and Sondra join the group. Royce, free for now, heads out to the apartment's stoop. "He ain't going nowhere," Kirsten says.

The family starts discussing the police. They were fortunate that Royce got picked up by two officers who know the Floyds—Royce's sister Charlotte, in fact, had met one of them at a school presentation. In this neighborhood, it wasn't unheard of for some "redneck" cop to pick up a kid, throw him into the system, and not bother to notify the parents for twenty-four hours. "They could come up with any kind of bullshit stories," John says.

This time, there's no one to blame but Royce. "Royce thinks that he could do anything that he want to do, and nobody has no right to say nothing to him," Kirsten gripes about her son. It's not that the young man doesn't have aspirations. He's mad about basketball. He practices every day; last summer he was playing in three local teams. But Royce doesn't seem to grasp that there are other worthwhile things besides basketball. He barely passes his junior high school courses and doesn't seem to care about getting into college, even though his granddad has assured him he'll have no shot at an athletic career otherwise. "He wants to be the shortest person in the NBA," John scoffs.

Kirsten is terrified that the neighborhood's bad elements will swallow her son whole. At his next court appointment, "I'm gonna tell them to put him away before something happen," she proclaims. "He's only fifteen.... If he don't wanna listen to his grandmother and grandfather, put him away. As simple as that. 'Cause ain't nobody gonna be out here looking for him all the time of the night with gunshots out here."

Their neighborhood might have its share of troubles—the kinds that come with popping noises—and yet Clinton Hill also has upscale new stores, a colony of Yuppie pioneers, and houses that sell for millions of dollars. Some of the wealth and success that now surround the Floyds has to rub off. So why can't Sondra persuade her grandson to make use of the opportunity? "Fifteen damn years of getting up in the morning, going through all this shit, and then [he] get throwed out," she snarls, bringing her already agitated mind to bear on Royce's dim academic prospects. "What damn difference does it make?"

"It's the system," D.J. insists, "the system."

"System, my ass. I tell you one damn thing—ain't [nobody] gonna lay up here on me and don't go to school. I don't give a shit. You don't care, brother, I don't care. . . . I just lost one out there. I'm not playing anymore. I ain't fucking around. I mean it from the bottom of my black heart."

The family is still grieving over the death of Aaliyah, D.J.'s daughter. A few months ago, Aaliyah, a junior at Yale, went to a pool party in Brooklyn. Two men, upset that they were being kept out of the private party, forced their way into the building and sprayed the pool area with bullets from a .22-caliber gun. Aaliyah was hit in the neck. By the time she arrived at the hospital, the bullet had lodged in her chest. The doctors opened up her chest, but Aaliyah suffered a stroke and died.

With the conversation turning to his daughter, D.J., already tipsy from the malt liquor he's drunk, becomes emotional. "It's hurting every day," he says in a halting voice. "Every single day." He starts to talk, somewhat disconnectedly, of his mother, who raised him with toughness and love. "I owe my mom all the praise in the world because I wouldn't be the man that I am right now" without her, he says. " 'Cause I ain't had no father, but I had a mother, and she was my mother and father." He begins to sob.

After a while, D.J. catches his breath and continues. "If you're gonna listen to anybody, listen to your parents, please," he concludes. "Listen to people that care about you." John concurs. The other grandchildren—Rasheea above all—seem to be heeding that important lesson. But for some reason, Royce won't.

Royce and Rasheea may be cousins living under the same roof, but in a sense they stand on opposite sides of a neighborhood rapidly being hewn in two by gentrification.[18] Like so many other young men in the ghetto, Royce sees the hustle of the street as a rite of manhood and a mark of respect. The same culture of gangs and drugs consumed many of the Floyds' children, and now it threatens the grandchildren. Yet Clinton Hill is changing. Its ghetto is becoming less of a ghetto; outsiders are breaking through the walls and staking out sections of the community as their own. The interactions between old-timers and newcomers are tense, if not violent; the rules of engagement are unclear, but segments of the community do benefit. Children like Rasheea, for instance, have had their eyes opened to the world beyond their corner of Brooklyn. This is the hopeful side of gentrification: the promise of success and prosperity in the next generation.

Indeed, the changing conditions of Clinton Hill are written upon the neighborhood's children, stamped upon their psyches like a genetic code waiting to express itself. For some kids, like Royce, it speaks to a past beholden to drugs and crime. For others, like Rasheea, it tells of a future of upward mobility and integrated communities. The influences at work here are not nature, of course, but nurture: the effect of the urban environment upon the children who grow up there, the behavioral patterns imprinted upon their pliable minds at an early age. This neighborhood DNA is being altered by the process of gentrification, and the result can be seen in kids like Royce and Rasheea—starkly different but emerging from the same family—twin faces of Clinton Hill past and yet to come.

By the time we catch up with the family again, in 2002, Royce has fallen even further from his grandparents' grasp. At the age of seventeen, he's skipped one too many classes and been kicked out of school. His uncle is now trying to help him get his GED, but the boy—who was hanging out with the Bloods until Sondra shipped him off to his godmother's—doesn't seem to care anymore. As for Rasheea, she is now applying to high school. Her once-perfect marks have fallen slightly— she has a ninety-one average, and her top pick, Brooklyn Tech, wants ninety-five and above—but she's joined her school's Mock Trial team and, at thirteen, is harboring ambitions to become a district attorney.

A child of Rasheea's talents, it must be emphasized, is a rarity. Her fierce determination to succeed in school sets her apart from many other kids—her cousin Royce, to be sure—who approach academics with attitudes that are lukewarm at best, antagonistic at worst. Rasheea's courage in brushing off peer pressure and focusing on her own goals is admirable, from any perspective. So is the dedication of her grandparents. Sondra didn't finish high school when she was young— growing up in a violent household with an abusive father threw her off any career track—but her passion as a grandparent is to make sure all the kids get their diplomas. It's what keeps her motivated in spite of her poor health. "The main thing is education. That is my main purpose of being here. Otherwise I'd be gone."

As for John, he has been a constant presence at Rasheea's school. He heads over there to demand that his granddaughter receive more-challenging assignments. He sits in on Rasheea's class and stays up —even when he can barely keep his eyes open—to help her with homework. John has even won a reputation for his culinary skills at school-sponsored events. For the end-of-the-year party that P.S. 444's fifth grade threw, he wheeled over a large red pushcart filled with several courses of professionally prepared dishes: fried and barbecued chicken, green beans, and potato salad, all cooked with love for his precious granddaughter.

It is a matter of common sense that involved parents lead to successful students, and no one seems to know this better than America's middle class.[19] Working parents often pride themselves on their ability, even after a long day of work, to correct their children's homework, show up for school performances, and meet with teachers. And when they can't spend the time, these parents spend the money to hire capable tutors and buy intensive private-school curricula and other forms of enrichment. Members of the Missing Class, however, do not yet have family coffers full enough to afford tutors or private schools. When they work such grueling workdays that they can't get home in time to do a second shift of home schooling, their children's academic performance often slips. But when parents can afford the luxury of time to sit

down for homework sessions and attend PTA meetings, their involvement pays off.

Rasheea's mother is hardly around and can't be bothered, but her
grandparents serve as the dedicated stewards of her academic career.
The fact that John and Sondra show up and stay up for their granddaughter is what distinguishes Rasheea from many of her peers. (In fact,
Rasheea fared far better than many of the other children we followed
during our fieldwork, *especially* those whose parents worked long hours
away from home.)[20] Yet Rasheea is not unique in her potential; a dedicated family like the Floyds was also able to produce a child like Aaliyah, the daughter of nephew D.J., who had made it to a prestigious
college and probably would have gone much further if not for a stray
bullet.

Clearly the efforts of caring adults, plus a modicum of talent and
self-discipline, make academic success possible for children like Rasheea and Aaliyah. But there are other factors at play here, too. If, as
politicians are fond of saying, it takes a village to raise a child, then
surely the neighborhood—the surrounding ecosystem of people, institutions, and resources—also shapes a child's prospects. And the part of
Brooklyn that the Floyds call home has undergone a complete transformation in the past few decades. When Hannah, Rasheea's mother, was
growing up, the streets were poisonous. It wasn't that Hannah was born
to be an addict and delinquent mother; as a child, she too showed promise. Sondra remembers how her daughter used to go to church every
Sunday when she was a teenager. "You didn't have to get her out of bed
or nothing!" But by the time Hannah showed up at her brother's fu-
neral, she was nothing more than a wraith, her once-full body wasted
by addiction. "She looked like a little old lady, bent over," Sondra says.

It is clear that the neighborhood still has its dangers, and too many
of its kids—Royce among them—continue to fall into the familiar ruts
of gang violence and drug use. Yet recent years have brought a percep-
tible hint of optimism to the attitudes of parents, teachers, and police
officers. The Floyds report that the police have cracked down on rampant drug dealing in the local housing projects, at one point going so far
as to evict entire families if one family member was involved in crime.
The recent wave of gentrification may have something to do with the
improved safety situation, John admits. After the whites started moving

back, they put pressure on the politicians to commit money to local infrastructure and policing. "I see more resources coming in," John says, "for the simple fact that [whites are] moving in."[21] Without these newcomers' conspicuous wealth to carry the day, the Franklin Avenue Shuttle—a line that the transit authority once wanted to abandon—would never have been rebuilt, he contends, and the area might still be in the hands of the drug dealers.

If gentrification has displaced many a poor family, it has also brought much-needed resources to those households that are somehow able to remain in the neighborhood, in the form of schools funded by a broader tax base, infrastructure given more attention by politicians, bureaucrats, and entrepreneurs, and neighborhoods policed more vigilantly. It's no surprise, then, that the local public schools—which once taught the Floyds' children and now their grandchildren—have improved in recent years. Once, substandard test scores consigned these schools to the dungeons of the city's percentile rankings; but now they are judged average or better. At Rasheea's new middle school, the parents are noticeably more involved, too. After citywide cuts shrank the school's budget by $200,000, they rallied to raise money and keep two favorite teachers from falling under the ax. "They could have let the teachers go," Sondra says, but "the parents' association took it upon themselves." Now that investors are plowing money back into the neighborhood and the tide of newcomers has lifted disposable incomes, local business has also rebounded—and along with it, employment for the younger generation. Charlotte, Royce's sister, was able to find a summer job for three years straight: as a messenger at a local hospital one year and as a day-care counselor for two years. Now she's three credits shy of her high school graduation and the law enforcement career she aspires to.

The community spirit is returning, too. Across the street from the Floyds' apartment is a garden tended by Joseph, an immigrant from Guyana. Joseph thought the neighborhood needed a garden and set out to plant one. In the beginning, however, he met resistance. "What is the West Indian man trying to do in this neighborhood?" people wanted to know. But now that the lot is thriving with vegetables and flowers, former skeptics are constantly inquiring about how to get plots. Joseph gives away bags of fresh produce and does it gladly, happy to be doing something positive for the community. (John is one of the garden's fans; just the other week Joseph gave him some turnip greens and scallions, which he raved about.) One bellwether of the changes in the neighborhood is the resurgence of community gardens like Joseph's. Where there are gardens, the streets are usually swept clean, and fewer men loiter on the corners.[22]

All these changes are good. But others are not, and at times John and Sondra can't help but feel left out. About a year ago, John was making extra cash managing a social club right across the street, where an older crowd gathered to shoot pool and play whist. But the rent rose too high, and the clubhouse had to shut down. Meanwhile, the places in Fort Greene where the Floyds used to go for an evening's entertainment have closed, replaced by chic bars for the young and artsy. They don't even bother setting foot in those establishments, Sondra admits.

With every passing day, the world the Floyds thought they knew becomes a bit more foreign. Their new neighbors look like they stepped out of a tattoo parlor in Greenwich Village. "People with purple and orange hair, they are here!" Sondra laughs. "They are here!" (The police never stop *them*, she adds pointedly.) Orthodox Jews from northern Brooklyn are moving in, too; the Floyds often spot them making the rounds on the block, quizzing people on whether they'll sell their home. Sometimes it's just too much. There's no rioting in the streets yet, but there's clearly a good share of jostling and jousting over what this neighborhood should be—a cold war with tempers and egos as its first casualties.

A Yuppie recently moved in next door. He parks his sleek black car outside, then walks up to his stoop with a pair of skis slung over his shoulder. "*Skis!*" Sondra chuckles derisively. "Don't know what he be doing.... You can tell he's a little cuckoo." This neighbor whines incessantly about all the "noise" her grandchildren make at night. But they're outside only until nine o'clock—ten, tops. The nerve of that man, to scold her and suggest the kids should play in a park. "You don't tell *me* where to take my kids."

The fact is, Alpine Man smokes reefers all day right on his stoop. Sondra gets dizzy just from walking through the smoke. "You ought to see him. He just don't shave sometimes. He always looks like he's high." There goes the neighborhood.

THREE

The American Dream, in Monthly Installments

Consumer spending—by shoppers of all kinds—is responsible for roughly 70 percent of the nation's economy.... The downside: Debt made much of this spending possible.... Personal bankruptcy filings in the United States rose from 1.2 million in 2000 to 1.6 million in 2004.
—*Atlanta Journal-Constitution*, February 27, 2005

THE CORONADO FAMILY

It is Miguel's birthday, and his family is having a party. Julia, Miguel's mother, and Sandra, his grandmother, have tidied up their apartment in Washington Heights for an evening get-together. His godmother has dropped by from next door, with two children in tow. Miguel's favorite uncle, Alejandro, is there, too, along with his wife and Miguel's four-year-old cousin, a bubbly girl with dark chocolate tresses wrapped into a ponytail. A few other family members straggle in, just in time to sing happy birthday.

Miguel has short-cropped hair, caramel skin, and almond-shaped eyes. Today he turns three. His godmother has given him a black-and-white suit for his birthday, and he's wearing it now, a dapper little man in his fancy attire. Little he certainly is—half the height of the leafy houseplant in the corner of the apartment, and still a good head and chest shorter than his older half-brother, Eduardo, who is eight. Eduardo is the well-mannered, thoughtful one; Miguel, as his grandmother puts it, "likes to play too much."

Julia—always the life of the party—is bustling about the apartment, playing the hostess. Her wavy brown hair falls down to her shoulders, and she shares Eduardo's laughing dark eyes. Her family members are

spread on her green leather couches, eating off her glass coffee table—
the one with the classy faux-marble edges she likes so much. Those
couches still have a new-leather sheen to them; Julia bought the entire
living room set last year, seized by one of her periodic bouts of shopping
fever.

And why not? Things have gone well for thirty-one-year-old Julia
Coronado. Once a below-minimum-wage factory girl, now she is the
office manager at a Manhattan health clinic. She left an unhappy marriage (her second) several months ago but still manages to support herself, her mother, and her two boys on little more than her white-collar
salary. Eduardo, with his third-grader's astuteness, puts it like this:
"She's, like, the holder of the house."

Right now the holder of the house is dishing out beef tortillas for
the guests. There are soft drinks, but Alejandro, a thinly built, thick-
browed man, decides it's time for something a bit stronger. He sends his
wife out for a bottle of amaretto.

On the other side of the room, standing in front of a large mirror,
is the family's Christmas tree. The decorations are stunning, but Julia
seems a bit disappointed. One year she spent $400 on a tree, decorating
it with a half-dozen gift boxes of pricey white ornaments. This year,
though, she can't spend as much as she's accustomed to. She shouldn't
be spending anything at all.

The fact of the matter is that Julia is deeply, dangerously in debt.
She has driven her credit cards into the stratosphere of $9,000 balances
and $300 minimum payments, and she is struggling mightily to keep
the rising debt from overwhelming her household. She has taken out a
bank loan for more than half that amount, canceled all but one of her
cards, and started bringing her lunch to work. Still, she frets. Julia isn't
sure she'll be able to pull herself out of this hole.

César, Miguel's father, calls. Sandra speaks with him, as do Eduardo
and Miguel, but Julia won't be bothered. She and César are separated.
They used to be on good terms. César continued living in the apartment while he looked for another place. Then César found out that Julia was planning to visit her new boyfriend in the Dominican Republic.
The morning of her flight, César stole her passport and airplane tickets.
Julia cut up his clothes in retaliation. "I wanted to chop up that man,"

Julia snarls. He's been banned from the apartment. The incident cost Julia a $738 charge to her credit card—$738 for a first-class ticket, because coach was not available—so that she could make it to Boca Chica and meet her boyfriend a day later.

The two latecomers to the party—Miguel's aunt and twelve-year-old cousin—leave, having had their fill of coconut candy. Send the birthday cake over to their apartment later, they say, as they wave their good-byes.

The party is already dwindling. Julia and her mother had been arguing about that. Why didn't you invite more people? Sandra had asked. They could have sent out invitations. They could have prepared more food. Julia reminded her mother that they couldn't afford a big party. Why invite people and spend money that she did not have? They didn't even have money for her son's gifts.

Julia's sister-in-law comes back with the amaretto. Everyone takes polite sips except for Alejandro; he's the only one who asks for seconds.

By now Miguel is grinning like a madman. A family friend has handed him his birthday present, and he holds it close, like a safety blanket, not even bothering to look inside. His four-year-old cousin pesters him to open it, and when Miguel refuses she starts peeling away at the gift wrap. Julia comes over and tells him, in her cooing mother's voice, that it's OK. "Open the gift, sweetheart, and find out what's inside."

It's a children's cassette recorder. A microphone is attached, for singing along to tapes.

The singing begins quickly, because Julia has turned on her stereo system—an electronic colossus housed in its own two-door, beige-colored cupboard. The two-foot-tall speakers are pumping out a throbbing mix of merengue and *bachata*, Dominican country music. Miguel starts singing to the songs with his microphone, then takes to the floor, jerking his little shoulders as the music pulses through his body.

Watching her son dance, Julia admits to a friend that she's long wanted to enroll him in a music program, but she hasn't been able to—it's too expensive, and even if it wasn't, there would be no one to take him there. Sandra runs her own one-woman day-care business and can't leave her two young charges to take Miguel anywhere.

If only Julia didn't have so much debt. If only she had a man to support her. Things could be better for Julia Coronado.

By now Julia's younger sister has returned from work. Julia has saved a few shots on her camera for more family photos. Sandra picks up Miguel, but the newly minted three-year-old squirms in her grasp, crying to be put down.

A few pictures later, and it's time to go. Eduardo and Miguel's cousin have already stolen his recorder. Alejandro has drunk all the amaretto.

Julia, the holder of the house, gets ready to clean it.

If there is a word to describe Julia Coronado, it is ambitious. The story of her rapid ascent from poor country girl in the Dominican Republic to welfare recipient in the American barrio to white-collar manager in Manhattan is remarkable and speaks to the resilience of the American Dream for some: the ability—even within this jaded postindustrial age—to rise from humble beginnings and secure an occupational perch far above the wretched fray of the sweatshop and burger hut.[1]

As the size of her paycheck has grown, so has Julia's desire for happiness—the kind that can be bought on credit. The unpaid balances on her credit cards have mushroomed with every passing month, fed by purchases of furniture, clothes, gym memberships, cell phones, plane tickets, and Manhattan-priced lunches and dinners. It is a simple matter to criticize Julia for her profligate spending—and, indeed, she is the first to blame herself. With the thousands she owes on her credit cards, she knows she could have bought that house she's always wanted in the Dominican Republic. "I have to start to think with my head," she mutters to herself.

Understanding her spending habits requires an appraisal of those earlier periods of her life when, quite simply, she had nothing. Julia was born in a small town in the Dominican Republic known for little but its tobacco crops. When she was a teenager, her parents separated. Her mother moved to Santiago, but Julia decided to stay in town to finish high school and moved in with the family of a friend, Magdalena. Before, when things were falling apart at home, Julia had often retreated there during the weekends, cleaning around the house in exchange for meals. She and Magdalena were close, and the family treated her as one of their own. When the girls went out dancing, she wore Magdalena's clothes.

Then Julia met Vicente Coronado, Eduardo's father. The two fell in love. She was sixteen; he was a stylish man with flashy clothes and wads of cash, a lover and a gambler. Soon after Julia graduated from high school in 1985, she and Vicente married in a fit of passion. But with time Julia learned that Vicente had little passion—for getting ahead. He did not like to work. He had no aspirations. "He was an animal," Julia says of her ex-husband. "He never talked. He talked when he was drunk." In time, Vicente developed a drug habit and a violent streak. He would take off on Thursday nights and come back days later. After two years of marriage, Julia left him.

Vicente moved to New York. Still enamored of his ex-wife, he offered to set Julia up with a U.S. visa. Vicente helped her with all the paperwork but balked when it came to paying for her ticket. Julia borrowed the money and caught a flight to New York.

The first job that Julia found was in a factory in Brooklyn, shearing stacks of linen to feed the insatiable appetite of New York's garment industry. She worked alongside other immigrant women, under a Dominican boss. She was never paid on time. Julia's boss did not have much cash flow—or so she said—and so Julia received her paycheck when, and if, her boss had the money. Julia didn't complain.

One day Julia sliced off the tip of her finger on the cutting machine. She bandaged the wound and went home. She didn't bother going to the hospital, didn't bother getting stitches. The next day she showed up at work. She didn't complain.

"Look at the way it is," she says, holding up her disfigured finger—which has a patch of scar tissue on top—for an observer's macabre appreciation. "Look at both fingers and see the difference." Julia could have sued, but back then she didn't know that. She kept her mouth shut. "I am really ignorant." Julia sighs.

She kept working, but not for long. One week of missed pay turned into two. Two turned into three. By then, even Julia had had enough. Three months into the job, she quit.

For a few weeks, she didn't have a job. "I was going nuts," she remembers. Julia would wander the streets near her apartment, looking for jobs along Brooklyn's Knickerbocker Avenue. Someone told her that a Jewish-owned factory was hiring. For six mornings, she waited at the factory entrance with other job seekers for the supervisor to arrive. For six mornings, he waved her off, telling her that there were no positions available. Finally, Julia decided to duck the crowd and approach the supervisor alone. She walked onto the floor where workers were sticking price tags on pocketbooks and handbags. "Have you ever done this before?" the supervisor asked. "Never," Julia confessed. She got the job.

Her luck continued. In one part of the factory, the workers—many of them Chinese—stuffed bags with paper nonstop until their hands were riddled with cuts. But for her assignment, Julia had only to take the handbag out of the plastic wrapping and attach the printed ticket. "I became really fast," she says. Even on a meager $3.35-an-hour payroll, Julia was not content to do just enough to get by. If she was going to be a bag handler, she was going to be the *best* bag handler. Julia was eventually promoted to a supervisory position—without extra pay—and was put in charge of the other women working the assembly-line table.

By now Julia had a new boyfriend, who found her a weekend job at a motel on Governors Island. Monday through Friday Julia worked at the factory, and Saturday and Sunday she did housekeeping at the motel. The pay was better there—$7.25 an hour—and in a short time Julia was managing the laundry work, watching over the other women as they hauled blankets into the washing machines and took them back, clean, to the rooms. On the job, Julia practiced her English. With the first paycheck she got at the motel, she sent her mother $400 to buy a new refrigerator.

It was just a refrigerator, but it was a sign of what Julia could accomplish. If anyone could succeed in America, it was Julia. She had plowed her way through a minefield of low-wage, dead-end work. She projected confidence at every workplace, and people—the motel manager, the factory foreman—noticed her. In Julia's case, low wages did not mean low potential.

Unfortunately, Julia was still having difficulty washing off the last smudges of her impoverished past. The prodigal ex-husband had returned. Having learned about Julia's new beau, Vicente abruptly ditched the woman he was seeing and came looking for her. In spite of all the abuse, broken promises, and heartbreak, Julia still had feelings for him. The two reconciled and moved to Washington Heights, into an apartment across the street from where she lives now.

Soon Julia was pregnant. Vicente forbade her to continue working at the motel. On the weekend mornings he would romance her and plead with her to stay home with him. Julia stopped going to work. "I was stupid or in love with him," she says. After a while, her boss gave up on her. "It was wrong," Julia says. "You are not supposed to quit like that."

In any case, Julia had other things to worry about. Her belly started to swell, and Julia knew she would soon have to give up her factory job, too. Her boss was sympathetic. He said good-bye to her with a $700 check. Her coworkers gave her a lavish baby shower, with enough presents to fill a van—bedspreads, a coat, a baby stroller, a cradle, and even a gold ring for the child. It was their way of saying thanks for her two years at the factory.

By the time Eduardo was born, Julia's marriage was disintegrating again. Vicente was selling and using drugs, but he refused to contribute to the household. Julia paid all the bills. Vicente would sink into deep depressions and at times lash out. Once, Vicente pulled a knife on her and slashed her. Julia never called the police. She loved Vicente, she says.

Then Thanksgiving came. Julia had cooked a huge meal, and Vicente's entire family was there. An argument broke out, and Vicente went wild. He kicked everyone out of the apartment, including Julia. She took refuge at a friend's place for several days. Vicente sent her a message that he was changing the locks. Julia was furious. That was *her* apartment; *she* was the one who paid all the bills. She marched over to the apartment and told Vicente to leave. The two got into a vicious fight. Vicente took a baseball bat and started whacking, smashing, and shattering his way through the apartment. Vicente slugged her; Julia hit and bit him back. Eventually, Julia called the police, and that was it for Vicente Coronado.

As she nursed her now-fatherless newborn, Julia tried to figure out how to make do without a husband and without a job. "I had no money,

not even for Pampers," she says. She was receiving half of her factory
salary—$66 a week—in unemployment, but it wasn't enough. Desper-
ate, Julia applied for welfare. The government started sending cash and
food stamps and paying for her rent. It was not what she expected when
she came to America, but she didn't have a choice. Welfare, she pointed
out, took the place of her derelict spouse. "You feel stable, like you had
a husband by your side," she says.

Eventually, her half-brother Alejandro found her a job at a restaurant on Dyckman Street. It was a tiny diner—just a counter and two or
three tables—and the work conditions were hellish. "Tell me about
those Sundays," she says, "when I was all by myself, and I had to wash
the sink—the steam!—and all the spoons. Wash and brush everything.
Oh, Jesus, I had no nails, and I was cut and burned everywhere on the
arms. It is an animal's job in the restaurant." Her pay was just $100
a week, $65 of which went to a coworker who watched over Eduardo
when Julia worked. But Julia, with her winning smile and coquettish
charms, soon befriended a number of customers. One regular, the
owner of a bank, would drink a cup of coffee and leave a twenty-dollar
bill. Another would have a $3.25 lunch and leave another twenty. "I was
not doing badly," Julia admits.

Julia met her second husband, César Reyes, at the restaurant. Three
months after they met, César moved in. He was the complete opposite
of Vicente. If Vicente was wild and unbalanced, César was reserved and
stable—perhaps too stable—a serious man who worked long hours at a
shipping company and didn't like to go out at night.

César soon persuaded Julia to leave her job at the restaurant. In
truth, Julia didn't need much urging. She was tired of all the years of
menial labor at restaurants and hotels and factories. "They disrespect
you, and you have to give them your life," she says. "I made my decision
not to work in a factory anymore. I said, 'I am going to college. I am
going to learn English. I am changing my life.'" In 1994 Julia started
attending Bronx Community College, majoring in computer program-
ming. Most of the one hundred or so credits she took were for remedial
classes. While in college, Julia also worked a variety of work-study jobs
—from telephone operator to receptionist to computer lab assistant—
which gave her a chance to improve her English and develop some office
skills.

César helped out, but Julia turned to welfare to support herself and her young son. It was good to know that there was always another check in the mail to blunt the edge of her monthly bills. And Julia knew she needed to avail herself of that help now. The government's requirements were getting stricter. Someday there would no longer be welfare to rely on, and when that day came Julia would need the skills to land a job that paid a living wage. "Let me go to college now that my kid is small," she told herself, "and they are going to pay and help me."

There was a price to be paid for staying on the dole, though. "People who depend on welfare live with a tension that is horrible," Julia says. "God forbid I will ever feel that again. You are always thinking that somebody will come to inspect your house, that they are going to call you for an appointment, that they might close your case.... I used to live waiting for a letter calling me for an appointment, who knows for what. And I was not alone. That is something all women on welfare feel. Living in agony."

Julia wanted an end to the uncertainty, the constant feeling that she was just barely treading water. But how was she going to do better? The money she had saved from her previous jobs was all gone. She didn't even have $5 for gas to find a job. And without a job, how was she ever going to leave welfare?

"Well, the most I can pay you is $5.15. You can't do much."

Julia is incensed. She has been called in for an interview at the employment agency, and the interviewer is telling her, bluntly, that she has no prospects. It's not that she even wants to be here. An agency like this one will charge her for any job they do get her—if she gets paid $10, they will take $2 or $3 for themselves. Parasites. But Julia is desperate.

"Next time don't go to an interview so badly dressed," the interviewer goes on. "And especially don't wear earrings." He is referring to the small second piercing in one of Julia's ears.

Cabrón! Jerks like him always seem to materialize when you're desperate for a job. But Julia isn't going to let him get to her. She and her friend Milagra have spent the last several weeks looking for jobs. Both are unemployed, and both are determined to find something quickly. They've bought a fax machine on credit. They've picked up the newspaper every day—the *New York Times*, the *New York Daily News*, and the

New York Post. They've scoured the Yellow Pages for employment agencies. They've swapped clothes for job interviews. "Lend me a skirt. Here, wear the blouse today, and I'll wear it tomorrow to go to an interview."

Julia is ready to swing at any pitch. Three hundred dollars for a six-day week, twelve hours a day? Sure, hook me up. Only later does she realize the job—working as an English-speaking cashier in a store in Queens—involves a brutal commute. In the end she declines.

Milagra has a stroke of luck when she finds a two-week job at a restaurant. One day a Jewish man walks in, sits down for a meal, and strikes up a conversation. As it turns out, he is a doctor at a Midtown health clinic. He leaves Milagra his business card. "We are recruiting now," he tells her.

The next day, at 8:30 A.M., Milagra and Julia fax in their résumés. Then they walk over to the gym to exercise. Julia, self-conscious about her weight, has taken up exercise with her usual can-do spirit, working murderously hard to keep her waist out of a size large. When Julia comes home, the doctor has already called twice. "Could you come on Friday, so we can learn more about you?" he tells them on the phone.

Julia is interviewed at 11:15, and Milagra at noon. The meetings are informal, and Julia—never one to let a conversation lag—soon is regaling the doctor with stories of her life in Santo Domingo.

The doctor sends the two women over to the clinic on Fifth Avenue. It is a multiservice therapeutic clinic specializing in illnesses of the brain. Friday happens to be one of their busiest days because the psychiatrist is there, seeing scores of patients over the course of the day. The space is your generic office setting—blue carpets, beige walls—but Julia loves it. Here people come to work dressed elegantly, in the distinctive uniforms of urban professionals, their only tools being the lattes they hold, casually, in their ungloved hands. "Oh my God, this is a nice place!" Julia tells her friend. "I hope I'll be hired to work here."

Tuesday morning, the two drive out to Midtown for a second round of interviews. But the car sputters to a halt on First Avenue. They have to leave it behind and rush over to the clinic. By then, they are late. Milagra is too ashamed to be interviewed. She refuses to go inside, and so Julia walks in, sheepishly, by herself.

They give her a spelling test—seventy-five words—and she has to

circle the ones that are right. Then there is a test on computer fundamentals. It turns out to be fairly easy; Julia used to work in a computer
lab, so she isn't afraid of an Excel spreadsheet. But then comes the writing test. She is supposed to write a memo to an employee who comes to
work excessively late (did they grasp the irony?). Julia hates writing. It
used to take her days to pen a short paper in college; how is she going to
do a professional memo? She tells the supervisor that she gets nervous
when others are watching. When the woman leaves, Julia starts to pray.

She passes the tests. Julia is called back for a third interview, and
then a fourth, this time with the office manager, Jennifer. Immediately
the two women click. "She asked me to write something on the computer," Julia says. "She made me feel nice." But Julia goes home still
wondering whether she got the job.

They told her to call the next week. Wednesday rolls around. Her
mother insists that Julia pick up the phone. She needs to know the out-
come, once and for all. Julia calls, and Jennifer is on the line. "It's good
that you called," she says. "I have good news for you."

"Yes?"

"You are the one that we selected."

"Are you sure I am the person?" Julia cannot believe it. A kid from
the Dominican countryside—a factory girl—a mom with two kids on
welfare—*she* is going to be working at a first-rate Manhattan health
clinic?

"Yes, you are the person that we selected for the position."

Julia leaps in the air. "Oh my God!"

The windfall of a white-collar job cannot have come at a more op-
portune time for Julia. A month later, the city calls her back to the welfare office—now renamed a "job center"—to tell her, like the hundreds
of thousands of other welfare recipients now running down their newly
established limits on benefits, that she needs to start looking for work.
Julia walks in holding a letter from her new boss.

"I am sorry," she tells her caseworker, relishing the words. "I am
working."

With rising income come rising aspirations for the good life. Often, the
expectations mount before the pocketbook can handle them properly.
Deferred gratification has been the rule as long as Julia can remember:

no clothes for the dance club, no cable for the Spanish-language shows, no exterminator for the cockroaches, no health insurance for the kids. Finally, she has grasped on—if somewhat tentatively—to a token of middle-class status. And she intends to cash it in.

After less than a year at the clinic, Julia has been promoted three times. Her new title is scheduling coordinator, and she has made herself into the administrative linchpin of the office. All the people who call in (half of them are Spanish speakers) go through her; Julia listens to their requests, certifies them to see a specialist, and arranges their appointments. When Julia first arrived at the office, the appointments were logged by hand—people would scrawl in new appointments, scratch out cancellations, and no one had a clue as to what was going on. Julia familiarized herself with a new computer program and single-handedly transformed the way the clinic did its scheduling.

Now Julia is making an annual salary of $29,000—$8,000 more than when she started. She learned just how indispensable she had become when she took a weeklong vacation. Without her in the manager's seat, the delicate order at the medical office fell apart: no one knew who was coming in or who was seeing whom. When she returned, her boss asked for a rundown of how many patients each clinician had seen. He was shocked by what he was told. When Julia was there, they each saw five or six new patients a day; but when she was gone, the load dropped to one or two a day. That didn't even cover their salaries. Julia got an immediate, retroactive raise.

More important than Julia's leap in salary, though, is her burgeoning self-esteem. "I used to think that a job that paid $7 was a good job," Julia says. "Not now. I feel I am a person with skills. My English has improved a lot, and I have learned a lot about the job, too. I feel I can do better." In fact, her rapid progress in the last year has only made her hungrier for further success—and less satisfied with her current pay. "Look, my salary is not a great thing either. Coming out from welfare, of course, it's good to start. But it's not a great thing. I have two children and my mother lives with me. So they have to consider that we are four people on a budget of $20,000-something."[2]

Julia has started to think she could do better in the romance department, too. Good-natured, kindhearted César—the man who supported

Julia when she was struggling to get through school, who once waited five hours for her on campus because Julia had forgotten to tell him she needed to take an exam—is suddenly not good enough. Yes, he is a good provider and works hard, but he is plodding and dull, a man with no personality or aspirations. Julia is an up-and-coming professional; she doesn't want to be stuck with a husband who lacks her ambition. César refuses to take classes to improve his English. He makes Julia pay the bills. He has been at the same job for ten years. When Julia comes home late from school, he gets upset. All they do is stay home and watch TV; there is no lovemaking, and no love. "I have not been lucky," Julia says. "The husbands whom I have had have been ignorant. They have not been what I want."

Julia tells her husband that they need to separate. César sleeps in the children's room for a while, then moves out. Sandra is not amused. Julia may find César boring, but her mother likes him. Here is a calm, honest, hardworking man, and what does Julia do? Leave him. She will regret it, Sandra says. Plus, how is she going to keep the household financially afloat without his salary? Julia should think of her mother.

Julia tries to assuage Sandra's fears. No matter what happens, you will not starve, she assures her mother. "I will never stop loving and caring for you. Everything I do for you, I will continue to do because you are my mother. It doesn't matter what type of man I am living with." Privately, though, Julia concedes that Sandra does have a point. César has just gone off to Puerto Rico for a vacation, and already Julia is missing his income dearly.

The truth is, Julia has accrued some major debts. Her purse has become loaded down with plastic, a veritable department store directory: Sears, Macy's, J. C. Penney. "Every time I saw something, I wanted it," Julia says. "I went to this place and bought blouses. I went to the Gap and bought clothes.... I bought so many clothes that I could not fit them in the closet." The bulk of Julia's debt, however, comes from buying furniture—enough to fill up every corner of the apartment. Bed? $1,000. Nightstand? $800. Floor tiles? $1,000.

Having grown up in poverty in the Dominican Republic, Julia has long wanted to live a respectable middle-class life—a health club subscription, a cell phone, Chinese food or pizza during her lunch hour—

and her new station in life has kindled that desire. Her first real buying spree, in fact, took place when she was attending college—she used her credit cards and her Pell grant to pay for a $2,000 sofa. Like many middle-class Americans, Julia wants a nice home that she won't be ashamed of showing to her friends and family. When she started her job at the clinic, she decided she needed a new floor for her apartment. She bought fine tiles at $58.50 per box for the living room and kitchen, decent ones at $45 per box for the kids' room, and discount ones at $7 per box for her own room—apparently following the rule that if the guests can't see it, why bother?

Julia wants the trappings of the average American's life, but her $29,000-a-year salary is not up to these demands. "How did I get in so much trouble? What did I do with the money?" Julia now asks herself. She spends as much as $300 on *minimum* credit-card payments every month. She admits that she doesn't think through her purchases. She goes into a gym and pays a trainer $10 for a workout. She buys a ticket for Santo Domingo. "It was like I didn't care if I spent because I knew I would have [money] to pay it with," she says. "I have fun. I go and get $50, $100 [out of my bank account], and I spend it. I don't think about it much."

After manning the phones and coddling M.D. egos for hours on end, Julia could use some fun. She's grateful for her job—she works hard and likes her coworkers—but she doesn't think of it as a calling. It's not surprising, then, that a good portion of her credit card bills comes from her frequent trips to the Dominican Republic. She charges $300 tickets for her two children to visit their family homeland. She shells out $2,000 for island hotel rooms for her mother, herself, and her new Dominican boyfriend. Santo Domingo spells relaxation, family peace, fun on the beach—everything that she doesn't have in her day-to-day life in Washington Heights.

What drives wanton credit card spending among Missing Class workers like Julia is a desire to lay claim to the material comforts that they have wanted but were not in a position to obtain, until now.[3] For these workers, running up card balances is not so much about acquiring things as seeking what everyone else seems to have: middle-class surfeit —on credit. Premium leather couches, state-of-the-art stereo systems with stadium-size speakers, stonewashed designer jeans, flat-screen plasma TVs that hang on the walls like fine paintings. This is the bounty that life has to offer. This is what they look forward to coming home to during those endless hours of office drudgery.

Cases of overspending as extreme as Julia's are, of course, the exception. Studies have shown that there is just as much frivolous spending today as there was a generation ago, and such excess is not primarily to blame for the recent rash in the nation's bankruptcy filings.[4] That said, the unique position that the Missing Class occupies—above poverty but below stability—puts it at special risk for the occasional bout of recklessness that can knock its families back down the fiscal ladder.

THE GERVAIS FAMILY

For Rita Gervais, a taste for the good life was not just a matter of long-deferred, pent-up desires. It was a job requirement. She was working at a bank on Wall Street, raking in about $60,000 a year and dressing the part. Being a professional meant no more shopping at Wal-Mart, a different pair of shoes for every suit, and power lunches followed by posh dinners. It probably didn't help that her husband, Henri, "spoiled" her by taking her out to upscale restaurants, the kind that wouldn't bother with the ninety-nine cents tacked onto each entrée price. She got so used to the treatment that when she went out to dine alone with her daughter, she had a habit of just walking out—until she sheepishly remembered the unpaid bill waiting for her on the table.

The pent-up desires, of course, were also there. The daughter of an alcoholic, absent Dominican father and a Puerto Rican seamstress mother, Rita lived a childhood of migration, shuttling back and forth with her five siblings between the Dominican Republic, Puerto Rico, New York, and the U.S. Virgin Islands, where a stepfather eventually lured her mother. On the island of Saint Thomas, where Rita spent her formative years, going to "town" meant walking over to the island's main drag, with its laughable strip of commerce that hurricanes bulldozed on a seasonal basis. After Rita's mother, Carmen, left the stepdad for good, the family's Puerto Rican identity meant safe passage to the American mainland. Once here, Carmen worked in a factory. Rita worked her way up to college. Her stay in Saint Thomas, an English-speaking former colony, had given her a proficiency with English that served her well in the business world. It had also given her a slight distance from Hispanic culture; she no longer wanted to live in a neighborhood that was completely Spanish-speaking. Though born in the Dominican Republic, she was raised more like a Puerto Rican and had "American" ways of thinking, speaking, and shopping.

Rita never earned her bachelor's degree, but she was fortunate enough to land a job at a bank with the help of Henri, then just a friend. Henri was also from Saint Thomas, but of French extraction, a well-groomed, cocksure older man who was making good money at the bank and sported the trappings of success: fine clothes and three failed marriages. In fact, Henri was married when they met but didn't disclose that detail to Rita. Early in their relationship, the two went to a club and ran into a short Puerto Rican woman who said she was Henri's wife. "Listen, I'm going home," Rita told Henri. She walked out, with Henri right behind her. He was furious. "Don't you dare do that again," he said. "You're with me . . . *casado pero separado*" (married but separated).

Rita stayed with her new lover. As if three failed marriages had not been a sufficient hint, Rita soon found out that only one member of the duo gave any thought to their future. Henri, the middle son in a gaggle of children, didn't want to have any kids. Rita told him that the two should look into buying a house, but Henri was not interested. He was content with his epicurean lifestyle. What was the point of settling down, once again?

Finally, Henri consented to having a child with Rita. When Tracy was born, the reluctant father became a doting dad. Rita left her job and took care of Tracy full-time. It was at this time that Rita learned that Henri, the man she had come to know as excessively secretive—in her words, "slippery"—had fathered another child whom he had never bothered to mention. One argument led to another, and by the time Tracy was three, the couple had separated.

Rita, the stay-at-home mom, did not see herself as defenseless. She wasn't willing to go on the dole, but she wasn't willing to go back to the bank, either. She wanted to stay at home with her daughter. Instead, Rita decided to convert her domesticity into liquidity: she started a day-care business. Even her friends were skeptical. "Everybody's looking at me like, 'Oh, she's nuts,' " Rita says. "All of a sudden it's open, and I got all these kids, and nobody believed it, you know, including my neighbor. . . . She was like, 'Oh, yeah, sure, she can't do that. That's too hard, you know.' "

But Rita did it. "Sometimes," she says, "I make it look like it's easy."

The bills—and the credit cards—started accumulating soon after. Henri and her mother had always criticized Rita about her profligate spending. Now that she no longer had a husband's safety net under her, those habits veered out of control. She worked her way up to seven credit cards, including two American Express cards (one for the business, one for herself), and several thousand dollars of debt. It was so easy. She kept getting offers in the mail for more credit cards, more painless purchases. Even magazine subscriptions were getting thrown at her, tokens of gratitude from her thoughtful creditors. "The credit cards, they're so good they give you like a chance to sample them, so I'm getting them left and right," she says. But now Rita was actually maxing out her cards. She would go into stores, pile up all her clothes on the counter, and then hear the beep of the credit card machine as the system announced her delinquent status to the whole world.

Thankfully, Rita no longer had an excuse to splurge on designer clothing. She still had her Wall Street tastes for trendy attire, but having transformed herself into a day-care provider, Rita was acquiring a new look—something above the artless drudgery of a babysitter and approximating the consoling, beatific appearance of a kindergarten teacher. Wide-framed eyeglasses, an unassuming pair of looped gold earrings, bangs of dark brown hair swept across her forehead—this new Rita could easily muster a gentle expression, from the pleasant laugh lines running down her cheeks to the tip of her slightly pudgy chin.

Rita saw herself as a small business woman, and she put all her white-collar skills to work, filing paperwork with the government agencies that paid the day-care fees for her low-income clients and negotiating with the provider networks that gave her subsidies for the meals she cooked for her children. She had the talent and expertise, but the problem, as always, was labor; she needed more of it. Rita's mother helped her with the day care, but other than that there was no one to turn to. When 5 P.M. rolled around, after a day spent running after children and diapering them, correcting their misspellings and cleaning up their accidents, Rita was spent. But then it was time to start cleaning the house, cooking dinner, and persuading Tracy to crack open her textbooks.

When she didn't have many children, Rita was less stressed out during the day but more anxious at night, as she looked over her bills and despaired. Before, she had managed to put away $100 every week for a new house, when and if it became a reality. At the moment, however, Rita was saving nothing.

Rita had been doing better financially than all of her siblings, and now she felt too embarrassed to ask them for help. Her brother Esteban, the juvenile delinquent whom Grandma used to spank for getting into fights, now had a respectable life as a teacher, but he had moved back to Saint Thomas. Her sister Susana lived nearby but could hardly make ends meet for her own family.

Then there was Ken. Of all her siblings, Ken was the one she most admired, the one she aspired to emulate, with his sunny California style and sharp New York wit. He was her little brother, the clown of the family, a fashion model who sported flashy clothes but whose razor-sharp intellect could savage anyone in an argument. When he lived in California, the two had chatted over the phone regularly, trading jokes and advice. He was a mentor to her at a time when she needed one. "When I spoke to him on the phone and I needed help with anything— if I was writing a paper or memo for my job—I would ask him, 'Hey, how does that sound?'" she says. "He would fix it. He was very smart." He was also gay, at a time of even less tolerance for this kind of identity, which was partly the reason Ken moved west—to escape his family's shame. Rita stood up for her kid brother. "I feel that he was born this way," Rita muses. "He was just that way. I don't know how people can say, 'No, you're not born [gay].'"

For all his good looks and charm, for all his intelligence and sophistication, fortune was not kind to Ken. He contracted AIDS. Today's lifesaving treatments had not yet been developed, and in just one year Ken wasted away. Rita was crushed. She remembers celebrating Tracy's first birthday with tears in her eyes. "He could die any minute, and I was there partying." Henri didn't want their infant daughter to be around her brother, and they argued about that.

Ken died a month after Tracy's birthday. The family buried him across the river, in Fort Lee. The beautiful clothes and shoes went to her brother-in-law, who could fit in them. Rita kept one memento: Ken's last message to her on her voice mail. "I could hear his voice," she says, "whenever he used to call me."

THE CORONADO FAMILY

It's a Tuesday night in the middle of January, and Julia walks the frigid New York streets merrily, fantasizing about her trip on Friday to the Dominican Republic. She is delirious with the thought of seeing her new boyfriend, Juan. They've been talking on the phone for half an hour every day, which has cost Julia about $35 a week in long-distance charges. Julia—whose debt on her Visa Platinum card alone tops $6,000—tells herself she'll start buying cheaper weekly phone cards. For the moment, though, she needs to prepare herself for some fun in the sun. She walks into a popular women's clothing store on 181st Street. Here, cost-conscious Dominican women can find cheap blouses for $10 and under while hunting for bigger-ticket leather coats and cocktail dresses.

Julia spends an hour stalking the aisles and popping in and out of the fitting room. She's brought along a friend to make sure she doesn't spend too much money. That's a tough task, as it turns out. In a matter of minutes, Julia has already picked out two metallic-colored pairs of jeans, one gray and the other blue. She descends on the bathing-suit section and spots a blue bikini—what a sight that would be on the pearly white beach! The sales clerk saunters by and eyes her figure. Why doesn't she try a large size, he asks. "Don't insult me," Julia snaps back, her laughing eyes betraying the joke.

In the end, Julia settles on the large bikinis—there aren't any medium ones. She adds a few more items to her pile: a shining pair of black slacks, leopard-spotted pants, another pair of jeans, and a few backless short tops.

With her friend and the sales clerk in tow, Julia starts going through the clothes to see how they fit. The sales clerk sounds like a perky answering machine, repeating over and over that the jeans fit Julia well, the top fits her well, the leopard-spotted pants fit her well, and so on. One pair of pants actually do complement her legs—hardened from gym squats—but they cost $40. Julia, remembering her next credit card payment, demurs. She spends a total of $100 on several blouses, a pair of jeans, a pair of sandals, and the leopard-spotted pants. An "admirer," Julia confides, is helping to pay for today's shopping, so she can indulge herself to some extent.

Julia and her friend leave and walk toward Saint Nicholas Avenue. The stores beckon, but this time Julia resists unsheathing another shopping bag. On the way back to the bus, however, she can't resist dropping by a new clothing store near Fort Washington Avenue. It has a pair of shiny gray pants that fit Julia well—show off those hamstrings!—and cost about $25.

As she's paying for her latest acquisition, Julia reminds herself that before her last trip to the Dominican Republic, in September, she also went on a shopping spree. Some of the clothes she bought then she ended up not wearing, and she has never worn them since. It'll be the same for this trip—but she's not alone on that score. What do most people do before they go on vacation? Buy things.

On the walk back to her friend's place, Julia's friend teases her about the person who offered to bankroll her shopping. Was it the owner of the store? Her new boyfriend? No, Julia says, it's another suitor. She had started working at a restaurant to make extra cash on the weekends. A regular there, a Mexican man, wants her company and is willing to pay for it. She loves Juan, but there is no money in that love, Julia says. She has to get money from somewhere. She has kids. She has bills.

She also has a flabby stomach. Did you see that bikini on me? she asks her friend. A size large, and still some of her stomach was hanging over the edge of the bikini bottom. It was a tight elastic band, her friend reminds her—anyone's stomach would be sticking out. When she gets home, Julia eats slowly, picking away unhappily at her lettuce, tuna, and chicken. If only her stomach could shrink before her trip on Friday. Six months of going to the gym, and this is all she has to show for it?

Later, she eyes herself in the mirror, poking at her pudgy parts. She has no other choice, she declares, but to get liposuction on her stomach.

Every day legions of plastic-windowed envelopes touting a utopia of limitless spending on credit ("Preapproved! Zero APR for the first six months!") wind their way into mailboxes across the country. Four out of ten Americans say they are solicited to apply for a new credit card every week. Awash as we are in offers, it may be difficult to appreciate that at one time credit cards were the playthings of the wealthy, carried by elite jet-setters, accepted solely by the most upscale of establishments. It was only in the early eighties that bankers began to foist cards on middle-class consumers. Later in that decade, they turned to college students and senior citizens; by the early nineties, even the working poor and the recently bankrupt were being wooed with zero-interest offers.[5]

The Missing Class has turned out to be especially fertile soil for the card companies to sow. Cash-starved households tend to do a worse job of paying off their credit card balances, which means they're a constant revenue stream for their creditors. "Credit card issuers make their profits from lending lots of money and charging hefty fees to families that are financially strapped," write Elizabeth Warren and Amelia Warren Tyagi.

> More than 75 percent of credit card profits come from people who make those low, minimum monthly payments. And who makes minimum monthly payments at 26 percent interest? Who pays late fees, overbalance charges, and cash advance premiums? Families that can barely make ends meet, households precariously balanced between financial survival and complete collapse. These are the families that are singled out by the lending industry, barraged with special offers, personalized advertisements, and home phone calls, all with one objective in mind: get them to borrow more money.[6]

Low-income households may be vulnerable to this lure, but Missing Class families are about twice as likely as the poor to own a credit card in the first place. In fact, if you split America's households into five groups ordered by income, it's clear that families in the second quintile—those Missing Class households wedged between the poverty of the first quintile and the middling incomes of the third—have seen their rates of card ownership rise at a faster clip than all other income groups.[7] Six out of 10 of these families owned at least one credit card in

2001, a jump from just 1 out of 10 in 1970.[8] Clearly, the Missing Class is a cash cow for the credit-card companies.

Part of the reason this segment of the market is so profitable is that many near-poor households simply lack the financial acumen to deftly juggle and dispose of their debt.[9] Julia is a case in point. Rather than using what's left over from her paycheck to pay off those monstrous balances, she decides to pay the minimum and sink the extra cash into a savings plan operated by Dominicans in her neighborhood. In one of these *sociedades*, or rotating credit associations, Julia and nine other Dominicans committed themselves to pooling $150 a week, with the arrangement that each will take the weekly pot—$1,500—when his or her turn comes. For immigrant families, *sociedades* are a reliable way to save money for big expenditures, imposing fiscal discipline until each individual is handed that lump sum. But in Julia's case, it just doesn't make sense. She is already strapped for cash, and the interest on her credit card balances is eating away at any new income.[10]

Julia isn't sure what she needs to do. She has seventeen credit cards—4 MasterCards (two of them platinum), 3 Visas, 8 store cards, 1 American Express, and 1 Discover. "I do not know if closing the credit line on all those credit cards will affect my credit," she tells a friend. "What is better, to keep the line of credit open or close it down?" She needlessly forks over $10 a month for a "credit guard"—paying a company to check her records for any change in her credit line. Even when Julia realizes she needs to get rid of all her cards, she finds it harder than she anticipated it. She cancels them, but then the companies call back, cajoling her to stay aboard.

The credit card companies have Julia in their crosshairs. She gets offers for new cards all the time and can't resist the temptation. She shops at Sears and Macy's, and they give her cards. She buys jewelry, and the store offers her another card. "When one does not have means" to pay for these things, Julia says, where else is there to turn? Julia doesn't want to depend on a friend or family member. "I'm going to do this on my own," she tells herself. Credit cards are such a marvelously convenient way to grab hold of the extra cash. Until the statement comes.

Eduardo and Miguel race to the apartment door. A family friend has arrived, and Miguel is already yammering away—he speaks more clearly these days, the friend notices, as she hoists him up into her arms. Sandra, Julia's mother, greets the visitor at the door and leads her into the living room, where they start chatting about the family's fresh suntans from a recent trip to the Dominican Republic. Julia, however, is nowhere to be seen.

As it turns out, she's hiding out in her room. Sprawled on the bed, she gazes mutely at the wildlife documentary on TV, a sour expression fixed on her face. Is she all right? Does she have a cold? Yes, Julia replies, but it isn't just that. The sorry state of her finances has made her depressed.

Energetic and gregarious Julia is not the type to have bouts of depression—as she herself makes clear. Yes, once in a while she feels blue, but it is normally a very temporary thing. But a deep gloom seems to linger over Julia now. "I have fallen behind in my credit card payments," she tells her friend. "I have been completely out of control. That depresses me." After months of shooing the worries out of her mind, suddenly Julia finds herself alone on the precipice, ringed in by mountains of credit card debt and rivers of unpaid bills.

She needs to cut her household expenses drastically. Julia earns $843 after taxes every two weeks. One of those paychecks has to cover the rent and transportation to and from work. The other has to cover household bills—utilities, telephone, child care (that is, her mom), and the mounds of food that Eduardo and Miguel devour. What she has decided to do, she says, is work out a new arrangement with her mom: Julia and Sandra will now split the expense of the telephone and electricity for the apartment. It will be an especially delicate negotiation because Sandra is no ordinary household dependent; she is the hired help who allows Julia to work all day with the knowledge that her children will be cared for.

As they struggle to juggle household expenses and pay down debts, Missing Class workers like Julia often find themselves navigating the family tensions that come with expecting—requiring—family members to contribute substantially to the common good. Middle-class families with stable finances enjoy the luxury of autonomous nuclear families and loving, unconditional relationships free of the taint of monetization, but those of lesser means have to beg, cajole, and guilt-trip their family members into sharing some of the burden.[11] They cannot outsource their needs to professionals—child-care workers, house-keepers—and so they rely on kin. And this is the root of the conflict between Julia and her mother. The two love each other, but neither denies the power that she wields: the child care that allows Julia to focus on her career and her personal life, the steady employment and housing that allow Sandra to stake out a new life in New York. Julia is frustrated that Sandra uses her low-cost child care as a threat to exert control over her daughter's life. Sandra, in turn, is fed up with Julia for thinking only of herself. When she comes home from work or play, Sandra notes, Julia eats and forks over some cash but won't "lift a finger" to help her mother, even when she is on vacation. And so Sandra is stuck with all the housework: not just caring for Eduardo and Miguel, but cooking, cleaning, washing, paying the household bills—in other words, playing the role of housewife to a couch potato husband.

But these days Julia has other things to worry about than pleasing her mom. She desperately needs to pay off her debt. "My error was not to get rid of the credit cards before this," she explains, staring down at her hands, "before all the responsibilities caught up to me. Now that I am thinking about it, it is too late. [I should have] taken $300 or $500 from my paycheck to pay credit cards. Or I could have gotten into a big *sociedad*." Until she sorts out this financial mess, all her plans are on hold. She can't go back to college, as she had hoped, to get her bachelor's degree. She can't put down a down payment on the house she dreams of. "Right now, with the financial problems I have, I have no money to do anything."

"I need to get rid of them," she says of her cards. "Pay them off. Not use them."

Two months later, Julia has brought some serious discipline to her pocketbook. She has sharply curtailed her spending, She has canceled all of her credit cards except for a single Visa. It has been a struggle to the very end—she is attached to those cards, and for a while insists that she needs two Visa cards, even if they perform exactly the same function—but Julia's inner voice of reason prevails.

Her efforts have borne a quick harvest. In September she had $9,300 in credit card debt and $800 in unpaid rent hanging over her head. By the end of November, she has paid off the rent. She has eliminated the balances on two of her cards. And she has slashed $2,000 off the $7,000 balance on her Visa Platinum, which holds the largest amount of debt. (Her saving grace, of course, has been the $5,000 loan she took out from Emigrant Bank, which charges her a fixed rate of $150 every month. The debt has moved from one hand to another, but with a lower rate of interest, it is a hand better suited for the holding.) Finally, her bills are manageable. Now, if only her brother will pay back the $1,000 he owes her. . . .

Things have gone so well that Julia—perhaps dismayed at the prospect of a safe, secure, and soporific future—has decided to plunk down a few hundred dollars into a less-than-certain business venture. Her boyfriend, Juan, has been in touch with a tobacco grower in the Dominican Republic who is willing to lend sixty acres of his land for nine months. While the land lays fallow, they can grow whatever they like—green peppers, melons, watermelons—and sell the produce at a profit. Juan and his father are contributing the labor and materials; Julia is paying the rent. She has already sent Juan $680—her mother, of course, knows nothing of the transaction—and the partners expect to make almost $5,000 in profit by the end of the season.

Meanwhile, Julia is barely saving up for her retirement. Out of her paycheck, she contributes 5 percent to her 401(k) plan. She wants to reduce that amount to 3 percent or lower; $790 every other week is just too little to live on, she insists. "It's a very good idea because I'll have money when I get old—but what about if I never get old? I don't care. So I'm going to put 3 percent. If I see that it's a lot, I'll go down to 1."

Two years later, Julia and her children are still living in the same apartment, but virtually everything else has changed. Her boyfriend, Juan, is now her husband and lives with Julia and the kids. Her children, ten-year-old Eduardo and five-year-old Miguel, now have a sister, Jacinta, born that year. Julia's mother, disgusted with her decision to divorce a second time, has moved out; Julia's father, ill with a heart condition, has moved in. Her last name has changed once again, adding Moreno to the repertoire of the Jara-Reyes-Coronado household, where Julia likes to joke "everybody's in a different party."

Julia has a new job, too. She works as the office manager at a psychiatric help line. She oversees three doctors and three administrative staff out of an office on Long Island. "I do everything," she says. "I'm in charge of everything in that place." And the remuneration for her labors, all things accounted for, has been pretty good. Julia finally has employer-paid health insurance for her entire family. She makes about $30,000 a year—only half of which her employer bothers to report to tax authorities.

What has not changed is Julia's tendency to fall into debt. After successfully clearing off over $9,000 in credit card debt, she now finds herself saddled with a $10,000 credit card balance—mostly from expenses related to her wedding and travel to the Dominican Republic. The debt does not frighten her as much anymore, however, because these days she's making more money and Juan has added another $20,000 to the family pool, which puts them squarely in the $35,000 income tax bracket ($50,000 if Julia reported her full income).[12]

Thanks to Juan's wages, the household is well out of the Missing Class. The two have been saving up assiduously to buy a house in the Dominican Republic, which will help certify their new status. "If you buy real estate, your money is secure," Julia says, echoing the middle-class mantra. She is convinced that buying property overseas will be a better investment. In the United States, you need a high income to support a house and all its expenses—water bills, heating bills, this and that—but in the Dominican Republic "all you have to worry about is the children's school and money to eat. That's it." In the next year, Julia and Juan want to make a small investment on the island—maybe buy a parcel of land, start building apartments on it, and earn some rent to pay the investment off. They hope to move the family there in ten years, but for now they're thinking small. "We'll go out and put down a grain of sand to start with," Julia says.

Marriage has brought big changes for Julia, the former "holder of the house" who now finds herself sharing decision-making responsibilities with her equally assertive husband. Her former husbands, Vicente and César, were pushovers, so it took some adjusting for Julia to learn to make collective decisions.

Julia has also learned to compromise somewhat in her work. Though she remains ambitious, she's not willing to kill herself for her job anymore. She gets to work at 9:20 and leaves at 4:30 without fail, "even if the world is ending," because she know she needs to catch the bus home on time. "I hate my job. I hate my boss," she says frankly. He's a pedantic, demanding man who doesn't care if he kicks some shins to get his way.

That's not to say that Julia cowers before him. She knows that she's invaluable in her workplace and that her boss will never fire her—he's even told her as much. Once, though, Julia had to put him in his place. Her boss had accused her of giving him the wrong address for an appointment, and the two quarreled. He used harsh words. She grabbed her purse and stormed out of the office. He called her at home. "Did you quit?" he asked.

"I suppose you want me to quit because you treat me as if I were your child," she snapped back. "I need respect....I need you to respect me as I respect you. You have to maintain a professional relationship with me."

Her boss promised Julia that he would never treat her like that again. "And he really hasn't done it," Julia says.

CREDIT'S OVERDUE

In Washington Heights a typical family will work grueling hours for a paycheck that will never wind up in an interest-bearing savings account, much less a stock or bond. It's not that these families don't know the value of a dollar or the importance of saving. Many simply don't have a bank account. They've never owned one. Instead, these families save by tucking rolls of bills under mattresses or stuffing them into shoeboxes. They take their paychecks to cashiers that charge hefty fees in exchange for handing out a week or two's hard-earned pay. They plow their savings into real estate or wire it overseas into the trusted hands of family members.

In an immigrant-dominated neighborhood like Washington Heights, there are many reasons that locals shy away from modern-day methods of saving their money. "Some people don't trust banks," says State Assemblyman Adriano Espaillat, a longtime resident of the neighborhood. Having grown up overseas, these workers prefer to hold their money themselves rather than entrust it to the ledger of some suspect institution that might shutter its storefront with any trembling shift in the economy. Or they just don't have any experience with banks, since back home banks cater attentively to the rich but shun wage-earning folk like them.

In Washington Heights the situation isn't very different. The major banking corporations have only a modest presence in the neighborhood, and the numbers of branches have dwindled over the years. Back in the early eighties, this neighborhood had about twenty banks; two decades later, it had half that number.[13] Where the banks once stood, you'll now find a wide variety of check-cashing stores, no-frills businesses where workers can bring their paychecks and, for a fee of about 1.5 percent of the face value, receive cash.[14] Some of these storefronts in Washington Heights, in fact, have been established by major banks like Banco Popular. "They recognize a lot of people don't use traditional banking here," says Espaillat.

Mark Levine has a less sanguine take on recent trends in Washington Heights. In 1994 he cofounded Credit Where Credit Is Due, a nonprofit dedicated to helping low-income families gain access to the kinds of financial services that most middle-class families take for granted— savings accounts, low-interest loans, and the like. The need is great. Across the nation, an estimated twenty-eight million people have no bank account, and more than forty million have a low credit score or none.[15] In Washington Heights the check-cashing stores, pawn shops, and loan sharks that abound have been holding families back, Levine contends. "It's a substandard set of services. People are being charged way more than they would [be] even at a bank in many cases."

As Levine sees it, part of the reason that families lack access to quality financial services in places like Washington Heights is that the major banks don't care to have them as customers. In an effort to cut costs, the banking industry in recent years has moved away from opening brick-and-mortar branches in favor of lower-cost electronic services: withdrawing cash from the ATM on the corner, transferring balances using a touch-tone phone, paying bills over an Internet-enabled home computer. "They don't even want you in the branches anymore," Levine says. The new options might be more convenient for educated, middle-class customers with high-speed connections, he adds, but they put lower-income families at a disadvantage. These families may not speak English, much less know their way around a computer. Some can't even read in Spanish. "So how are you gonna do an ATM machine?"

Customers at a typical bank are required to hold a certain amount of money in their accounts—typically $1,000 or more—lest they get hammered with monthly fees.[16] Add the ATM surcharges and account fees and other fine-print subtractions from an already diminutive balance, and it's no wonder that many Washington Heights families prefer check-cashing stores. The cashiers may charge even more, but at least they're upfront about it, and they genuinely want lower-income families walking through their doors. "If you got three hundred bucks in your account in Citibank," Levine says, "they don't even want to basically know you."

Those who cash their paychecks, however, are handicapping themselves in the assets-acquisition game. "You keep your money at home," Levine notes. "You get no savings. No relationship with a financial institution. Mad fees." Many check-cashing stores also offer so-called payday advances, which provide the customer with cash now with the stipulation that the loan will be paid back—often at an exorbitant rate of interest—when the paycheck finally arrives. Those families who are uninformed or desperate enough to consider this option can quickly fall into a sinkhole of debt.

Families without access to traditional banking accounts suffer in other ways, too. They normally have to purchase money orders, which cost $1 or more each, to pay their rent or gas or electricity bill, tacking on another several dollars a month in expenses in already cash-strapped households. The most serious problem, however, is the difficulty that these families have in accessing lines of credit. "Banks really have no interest in lending to someone who's got no credit history at all," Levine says. "Forget about a mortgage or even financing a car loan or anything like that. You've got to have a foothold on at least the first rung in the ladder to go up to that next level." The market, after all, is stacked against the small borrower. It costs the bank the same amount to make a $500,000 loan as it does to make a $5,000 loan, Levine points out.

"They gotta pay some staff person to sit down and do the paperwork. So obviously, they'd rather make the big one."

With legal borrowing out of the question, Washington Heights families have no choice but to turn to loan sharks in order to finance their start-up businesses, pay their medical bills, purchase their first home computer, or cover their tuition at vocational schools. Once desperation brings them down that path, they're forced to fork over weekly interest payments that add up to 300 to 400 percent a year—not including the threat of violence for delinquent payers, which the sharks provide for free.

THE GERVAIS FAMILY

> Too poor to buy a townhouse or apartment but too rich to qualify
> for traditional affordable-housing programs, they feel cheated out
> of the American dream's promise of homeownership.
> —*Washington Post*, December 8, 2005

It's 2:45 P.M., and the day is almost over, but in a way it hasn't yet begun. Rita has stowed Ash, the South Asian two-year-old, in his high chair, where he chews over his apple and stares fixedly at the TV, absorbed in the antics of Mickey Mouse. The other child, a four-year-old, is snuggled up in his portable bed in the living room. All quiet on the day-care front, Rita puts her mother, Carmen, in charge of the children while she walks over to the local public school to pick up her afternoon charges.

The playground is a chaotic scene, the bottled-up energy of a day spent behind the school desk uncorked onto the tarmac. It takes about ten minutes to round up five of the six children Rita normally picks up: two second-graders, two first-graders, and a kindergartner. (The sixth child, fifth-grader Steven, hasn't been set free from school because his father is coming by to talk to the boy's teacher about some behavioral problems.) Almost all of their parents work at Columbia University Medical Center, just a few blocks from Rita's apartment and day care. They are the nurse's aides and orderlies who man the lower rungs of the hospital hierarchy, lower-wage workers who need cheap day care within walking distance of the hospital.

Once Rita has corralled the children, it's a block's walk to the bus stop, where another first-grader arrives fresh from school. Rita scolds all the children for misbehaving but saves her sharpest words for Paul, a second-grader who is new to the group and hasn't learned her rules. Eli, on the other hand, is a little gentleman, carrying the girls' book bags on their way home. He is the son of a single mom who lives in New Jersey and works at the hospital. His father is a deadbeat dad; whenever the authorities force him to pay child support, he stops working.

It's a frigid November day, and so in spite of pleas from the kids, Rita decides to postpone a walk in the park until tomorrow. Instead, the group walks back to Rita's apartment, where Ash is still cooped up in his high chair. The kids put their coats away, and Carmen sends two at a time to wash their hands. Then Rita sits them down, each to a chair around the table, to eat a snack and do homework. Carmen is their taskmaster, encouraging them to eat and drink, while Rita attends to Ash. The toddler hasn't been causing any problems lately, but Rita insists that she needs to keep him in the high chair because otherwise he'd fight or take things from the other kids. In any case, it's a lot easier for Rita and Carmen not to have him running around. After fifteen minutes of further purgatory, Rita frees the two-year-old from his perch, though with stern words that he will be sent back if he starts fighting or running around. Ecstatic, Ash jets off with another kid.

P.J., an African American first-grader who attends a gifted-and-talented program, is working speedily through her Spanish assignment. She has to write three sentences in Spanish about a friend. "*Por eso es que pienso que mi amigo es una persona agradable*" ("That's why I think my friend is a nice person"). Then it's on to her math assignment, where P.J. has to write down all the possible combinations for packaging seven apples in two bags. By now, she's getting sluggish and droopy-eyed. Rita remarks—in front of her but in Spanish—that P.J. is a somewhat antisocial child who always appears to be in a bad mood.

By now, three of the kids—Eli, his younger brother, and P.J.—are leaving with their parents. Ash is, unsurprisingly, back in his high chair in the kitchen, with Carmen standing guard. He is bored, fidgeting, and crying for "teacher." With so many kids for Rita to take care of, it seems that Ash spends many an afternoon in his high chair.

Rita has her hands full right now working with three of the children. Art is coloring, pasting, and studying the letter "e." Paul is playing with blocks inscribed with the numbers one through ten. He tends to rush through his work, and Rita has to chide him about being too hasty. Paul needs a lot of help, Rita admits. Before coming here, he attended another day care in Washington Heights, which, Rita believes, didn't do a good job: Paul entered school this fall not knowing his colors. That would never happen at Rita's day care, where she makes sure that all her prospective kindergartners know their colors, numbers, alphabets, and letter sounds.

Steven has arrived, dropped off by his dad. Rita puts him to work pasting pictures from a magazine—it's supposed to be part of a school assignment, but Steven sputters when asked what the point of the assignment is. Rita tells him she can't help him if he can't tell her what he's supposed to do. Steven and his brother, Art, are the children of an attractive couple, Rita notes, but one that is on the verge of a breakup. The mother, who does janitorial work at a local bookstore, has talked to Rita about leaving her husband. The couple recently had a fight, and since then the husband hasn't been staying at the house.

Steven's parents have been planning to buy a house. If they can commit to this goal, Rita reasons, perhaps some of their difficulties will go away. Their problem is a lack of focus, she says. They need something to show them the value of family.

With persistence, Rita has tackled her credit card problems. In the past few months, she has "hustled" like never before at her day care. She used to have strict standards about which children to accept—which ones would add to the center's ambience of care and cleanliness, and which ones would cause problems. Now she is taking anyone she can just to push her monthly payments above her monthly debts. "If I want this setting to be nice, I interview parents and I'm saying, 'Wait a minute, this child isn't gonna fit in, so I won't take him,' you know?" she says. "But if I have bills and I want to get rid of them, I would just take anybody that comes in."

The fruits of this strategy are obvious: $5,000 worth of debt wiped away. All but two of her seven credit cards stripped of their balances.

No more minimum payments, ever. And $100 to seed her bank account with, each and every week, in anticipation of that big down payment on her new home. In fact, her credit rating is better right now, she boasts, than her ex-husband's. Rita is making about $20,000 a year, after expenses, from her day care. It's barely enough to clothe and feed herself and ten-year-old Tracy and pay their rent, but with Henri's extra infusions of cash—for dinners for her and Tracy, gifts, ballet classes, and so on—she and Tracy are surviving. Rita knows people who have dealt with massive credit card debt by declaring bankruptcy. Rita isn't going to do that, she resolves.

In June Rita tentatively announces her plans to buy a home. Nothing too extravagant. She admits to being nervous about approaching a real estate agency, but she is working her way up to that. The first step is buying a book on all the things a home buyer needs to know. Rita wants to live in New Jersey, maybe in Bergen County, just a short jaunt across the George Washington Bridge from Manhattan. She plans to keep her apartment in Washington Heights to house her day care.

For most American families, the home is the most important asset —in fact, the only substantial savings many of them have. Two-thirds of Americans live in homes they own.[17] Home ownership means more than staking out a plot of privacy and comfort in the urban or suburban wilderness. It is also about accumulating equity and amassing a substantial net worth that opens possibilities in this consumer society. Beyond that, a home is an important symbol: the ultimate marker of "making it" in a competitive market economy, the cornerstone of the American Dream. Not surprisingly, rates of home ownership among both the poor and the Missing Class are substantially lower than among more affluent households.[18]

Rita understands the significance of becoming a home owner all too well. It's all about providing for her little one, *por la chiquita*: "When I'm not around she has a roof over her head." Tracy isn't going to be raised as some poor Dominican kid in Washington Heights; Rita has invested far too much in her only child. She's determined that Tracy will grow up in a good neighborhood. What Rita doesn't know is how to go about buying that piece of opportunity. Before, Rita didn't even realize she needed a mortgage. She just showed up at the real estate agency expecting to be served. Angie, the mother of one of her day-care charges, has helped set Rita straight. Angie and her husband just went through the process of buying a home, and now she is guiding Rita through the twists and loops of the mortgage process. The first step, Angie confides to her, is getting preapproved for her mortgage.

Three months later, Rita decides she is finally ready to take the leap. She knows that with an income of $20,000 a year, she has no hope of obtaining a preapproved mortgage for a two-family home in New Jersey. She needs a cosigner. Rita decides to turn to a good friend from her college days, Gwen. They've known each other for years, and though they've had their quarrels, the two are tight. Plus, Rita knows that Gwen has a lot of money in the bank and doesn't have any heavy bills or debts, so she can handle such a request.

When Rita finds an opportunity to pop the question, though, her friend balks. "Oh, I don't like to do these things," Gwen says. "I'm sorry. I've been told before that if you don't pay, then I have to take it over."

Rita says she understands. But now she doesn't have any options—except for Henri.

She has been dreading the idea of approaching her ex-husband to cosign the paperwork. It isn't that she needs him to put out any real money. All she needs is his signature so that the mortgage companies won't throw her application into the recycling bin. But Henri is the one who has always harangued Rita about her finances. He makes $50,000 a year at a big company, and he is an accountant to boot. He's sure to give her an earful.

Rita finally musters the courage to talk to Henri. Her worst premonitions are confirmed the moment she finishes her spiel. Henri opens his mouth to speak: "Well, let me tell you this—"

"Listen," Rita says, interrupting him. "Tell me yes or no."

She's sweating, half expecting Henri to continue his lecture. "Yeah, OK," he finally blurts out. Forced to make a decision, Henri decides to underwrite his daughter's long-term future. The house, after all, is really for Tracy.

By the beginning of 2000, Rita has closed on a house. The mortgage is $176,000; her monthly payments are $2,000. The new home is in northern New Jersey, where she has long wanted to live: an inner-ring suburb of New York where middle-class families head to raise their children.

Two years later, Rita and Tracy have settled into their new home in New Jersey. Now twelve years old, Tracy has shot up to Rita's height and has taken to wearing her hair long and straight—the salon bills attest to it. Rita is fifty-two and admits to feeling her age. She recently hurt her back picking up a child at the day care. At one point, the pain was so bad it took all her strength to hobble five feet. Since then her condition has improved, though the doctors are still dumbfounded about the cause of the pain; X-rays of her back revealed no injuries. To make matters worse, the diabetes that Rita had when she was pregnant with Tracy has come back, and though it isn't severe, she has acquired a bad habit of not keeping tabs on her blood sugar because of her hectic schedule.

As for her new neighborhood, Rita has laid down roots. Here in New Jersey, neighbors look out for each other's property. They borrow each other's parking garages. They have a sense of loyalty to one another that her more anonymous neighbors in Washington Heights didn't express. She's glad that she no longer has to shop at the city Pathmark, where the cashiers had nasty attitudes and customers would occasionally get into shouting matches with them. These days she can stroll into any twenty-four-hour supermarket and find those delicacies she always craves: blueberries, honeydew melon, French cheeses.

This is the life she has dreamed of. If she can continue making those mortgage payments, she'll be able to keep it.

FOUR

The Sacrificed Generation

But come now—the Community Reinvestment Act of 1977,
the CETA jobs program, the national debate after the Rodney
King riots, Enterprise Zones, workfare, Bill Clinton's National
Dialogue on Race, welfare reform, No Child Left Behind, the
Faith-Based and Charity Initiatives—can we really pretend that
[Hurricane] Katrina is showing us that America has "ignored"
black poverty? What Katrina revealed was the result of one
especially unsuccessful attempt to address black poverty:
30 years of teaching poor black people not to work for a living.
—*National Review*, September 25, 2006

THE WAYNE FAMILY

The rabbit's warren of weather-beaten desks is filled to overflowing with paper and index cards, colored forms and Post-it notes. Battered three-drawer cabinets disgorge files that are several inches thick and filled with the sagas, complications, complaints, late notices, and bright red stamps indicating "case closed" that are the stuff of a New York City Human Resources Administration office, known to its clients simply as "the welfare." Whatever the official name—AFDC or TANF—it is the same old story to the women who appear at the threshold, muttering under their breath, hoping to break a bureaucratic blockade that has curtailed their housing assistance or stymied their Medicaid cards.

A young Latina approaches one of the small brown desks and asks to speak to Danielle Wayne. "Danielle is out," she's told in a tone that suggests she shouldn't ask again.

"I'm having problems with my child care," the woman pleads. "The vouchers aren't coming anymore." It seems the babysitter who has been looking after her kids is no longer content to do so without being paid. How is she going to go to work, she asks, if she can't pay the child-care bill?

The caseworker filling in for Danielle, a smartly dressed black woman, explains that while center-based child care is a possibility in theory, in practice it is a distant prospect. "The wait lists are thousands long," she says without emotion, having pointed this out hundreds of times this month alone. Crestfallen, the client tries to explain again that the babysitter won't work for free.

By now, Danielle has returned to her desk. "That's just terrible," she tells the client after hearing the story. "I know where you're coming from. I didn't get any money for child care for the whole summer."

"They don't understand," wails the client; the sitter just wants the money. Danielle looks at her with a sympathetic eye but can do nothing more than give her a form to fill out, restating her request for funds. Another disappointed customer turns to leave.

Danielle has been there, on the client side of the desk, for more years than she cares to remember. Today she is part of the welfare machinery itself, and her job is to keep it well oiled. Wearing an ankle-length black skirt and a matching jacket with gold trim, her hair wrapped tightly in a bun beneath her black scarf, Danielle is every inch the respectable Muslim convert and prim professional. Pictures of her three children adorn her desk. A small gold clock with her name engraved at the base ticks quietly while Danielle shuttles back and forth from the filing cabinet to the desk. Her coworker, a young woman in jeans, asks how to complete a claim form. Danielle motions for her to sit down next to her so that she can explain the process.

Fifteen minutes later, the manager of Danielle's work group, a black man in his forties, strides into the office. He spots Danielle sitting at the larger desk. "You taking over?" he asks with mock indignation. Smiling, Danielle points out that since there was no boss in the room, she thought anyone could sit there.

The truth is, Danielle *is* moving up. For the last six months she's been part of the city's Work Experience Program, which sends welfare recipients to work for their benefits. Apart from these "workfare" payments, she hasn't received a salary since she started this job. But that will soon change. Having impressed her higher-ups, Danielle is about to make the transition from workfare peon to salaried civil servant.

In 1996 Congress overhauled the nation's welfare system, imposing time limits on aid and pushing recipients into the workforce. Over the last decade, Danielle's experience has been shared by hundreds of thousands of poor women in this country. Many are now working poor rather than welfare poor. Others, like Danielle, have moved up into the Missing Class. Between 1995 and 1998, the number of New Yorkers on welfare dipped from 1.2 million to 810,000, more than half of whom were children. At first, those leaving the rolls had a hard time finding work. Unemployment was high; their skills were weak. By the late 1990s, around when we first met Danielle, the situation had begun to improve.[1] In fact, the United States saw record levels of employment; labor markets were so tight that employers began to look harder at applicants they had previously dismissed.

Danielle's job is not perfect, but it's a vast improvement over any of the positions she has held before. She now has the chance to exercise her judgment rather than just follow orders. She is responsible for the lives of others, which makes her feel more valuable than when she was packing food trays for airlines or cleaning bed pans in a mental hospital. Doing important work has elevated Danielle's self-respect. It has transformed her from a frightened, unsteady, and clinically depressed welfare recipient into a capable employee, comfortable enough in her own skin to protest being overworked and underpaid. In other words, Danielle sounds just like everyone else in the real world of clerical work.

A Puerto Rican colleague drops by her desk. "You have to deal with a lot of crazy people in this office," Yolanda confides.

"I know what you mean," Danielle replies, her voice just above a whisper. She relates several episodes to prove her case that people in the office are superficial in their concern for others, insincere, and—worse —back-stabbing.

"It's better here than on the fifth floor," Yolanda notes. "Up there, there's a lot of friction," and some of the worst offenders want to put Yolanda in the middle of it. "I'm a grown woman. I don't need to deal with that. No one is going to drive me to a nervous breakdown." She wants to be transferred, perhaps to an office in the Bronx, where she lives.

"I could probably help you out there," interjects Chanida, who's in the office hunting for some records. Decked out in a striking yellow

suit, Chanida supervises yet another section of the vast Human Resources Administration empire. "Do you have good secretarial and
math skills?" she asks Yolanda. "Because that's what I need over in the
other building."

Chanida walks away without a definitive answer. Yolanda leans over
to Danielle. "That offer sounds nice, but I hope they don't expect me to
dress up."

"I don't know," Danielle replies. She remembers hearing the managers talk about some kind of dress code during her orientation. Yolanda rolls her eyes and points out that she is raising a child by herself
and barely has enough money to buy underwear, let alone business
clothes.

Chanida returns to the conversation just in time to hear mention of
the dress code. Another coworker asks Chanida if it's OK to wear the
kind of blue jeans she has on right now. "That's not really what we want
to see employees wear," Chanida replies. "We want the people in this
office to look professional." Chanida's theory is that caseworkers will
command more respect if they look the part. And respect is a serious
issue in this office. Clients are inclined to see caseworkers—especially
those in blue jeans—as arrogant, demanding more deference than they
are due. The tension is heightened by the negligible social distance between welfare client and caseworker. But for the grace of a single bureaucratic decision—to open workfare positions in Human Resources
Administration—Danielle, Yolanda, and dozens of other women in the
building would be sitting on the other side of the table, sharing in that
humiliation.

In fact, although Danielle happens to have a workfare assignment,
her struggles are far from over. She is not getting support for child care
and has to make do, patching together a contingency plan of after-
school sessions and whatever help she can get from her ex-mother-
in-law, who looks after Safiya, Danielle's two-year-old. But since there
is little she can do to change the lot of her clients, the anger directed
at her—the visible representative of a system in which she is herself
enmeshed—just makes her feel defensive. By the end of the day, she
gets a tad upset and, truth be told, does feel slightly superior to the sad
cases that present themselves in her office. After all, in less than a

month, she will be an official civil servant, with benefits like health insurance and vacation pay. It will be the best job Danielle Wayne has ever held.

A world away from Danielle's Midtown office, on a rundown street running parallel to Harlem's main thoroughfare, sits one of the hulking high-rise towers common to this neighborhood. The gray concrete structure reaches up twenty-five stories, with metal bars around the bottom floors and air conditioners poking out of the windows, their familiar hum stilled for the winter months.

None of the buzzers that are supposed to signal the arrival of a visitor is working, but the security guard knows Carla Wayne—Danielle's former mother-in-law—because she's lived in apartment 6B for the better part of a decade. This public housing building is better than many of its kind, since the hallways are largely free of graffiti and most of the overhead lights work. One wouldn't want to linger long in the elevator, though, which smells vaguely of urine.

Sixty years old now, but surprisingly spry despite her weathered face, Carla Wayne opens the door, surrounded by three of her charges, all under the age of seven, who hold on to her skirt and trade furtive glances with an unfamiliar visitor. Safiya, Danielle's two-year-old daughter and Carla's youngest grandchild, is particularly skittish, but she flashes a smile before yelling at the top of her lungs her one stock phrase: "SHUDDUP!" If you ask Safiya how she's doing today, "SHUDDUP" is all you will hear in reply.

Carla's apartment is modestly furnished with a living-room set, a small dining-room table tucked in the corner, and chairs that are torn and stained with years of spilled cereal and milk—the physical traces of her off-the-books child-care business. Toys are jumbled into a pile on the floor, having been pulled off the shelf that holds two televisions, one on and one off. A woman half Carla's age sits on the sofa quietly watching the raucous happenings on the *Jerry Springer Show*. She doesn't appear to find Springer all that funny, but the kids gravitate toward the screen to see what all the noise is about. They aren't too sure what to make of Springer's topless women, their breasts blurred on the screen.

A two-year-old boy named Jason runs around the room, followed by another boy of about eight. Safiya stares at them but does not join in, perhaps discomfited by the presence of unfamiliar people. Sadiq, the oldest in the group, is sitting at the table writing on a piece of paper. She *is* interested in company. Sadiq introduces herself and shakes hands.

"Are you getting your homework done?" Carla asks. Sadiq sits back down and returns to her third-grade math work sheet. The woman on the couch explains that she has four children of her own: 14, 15, 16, and 18. Are they in high school now? "The boys live in the Bronx," she explains, but she offers nothing further and looks a little sad around the edges.

"Sadiq was my first child in care," Carla notes. She is the child of one of Carla's daughters and started staying with her grandmother when she was three months old, nearly eight years ago. Carla was glad for the work, for she had been forced to quit her previous job as a home health aide when she developed glaucoma. She didn't have any training or experience in child care other than being a mother four times over herself, but that seemed like credentials enough from Carla's point of view.

Sadiq is the oldest, with a wide gap between her and the little ones. She comes to Carla's place when school gets out, often walking the blocks from P.S. 57 to the apartment by herself. On some days the girl is also given the task of retrieving Carla's other part-time charges from school. It's a big responsibility, given the dangers that lie in between, for this East Harlem neighborhood is a drug-dealing paradise for everyone except the law-abiding citizens who live in the same apartment buildings. School authorities refuse to release children to anyone but their parents or a lawful guardian, so at times Sadiq has to persuade one of the adults waiting outside the school to play that part. She is clearly nervous about having to lie. On the other hand, some teachers don't check too closely on the relationship between the adult and child, since they have grown accustomed to the fact that these faces change fairly often.

Danielle has been dropping her daughter off at Carla's place ever since she started her workfare job. Lacking the money to put Safiya in a child-care center, Danielle was relieved that her ex-mother-in-law was willing to take the girl. Without her, Danielle would have been standing in line at the welfare office like the dozens of clients who now visit her, complaining that they can't find a willing relative like Carla and can't pay whomever they have found.

Thank God Carla is completely reliable and charges only $50 a week. That's a big chunk of Danielle's welfare stipend, but since her ex-husband, Julius, Carla's middle son, actually comes through with child support most of the time, she can manage, if just barely. Danielle would rather sever ties with Julius, since their marriage was troubled almost from the start, but she needs his mother to make it through the workweek. And she needs that child support. The family budget will improve immeasurably when Danielle starts to receive her civil service paycheck. She'll be taking home $1,400 a month after taxes, and it cannot come a moment too soon.

About an hour into the visit, two men in their late twenties or early thirties turn up at the door. They grunt a perfunctory greeting, to which no one replies, and make their way to the room in the back, next to the one the kids use as a playroom.

Clearly restless, Jason dribbles a small plastic ball down the hallway between the playroom and the living room until Carla reminds him firmly that he is not supposed to play ball in the house. Safiya wanders into another room and tries to climb up on the full-size bed that sits to one side. She cannot quite reach the top of the bed, but when asked if she wants some help, Safiya just grunts. Unlike other two-year-olds, who incessantly spout questions, point at objects, and make demands, Safiya seems unable or unwilling to engage other people. She has a two-word vocabulary—"NO! SHUDDUP!"—shouted with the kind of vehemence that makes you wonder whom she might be imitating.

The unmistakable scent of marijuana drifts from the room where the two young men are hanging out. Carla never speaks to them or about them, and it's not clear what their relationship is to her. She is willing to talk about her middle daughter, though, who turns out to be the young woman sitting silently on the couch in the living room. Carla's voice softens to a whisper as she confides that Jasmine is a "crackhead." A longtime abuser of alcohol and pot, Jasmine has in recent years started smoking crack cocaine, a deadly habit that has already cost her custody of her four children. A month ago she turned up on Carla's doorstep, clutching a few bags of belongings and asking if she could stay there.

"Where are your kids?" Carla remembers asking Jasmine. When she didn't get an answer, Carla quickly realized that her daughter "didn't seem right."

Two weeks later, one of her grandsons showed up unexpectedly and asked if Carla had any idea where his mother was. The boy had no clue that Jasmine had moved in with Carla. When he found her sitting in the living room, Dwane asked his mother what was going on, but Jasmine barely replied. Carla sat her grandson down at the same table where Sadiq is now doing her homework and explained the situation. Their father had been in and out of jail, and Carla knew he was a bad bet to replace Jasmine. Basically, the boys were on their own. "You and your brothers have to watch out for yourselves now," she told Dwane. That was the last that either Carla or Jasmine has seen the boys.

Jasmine receives about $400 a month in SSI—the government's disability benefit—but she keeps that amount to herself. Once Carla asked her if she could contribute something toward the rent or food, but the request didn't go over too well. "I'm not gonna pay your bills!" Jasmine snapped. Carla is at a loss about what to do for her daughter:

> All she does is sit on the sofa all day watching TV, eat something, and sleep. When her check comes in the mail, she cashes it and then runs with her money to a crack house and smokes for days until it's all gone. When she passes out, people steal the money she has in her pockets. I know where that crack house is because some of my friends' kids are going there and doing the same stuff.

Grandmothers like Carla are picking up the pieces, raising the third and sometimes fourth generations. Some are bearing this load while their own children are smoking up the resources they have. Others are helping out their working daughters (or daughters-in-law) who don't earn enough money to afford professional day care.

Carla isn't worried about the people Jasmine associates with when she is out of the house. "She's an addict, but she's not dangerous," Carla says. "She knows better than to bring those people to the house."

Carla knows that people in the crack house have passed the word to "leave Ms. Wayne and her people alone." So far, Jasmine hasn't stolen anything from Carla or anyone else. On the grand scale of things, this is a plus. Other elderly women in Carla's circle wake up to find their drawers rifled, their jewelry missing.[2]

The families who leave their kids at Carla's day care seem to be satisfied, at least enough to bring their siblings when the need arises. Carla feeds her charges; she gives at least a glancing nod to their homework obligations. When the spirit moves her, Carla takes them to the park. While the kids play, she sits on a bench with all the other grandmothers who work off the books. As for Jasmine and the men in the back room, the children under Carla's care treat them as inanimate objects that they need to navigate around. They are too young to register the fact that there are drug users in the house, and in any case they have enough company among themselves to ignore grown-ups most of the time.

Even so, it's clear that this isn't the best place for little Safiya to be spending her days. Nobody is learning his or her ABCs from *Sesame Street* in this house.[3] When Safiya starts kindergarten, she is going to have trouble if all she can say is "NO! SHUDDUP!"—even if she does muster her devilishly cute grin. She is far behind in her cognitive development compared with where her eight-year-old brother, Keith, or nine-year-old sister, Elesha, were at the same age. When they started school, Keith and Elesha knew their letters, numbers, and colors. Danielle saw to that.

Danielle grew up in Jamaica, Queens, at a time when the neighborhood was predominantly white but trending toward black. She started her work life at the age of sixteen in a summer youth program, dutifully turning over her extra money to her mother to help with household expenses. Once that summer ended, she shuttled between a number of short-term jobs, working for a while at the post office, just like her mother. Many of her relatives would have considered such a job a major accomplishment, but Danielle was unhappy working in a dungeon with no windows. She quit and found work at a mental hospital. By then, she was married to Julius.

When the subject of her marriage arises, Danielle withdraws into a cocoon. Her voice drops to a whisper, and she cannot look anyone in the eye. In the beginning things were "all right," she allows, but they never seemed to get better than this low benchmark. Julius was in and out of her life and her home almost from the beginning. As Danielle puts it, "We go way back on being separated. We were together for so long trying to make things work." At eighteen, Julius already had a steady job as a security guard but couldn't be bothered with paying bills. Danielle lost patience with his failure to contribute, kicked him out, moved in with her mother, and began her first stint on welfare.

On and off welfare for the next decade, Danielle found her own place, courtesy of the federal government's Section 8 housing subsidy. Though she and Julius never made a long-term home together after that, they didn't lose touch for very long. Danielle's three children and the four miscarriages she suffered along the way reflect his presence, though less as a resident and more as an intermittent guest. The old welfare regulations discouraged men from staying with their wives, but that was only part of the reason for his distance. Danielle was not happy enough to want Julius to park his shoes under her bed for very long. He returned the suspicion with escalating levels of physical abuse, which got worse when the babies were born.

Danielle decided to get out of Queens. In 1995 she moved to Washington Heights, which seemed safer than any of the alternatives. Around the same time, Danielle took out loans to pursue a license as a beautician. "I didn't finish," she explains with regret, "because I couldn't get into it. At first I thought I would like it. I love to do hair, but studying wasn't for me." She still owes the lender about $2,000.

She has not regretted the decision to move to Washington Heights, however. The neighborhood is teeming with three-generation Dominican households that spill out onto the concrete courtyards of the apartment buildings, their laundry lines flapping in the breeze that slips off the Hudson River to the west. Danielle can't speak more than a phrase or two of Spanish, but she feels safer having all these people around her. On her block, the presence of these "Spanish" families, with grandmothers watching over grandkids, street vendors selling their wares, and kids playing soccer in the courtyards, means that there are a lot of eyes on the street.[4] Deserted spaces make Danielle anxious. She knows what corners to avoid, and with that navigational sixth sense—one she is working hard to convey to her kids, now that they're going outside on their own—she manages.

The Section 8 apartment they call home is modestly furnished and orderly, but it is dark; almost no natural light penetrates the rooms because the apartment sits alongside the building's air shaft. One window looks out on the sky, in the bedroom Danielle shares with Safiya. The place is affordable only with the help of "the welfare," and although it is safe, it's not what Danielle wants. Darkness makes her feel gloomy; four walls bottling up three rambunctious kids made it hard for her to muster the energy to get out in the world and find a job, something she wanted to do long before the pressure of welfare time limits pushed her into it.

It has been an ongoing battle for Danielle. During our six years of acquaintance, she crashed into a wall of depression many times. She found it a struggle to leave the house; worried about how to make it to the end of the month on her meager resources; felt bad about her lousy marriage; and was simply worn down by the demands of caring for three kids.[5] A fearful person by nature, Danielle has few friends. Most of her family lives in North Carolina now, so there isn't much of a support network for her to turn to locally. She had a best friend once, but that relationship dissolved after a disagreement, and Danielle has not been close to anyone since.

To her credit, even in the depths of her depression, Danielle never let her mind-set interfere with her parental duties. But she did lose her temper with the children, and they felt the hard edge of a belt from time to time. Danielle is a strict disciplinarian. It is the only way she knows to be a responsible parent, to distinguish herself from the many mothers she meets at their elementary school who don't seem to care one way or the other what their kids are doing. When the kids misbehave, it is her job to pull them back in line—especially her son, who has a knack for riling her up.

A gifted artist, Keith is shy before strangers with everything but his artwork. He has to be coaxed out from behind the living room couch, but he will show off the drawings he has done, which are vastly more sophisticated in technique and accuracy than the stick figures most boys his age draw. Remarkably, the eight-year-old seems to have figured out how to represent distance through perspective all by himself. Perhaps discerning in him a likeness to his father, Danielle thinks that Keith needs constant surveillance and has made it clear that she will drop by his school if she hears that he has been out of line. Her iron control may be one reason that Keith wants to visit his dad in South Carolina.

Those worries aside, Danielle is almost unrecognizable from her days as a persistently depressed, socially isolated mother. Today she is a poster child for welfare reform—a civil servant with vacation pay and medical insurance—a bona fide member of the Missing Class. When Danielle gets up in the morning and puts on her head scarf, she feels like a proper working woman. When she gets on the subway with the rest of the morning crowd swarming into Midtown, she is pleased to be part of the rush. And even though she is tired at the end of the day and grumbles about her boss, in this she joins millions of other Americans. She can see a future ahead of her.

Down the cinder-block hallways of her children's school, painted royal blue with green stripes running down the linoleum floors, the walls are plastered with kindergarten handprints, life-size paper bodies with string for hair, and third-grade autobiographies. At the end of the twisting corridors is a cafeteria teeming with students. School rules call for silence during lunch, a last-ditch effort to control what has been a run of food fights and back talk.

No one seems to be paying the rules much mind, although Danielle is stationed in the back trying to assist the official school aides in keeping a semblance of order. It's a rainy day, which means everyone is cooped up inside. There is nothing quite like 350 kids under the age of ten stuck in a room and squirming in their seats to make a grown-up long for the sun to return.[6] Danielle pulls one kid off the floor and tries to find out why the little girl in pink pants is crying her eyes out.

Danielle enjoys her role as an enforcer of school order. "When I come down the hallway," she says with some degree of satisfaction, "[the kids] know they can't do what they want. If they talk back to these teachers, in a minute I'll say something. I'll say, '[You there], make a U-turn.'" More important, her duties at the school allow Danielle to spend time with her children's teachers. "I want to know who is going to be taking care of my kids," she says. "There ain't nobody here that don't know me. And if they don't know me, they're going to get to know me because I'm going to come and find out who you are."

Parental involvement is a rarity at P.S. 57. Most families keep away from the classroom; assaults on teachers and fellow students are common, and the police are constantly fielding calls from the assistant principal, who often does not last through the school year.[7] Although it cuts off at fifth grade, sending its graduates to even tougher, more unruly middle schools in Harlem, P.S. 57 has students as old as thirteen who have been held back. Those boys—and it is nearly always boys—are the worst offenders when it comes to disrupting the classroom. Already they have little use for school, and if statistics tell us anything, they are on the glide slope that leads to the dropout line.[8]

Danielle sees plenty of blame to go around. On the one hand, it's clear that the teachers at P.S. 57 are faced with an overwhelming task. They can barely teach, since they are consumed with trying to keep basic order.

> A lot of teachers, they came to me crying on my shoulders and sharing their problems with me. Some are having problems with each other, and you have kids coming to school acting the way they do because you have parents coming and acting foolish, ready to fuss and fight. Teachers in our school done got hurt by parents!
>
> If it's not the parents, it's the kids. The kids and their gangs.... These days a lot of the parents have to go out and work. So the kids are really left on their own, no guidance to teach them what's right. A lot of the kids over there, six or seven, is going to school by themselves. You even have a nine- or ten-year-old walking babies to school....
>
> Then you ask yourself why does the kids come out the way they are? Because the parents train them to be that way.

From her volunteer work for the PTA, Danielle knows that the school's parents tend to be unresponsive, despite entreaties to get involved. "You send the kids home with notes," she complains, "and the parents are not looking into the [backpacks] or are just not interested in coming to the meetings." And when they do, tempers flare. The PTA meetings at times turn into shouting matches. "When you're arguing, you can't listen to that person making a point. You walking out of the school with arguments, not achievements."

While she is genuinely sympathetic to the difficulty of managing a school that seems overrun by disorder, Danielle is not one to side with the administration, either. She vehemently condemns then-mayor Rudy Giuliani for cutting the after-school program. "That's not right!" she insists. "Our children need that program. And he wants to take away pre-K. That would really hurt." Would these cuts have been avoided if more parents had been active in the school? She is sure of it. Would the school work better if the teachers and the principal were on the same page? Absolutely.

> We don't have the teachers supporting the principal like they're supposed to, so it's like an attitude thing going on around in this school, not only in this school but in this district.... When I run into people coming from other schools in this district, they say, "We're having the same problem."... There's so much conflict between the teachers and the principals, and that's why the kids are so frustrated. They're loud around here.... You can see the kids running around the lunchroom.... We get mad when we see these people [teachers and other staff] let the kids do what they want to do.

Danielle has given serious consideration to yanking her children out of this school, but she isn't sure she can find something more secure. In fact, it can very well be worse, she points out. Her best bet is to minimize the negatives and maneuver to get the best out of the situation. "I'm not going to run my child from school to school to school," she says. "They could be running the rest of their life. I can just stay right here and get the best of the teachers.... And I already know who is the best. I know who for each grade." All her inside knowledge of the school, however, has not saved Danielle's oldest child from the harsh justice of standardized testing: Elesha was held back in third grade, having failed the state reading assessment.

Sadly, Elesha has a lot of company, both in New York City and the nation as a whole. Between the ages of nine and eleven, a gap opens between white kids and their black and Hispanic counterparts: 5 to 10 percent more minority kids than whites are held back. These differences, which widen at the high school level, reflect the pressures that poverty places on educational performance. If everyone graduated in the end, perhaps this would not matter very much. After all, our European counterparts start their children in school later than we do, and they finish their secondary schooling at a later point as well. Unfortunately, the practice of "grade retention" in the United States seems to harm children more than it helps. Those kept behind tend to have lower test scores and much higher dropout rates than similar students allowed to move on.[9]

In the area where Elesha goes to school, nearly a quarter of the students fail the state reading exam every year and a third score too low in math. One in ten is mandated to attend summer school and therefore identified as "at risk" for being held back.[10] These failing students are hardly a random group. Kids held back a grade, like Elesha, are overwhelmingly from single-parent households and have typically grown up with parents who are not well educated themselves. They arrive in kindergarten with a long list of deficits that reflect their parents' own educational weaknesses.

Dedicated parents can make a difference even if they aren't highly educated themselves. Danielle's reaction to Elesha's academic problems was to enroll both of her older children in reading clubs sponsored by the local branch of the New York Public Library. Each child in the club had to read a minimum of one book a week. In the summer, the library program requires the children to write short book reports on every novel or nonfiction book they have read. Danielle has high hopes that all this extra work will help Elesha catch up in school.

The emphasis that Danielle places on reading at home is all the more interesting given that she has only a high school degree. (She comes from educated stock, however; her mother retired from the post office earlier this year to pursue a master's degree in religion, and she has sisters who attended college.) Danielle may not talk to Elesha or Keith about the content of what they are reading, but she coordinates their book time with almost industrial efficiency, ensuring her kids far exceed the expectations of the librarians in Washington Heights. The result is a large collection of gold ribbons and plaques on display in the Wayne family living room. In the summer alone, Elesha mastered 25 books, Keith plowed through 16, and Danielle read 10 books to Safiya. "A lot of parents don't have their children reading like they should," she notes a little smugly.

Danielle used to do much more for her children. Until she started her workfare job, she was the treasurer of their school's PTA and spent nearly thirty hours a week volunteering there. It was a labor of love but also a cause of frustration. Sometimes only ten people would show up for meetings—in a school with seven hundred kids. Though Danielle found plenty to gripe about, she wasted no time mustering a constructive response. Making a difference at P.S. 57 became her mission.

Ironically, it was her very freedom from work that allowed Danielle to become a fixture at the school. Because she didn't have to clock in at an office, barely a day went by in the late nineties when she wasn't at the school, working in the library, going over the PTA accounts, helping out with playground or lunchroom supervision. She visited with the teachers, became a conspicuous adult presence during dismissal, dropped in on the principal most mornings as kids climbed off the school buses, and made sure that she was present to fight for the cause at every District Five school board meeting. For someone fighting depression, her devotion was impressive.

It was also pragmatic. "If you're not involved with what's goin' on behind doors, then you don't know what's behind [them]," she reasoned. She has seen teachers yank kids by their clothes, push them against the wall, and scream at the top of their lungs. By inserting herself into the school hierarchy, Danielle made sure she could protect her own.

Danielle's proactive presence at P.S. 57 was not without its detractors. Whenever her name came up, school security guards would roll their eyes skyward. Some of the Latino parents thought she was highhanded. Even the PTA president, someone Danielle worked with fairly closely, denounced her on occasion. "Are you a crackhead or something?" Yvonne, the president, yelled down the corridor during one of their dramas. When Danielle retorted with an equally unpleasant rejoinder, Yvonne told her in no uncertain terms whose ass she could kiss. The whole incident left Danielle so steamed that she considered quitting the PTA and pulling her kids out of P.S. 57. In the end she decided against it. The school had become her avocation. She knew enough about its inner workings to guarantee a certain level of attention for her kids, and she couldn't give up that advantage. Still, the episode taught Danielle that you really can't rely on anyone but yourself. Nobody covers your back. On the other hand, nobody covers your kids either. That's a mother's job.

Until welfare reform pushed them into the labor force, mothers on welfare like Danielle were the mainstay of many Harlem elementary schools. They were the helpers whom every school depended on to keep things on track. In middle-class suburban schools, this "job" falls to nonworking moms (and a few dads) who organize the bake sales, publicize the school play, ride along on the bus when kids take field trips, and drum up class representatives for as many grades as they can manage. Principals and teachers depend on these parents to keep the institution running, and in big cities, where budgets are always tight, they have become ever more important for maintaining basic order.

When there is no money for official, paid classroom aides, nonworking moms—often on public assistance in poor communities—do what Danielle did. They watch the hallways and the lunchroom and pitch in during bus-boarding time, dismissal, and those Friday afternoons when, to hear Danielle tell it, the whole school goes "off the hook." They make sure that kids return the forms that qualify them for free school lunches, which provide nutrition that is better than what many families can afford.

Welfare reform put an end to this volunteer workforce. Danielle and thousands of other mothers like her now spend their days toiling at the office or sweeping the city park and struggle to find the energy to get to evening school meetings when they can. Their days as hallway monitors are over.

For the time being, however, Keith and Elesha will continue to benefit from the residual reputation of their mother at the school. She will still be able to influence their classroom assignments, maneuvering to get the best teachers available. Danielle would like to remain in the know so that when little Safiya graduates from Grandmother Carla's care—surely lacking the vocabulary and conceptual development that her peers at day-care centers will have—she can be there for her, too. But now that she's working, her knowledge of the school is getting stale and the people on the PTA board don't listen to her as they did when she was the treasurer.

More serious, perhaps, for Safiya's cognitive development are the consequences of Danielle's absorption into the labor force.[11] One of the reasons that Danielle has placed Safiya with her grandmother, apart from the affordable price tag, is that "she just doesn't know how to talk." It wouldn't be a wise decision, as Danielle sees it, to send Safiya to a proper day-care facility if she cannot communicate. "You want to send your baby [to day care] when she's talking and so she could come back home and say, 'Mom, that person pinched me.' "

What Safiya hears all day is Jerry Springer on the tube. Very little conversation is directed at her.[12] Danielle used to read to her daughter and still tries to do so, but she has less time and energy for the task, now that she is a full-time worker. From the look of Carla's day care, it is hard to imagine that this toddler will start kindergarten with the kind of head start that Danielle gave her older children. And it is anyone's guess whether Keith and Elesha will remain motivated to do well in school, now that their mother is less of a presence.

To be honest, there were no guarantees even when their mother was around all the time. Elesha was already in trouble and repeated a grade. But it is fair to assume that she would do better with the kind of attention she received when Danielle was a stay-at-home mom, even if it was limited to ensuring that Elesha was spending "time on task" reading library books. These days Danielle is exhausted by 7 P.M. What's more, now that she is working, Elesha has had to shoulder some of the chores. The nine-year-old is charged with taking care of Safiya in the evening so that Danielle can make dinner and recharge her batteries for the next day in the office. Elesha gives Safiya her nightly baths; if Safiya needs a diaper change, it is Elesha who gets up to do it.

If you ask Danielle whether she's a happy person these days, she will pause to give the question serious consideration. On balance, she feels good. Even with all the office politics, she likes her job. The income is a godsend, the stability of a real job an almost unbelievable stroke of good fortune, and the fact that she spends her days doing what grown-ups are supposed to do—work in an office with other adults—has returned to her a sense of efficacy that was submerged for more than a decade when she was on welfare.

Leaving the ranks of the nonworking poor, Danielle took up membership in the Missing Class in 1999. She is determined to hold on to this hard-won upward mobility. Less certain is whether her kids will get the education they need to repeat—much less surpass—her success.

TEACHING THE BASICS

Mr. Blatchford sits behind the desk in his classroom, waiting for his next appointment to file in. Intermediate School 25 in Washington Heights is holding its parent-teacher conferences, and Mr. Blatchford, a handsome, young D.C. native one year into his new career as a New York City public school teacher, is still figuring out the best way to deliver bad news. He teaches eighth-grade social studies and language arts, but some days it feels like his only course of instruction is discipline.

An African American student by the name of Latoya Greene walks in, accompanied by her mother. Latoya, the teacher announces, received a 70 in social studies. She clearly could do better—she received an 80 on a project, another 80 on a test—but because she missed four homework assignments, her grade dropped.

A worried look crosses Ms. Greene's face, but she seems to accept the teacher's verdict without protest. She says she tries to review Latoya's homework every night, but there are some days when she gets home too late from work. She vows that she and her daughter will work together to finish all the assignments in the new grading period.

The next student is a timid Latino boy by the name of Ramón Mendoza. He's followed by his mother and his older brother, a young man in his twenties who's dressed for a basketball game, a do-rag covering his head. Mr. Blatchford starts his routine, running down a list of

Ramón's social studies grades. Test? 78. Quiz? 44. Homework? 11 out of
25 points. As Mr. Blatchford reads off the assignments that Ramón
never completed, his mother pipes up.

"Answer me," she snaps at her son in Spanish. "Do you have an ex-
planation? Do you think I am a jerk?" She hisses the questions through
grinding molars, not waiting for Ramón to answer one before launch-
ing into another.

Ramón finally ventures to explain himself. "I have problems in my
head—"

"Are you taking me for a fool?" his mother interrupts. "All this time
telling me that you did your homework? Explain to me, why?"

Tears roll down the mother's anger-flushed cheeks. Ramón gazes
back with wide-open, terrified eyes, looking plaintively at his mother
and then at Mr. Blatchford.

Ms. Mendoza finally calms down again, and Mr. Blatchford moves
on to the language arts grades. Ramón received 91 on a test but had an
overall grade of 40 for his homework. This latest revelation enrages Ms.
Mendoza once again. She grabs the boy's hand and twists his thumb, vi-
ciously. Ramón cries out.

Mr. Blatchford tries to intercede. "I think we can work something
out, Señora. I think there is a way to improve the situation." Ms. Mendoza lets go of Ramón's hand.

Ramón is not stupid, Mr. Blatchford points out. He can do the
work. Already in this new quarter, he has earned an 85 on the first project. If he keeps up with his homework, Mr. Blatchford says, Ramón will
be able to pass the class.

Mr. Blatchford asks Ms. Mendoza if her son will be able to attend
the upcoming class field trip to Gettysburg, the Civil War battlefield.
At first she says no; she doesn't want this lying, loafing son of hers to enjoy himself. The trip will be fun, the teacher concedes, but Ramón will
also benefit a great deal from going. It's not just about the history lesson. Travel has the power to change young people's lives, as Mr. Blatchford knows well.

Within the week leading up to my first few days of school, our principal was dismissed from his job here and moved to a job in the

Bronx. So we started the year without a principal and went really the entire year without a principal. One of the assistant principals took over for a short time. And she left. And we had another man come in to run the school. He came for a short time, couldn't handle it, and left. And then we had the district deputy superintendent come in for a little while to run the school. And then he left. . . . The student schedules changed twice in the same year. They started with one, they changed it, and then they changed it again. The honest answer is, people didn't really know how to run the school. . . .

Parents definitely care about their children's education. But in terms of getting parents involved in the school community here, it doesn't really happen. . . . The school doesn't make an effort—intentionally—to get parents involved. 'Cause if parents were to walk down these halls right now, some of the parents wouldn't be too happy about what's happening. And I know if I were a parent, I would raise hell about this place. I'd be very concerned about my child's safety here.

The student body here is between 75 and 80 percent Dominican. Close to 90 percent are eligible for free lunch. So I think we're primarily talking about relatively poor families, immigrant families. . . . Some of the parents are not involved here because of a kind of a fear factor. . . . If it's a recent immigrant family that hasn't become legal yet, they might not want to raise too much hell in the school.

I wanted to take [my students] out of state to a Civil War battlefield. So I called Gettysburg, asked them if we could come. They said sure. Last year, as soon as we started crossing the George Washington Bridge, the whole bus erupted with applause. We're going out of state. We hadn't even crossed the bridge yet, you know?

In fifteen years how many kids are gonna remember what the three most important events leading to the Civil War were? Very few will remember that. But how many will remember walking across the battlefield at Gettysburg? You're gonna remember those things forever.

THE GUERRA FAMILY

Omar Guerra needs a haircut. At age fourteen, he is self-conscious about his appearance and thinks his hair—which is frizzy, black, and generally unruly—makes him stand out from the crowd. Stuffing it under a baseball cap brings the problem under control. But hats—particularly those in gang colors—are against the rules at I.S. 25, the brand-new middle school in the heart of the Dominican neighborhood of Washington Heights. With its sunlight-flooded windows and gleaming floor tiles, its stairwell mosaics and softly painted walls, I.S. 25 testifies to the investment the city is making in schools for its burgeoning immigrant population.

Mr. Mercado, the principal, has confiscated Omar's hat and wants his mother, Tamar Guerra, to come and pick it up. They should have a little talk about Omar, he says. Mercado has a box overflowing with hats he has pulled off the heads of seventh-grade boys. Where he finds time to enforce this rule is anyone's guess. I.S. 25 has over two thousand students and runs on double sessions. Fifth- and sixth-grade students start their day at 7:30 and leave at 1:30. Older kids, like Omar, arrive at 10:30 and leave at 5:30—which is news to the police, who sometimes pick them up as truants. Between periods, the hallways and stairways are clogged with students dragging their backpacks from class to class. Lunch is served in staggered shifts, starting with the youngest kids at 11:00 and every half hour thereafter until 1:30, when the oldest finally get to eat. Police patrol the hallways. Five of them have been assigned to help maintain order, a legacy of Mayor Giuliani's victory over the chancellor, who insisted that school security staff were up to the task.

Tamar isn't very happy about having to visit Omar's school once again. He tells her that he's doing fine, but she receives a regular raft of notices suggesting otherwise. Although Omar is officially in seventh grade, his test scores show that he reads at the third-grade level and writes like a fourth-grader. Attention deficit hyperactivity disorder (ADHD) is clearly part of the problem. Concentration is not Omar's strong suit. He forgets about the beginning of sentences by the time he gets to the end. He was diagnosed at the age of five but didn't get help for his learning problems until he was seven. Little has improved over time.

When we first met Omar, he had been a fixture in special education classes for many years. In middle school his placement became a source of shame. Nothing could be worse than being publicly labeled a "SPED" student, and he fought the classification with all the indignation a fourteen-year-old can muster. "I can do the work in regular classes," he protested. "Just gimme a chance!" In truth, Omar didn't like school very much. He preferred to work. He started sneaking out of school as often as he could get away with it, mostly to pick up odd jobs.

Tamar was ambivalent about the whole matter. The ADHD diagnosis entitled her to SSI disability coverage for Omar, which made a big difference in Tamar's finances. With that monthly support, she could refuse the worst factory jobs and spend more time helping Omar and his two younger brothers, nine-year-old Saúl and four-year-old Manuel. She worked on the side (and under the table) to make ends meet—picking up a neighbor's kids from school for $25 a month, babysitting elderly people. With the consent of her husband, Víctor, she partitioned the living room of their Washington Heights apartment, creating enough space for a boarder. That brought in another $50 a month.

Tamar never told Omar that she wanted him to remain in remedial classes for the SSI benefits, and it would be unfair to suggest that she wanted anything less than the best for her son. In Tamar's opinion, Omar had no chance of doing the work expected in regular courses. Her intuition turned out to be correct. In February 1999 Omar decided to forge her signature on transfer papers that authorized his release from special ed. Tamar was visiting her family in the Dominican Republic at the time. When Tamar came home and found out what had happened, she flew into a rage. She declared she was heading to school to reverse the transfer. Omar got on his knees and pleaded with her not "to do this to him." Tamar relented.

Now, as she sits outside the office of Alana Gonzales, Omar's guidance counselor, waiting to endure another barrage of criticism of her son, it's clear to Tamar that she made the wrong decision. Just look at his test scores or, worse yet, read the notices coming home from teachers who regularly complain that "Omar is not doing his homework," "Omar did not complete the science project," or "Omar does not have his workbook." She has a regular correspondence course going with those teachers. Since Tamar's English is weak, she is hardly in a position to supervise his homework from a quality standpoint. All she knows is that when she insists, he opens his books. Otherwise, the homework stays in his backpack. Vigilance is required at all times, and even that is proving insufficient. Omar is pulling down regular tours of duty in detention; his report card is a sight not for the squeamish.

"Do you want to get left back?" Tamar asks him. Omar is terrified of the prospect. Having to repeat seventh grade while his friends move on is a social catastrophe too damaging to even contemplate. Tamar understands his worry all too well. She was held back herself in seventh grade in the Dominican Republic and remembers how her teacher told her that she could just forget about going to college. Right then and there, she lost whatever enthusiasm for school she had ever had. "I don't want that for Omar," Tamar whispers.

The door opens and Ms. Gonzales ushers them inside. Once they're seated, she launches into a litany of complaints that take a full thirty minutes to deliver. Omar has failed to do a shred of homework this semester, she begins. His history teacher says that Omar doesn't have any idea what they are studying. It's not just that he doesn't understand colonial New York; he doesn't know that this is the topic at hand. He sleeps at his desk in math and cannot manage to bring his grammar workbook to his English class.

"*Creí en ti.* I believed in you," Tamar says accusingly to her son. "You are going to end up working in a stinkin' factory if you keep this up."

Tamar knows whereof she speaks, for she has often had no choice but to take jobs that offer low pay, with bosses that ride her back. With no education and a weak grasp of English, this is all she can find. She doesn't want Omar to settle for so little. But her teenager isn't listening. He slinks lower in his plastic chair, fiddles with the silver chain hanging from his waist, and avoids eye contact with either his mother or his counselor.

"Your academic record is a disaster, Omar," says Ms. Gonzales. "You are in real danger of being held back to repeat seventh grade. If your grades don't improve, I will have no choice."

Omar starts to protest. The classroom is too chaotic, he complains. Kids are yelling or sleeping at their desks. Teachers "don't do nothin'."

Alana Gonzales acknowledges that he has a point there. The classrooms *are* often out of control: overcrowded, underresourced, with teachers who cycle on and off the faculty at a dizzying speed. But Omar can find help if he looks for it, Ms. Gonzales adds. One of his teachers has offered to give up her lunch hour to work with him.

"What about *my* lunch?" Omar wants to know.

Alana shakes her head. "Omar, you have to sacrifice. Your teacher is willing to sacrifice."

It's no use, Tamar frets. Omar belongs in special ed. She knew he would fail in regular classes.

Ms. Gonzales disagrees. He has the brains to rise to the challenge. What he lacks is motivation. Perhaps fear will light a fire under Omar Guerra.

Tamar thinks her son might learn something from her own work history about the value of an education. In the spring of 1981 she arrived in New York, another fresh-faced immigrant teen looking for work. Almost immediately she found a factory job on Long Island for $3.25 an hour. When September rolled around, she enrolled in a special program for non–English speakers at a notoriously rough public school in the Bronx. Dominican kids fought pitched battles with black kids, and the Puerto Ricans were none too happy with either group. Tamar left the school one step ahead of a gang of African American girls who proclaimed loudly that they wanted to kill her. Tamar eventually wound up at the International Career Institute, where she picked up her GED.

Her education did not pay off in the job market. The only position she could find was in a clothing factory that paid her 10 cents for a completed collar. She earned $30 and then quit. Tamar is not a quitter by nature, and the next job she found, at a clothing store in Washington Heights, lasted for seven years, right through her pregnancy with Omar. His father was a scoundrel and had no intention of helping her out with this child. She hasn't seen him since the boy was six months old.

Víctor, her husband and the father of her two younger sons, is a better provider. They have been a couple for eleven years now, though they married only a year before our fieldwork began. His part-time job at his brother's discount store brings in the official cash, but Víctor also hawks socks and men's underwear on the street and operates a secretive business selling asthma medications to people who can't afford prescriptions. Putting all his gainful employment together, Víctor probably hauls in about $25,000 a year, though the exact number is anyone's guess—and certainly not information Tamar is privy to.

Víctor has always disapproved of Tamar's desire to work, but when Omar took himself out of special ed and lost his certification for SSI payments, Tamar had no choice but to make up for the lost income. Finding a job, however, turned out to be surprisingly hard. Though factory jobs had been plentiful in the early 1980s, they were scarce by the late '90s. Dominican neighbors told Tamar that the only places hiring were out in New Jersey, many of them two hours away. She landed a position ironing clothing for a dollar below minimum wage, but the cost of the private van that shuttled Tamar to the factory was $25 a week. That lasted about a day, just long enough for her to calculate how little she was going to pocket. She tried other factories closer by, but they were paying ridiculous wages, even lower than the ironing job, and illegal immigrants by the dozens were lining up for them anyway. "I'm better than this," she thought, and then remembered the cable bill, the electricity bill, and the telephone charges, all mounting up .

Deliverance arrived in the form of a cosmetics factory in New Jersey. An acquaintance said there might be openings and told her to head over to the factory's employment agency on 188th Street at 5 A.M. When Tamar arrived, the office personnel checked her green card and asked for her Social Security number. She was saved the bother of filling out an application; someone in the office did that for her.

On her first day of work, Tamar boarded one of three vans leaving from Washington Heights. Of the sixty passengers on those vans—all Dominicans hoping to find work—only thirty-two would be hired, her driver noted pointedly. An hour later, the vans deposited their passengers in front of an enormous corrugated-iron complex. Tamar could hear the morning whistle sounding the beginning of a new shift. Inside the facility, the walls climbed up twenty feet and the din from the conveyer belt made talking difficult. The place was so cavernous that it took Tamar almost the duration of her ten-minute break to get to the bathroom and back.

Between 7 and 3:30, Tamar and six other Spanish-speaking women packaged bottles of hair spray on a conveyor belt. Two of them placed the bottles in the individual containers, while the other four arranged the packaged bottles into boxes, closed the boxes shut, and sent them on their way to the pallets waiting at the end of the line. Thirty-five thousand bottles per day passed through their hands and were packed into containers for shipment to retailers across the country.

With just two ten-minute breaks and twenty minutes for lunch, the pace was breakneck. A Mexican coworker, whose name Tamar never did quite catch, tried to teach her to keep an even pace. "Don't slow down and then speed up," she admonished Tamar.

Bone-weary at the end of the day, Tamar slumped into her van seat and kept her mind on the money she was earning. "Thank God they want me back another day," she thought just before falling asleep.

After several weeks on the job, Tamar now feels more like a veteran. Divining the special tricks of survival on the factory floor has taken some time, but Tamar has figured out that the key lies in getting on the good side of the swing-shift bosses. Workers rotate through the plant—working on a Calvin Klein order one day, then shifting to J. Lo's new perfume. Some assignments are harder than others: the bottles are heavier or the shape more awkward to package. (Some assignments are also more dangerous than others; one week a worker lost the tip of her finger in one of the machines when she tried to retrieve a lid that had fallen in, threatening to jam the line.)

Winning over the first-line management ensures better placements. Tamar figures that of the twenty supervisors in the plant, she has converted three into fans, partly because she takes them up on overtures to buy things they are selling. One boss sold her a pair of pants that turned out to be a waste because they were too big for Manuel and too small for Saúl. Another boss sold her some raffle tickets. These little side deals seal the solidarity between Tamar and her bosses and help her hold on to the easier assignments. They also protect her when periodic sweeps of the workforce blow through the plant, resulting in mass firings. One week fifteen people were let go. Tamar doesn't know why; she is just glad she has some protection.

Not everyone is so fortunate. Two months into Tamar's tenure at the plant, a violent confrontation erupted on the shop floor. A coworker got in trouble for being too slow in moving bottles of cologne off the conveyor belt. Her supervisor pulled her off the line.

"Lady, you do not listen!" the line manager shouted and started hitting the worker on the arm with a roll of papers. By that time, the woman was frozen into what Tamar thought was a nervous breakdown. "She was stiff...like a cement block," Tamar recalls. Paramedics rushed to the shop floor but couldn't pry the woman's fingers open. The terrified supervisor pleaded with the victim to calm down but didn't succeed. The supervisor was fired the next day, her demise hastened by the fact that visitors from Estée Lauder were on the factory floor and had witnessed the incident.

Tamar hasn't had any accidents yet, but the job does take its toll on her. She arrives home at 6 P.M., makes dinner for her family, and passes out in the armchair. "My whole body hurts," she complains. "I didn't get to sleep until 3 A.M. last night, and Saúl woke me up at 5:30. My back hurts, my shoulder, my arm and wrist, and my knee here," she says, pointing to her swollen joint. Víctor thinks she is nuts for working this job and urges her to quit. "How can I quit?" she asks.

Tamar feels obligated to pay for things her kids want. If Omar asks for sneakers that cost $55, she wants to get them before he changes his mind and asks for a name-brand version that is even more expensive. And when the two younger boys see what Omar has, they want some of the action as well. "You don't love me, you only love Omar," Saúl complains.

It is true that Tamar shows Omar special attention. Because he is not Víctor's child, Omar cannot command as much of his stepfather's interest as his brothers can. Víctor never tells Tamar that he won't pay for Omar's sneakers, but she has a sixth sense that tells her not to push the boundaries of his largesse, so she doesn't ask.

When September arrives, Tamar has to buy school supplies for the kids. She asks Víctor for $50 and adds it to the $160 from her own earnings. Then she ventures out to find a Pokémon book bag for Saúl and a gold ring with his initials on it for Omar. Little Manuel, who spends the workday with Tamar's mother, isn't old enough to demand very much, but his older brothers understand the connection between Tamar's job and these goodies. That's why Saúl shakes Tamar out of bed at 5:30. "You gotta get ready for work, Mami," he tells her.

Yet some things Tamar cannot do for her family precisely because she is gone much of the time and completely sapped when she is at home. Víctor has never taken much of an interest in the kids' schooling. He looks after Manuel in the early morning but is perfectly happy to turn him over to Tamar's mother by 9:30. Rarely will Víctor ask Saúl or Omar about homework. Tamar used to do so before she started the factory job, and she still tries to show some interest. Yet the kids sense that her mind is not focused on their academic performance, and that's OK with them.

The sudden loss of Tamar's vigilance is showing, though. A year before Tamar started working in Jersey, Saúl was doing so well that his teachers recommended he skip third grade and go directly to fourth. Tamar and Víctor declined that option, but they came out of his parent-teacher conference glowing with pride. Saúl's teacher said that he was one of the two "most brilliant kids in this class." The lowest grade he received was an 85, and that was only because he didn't sleep well the night before the test. He had a near perfect homework record. To help him with his math, Tamar stuck copies of multiplication tables all over the house, but it turned out Saúl had already committed them to memory.

Now, within a few months of Tamar's employment, Saúl has fallen to below-grade-level performance in some of his third-grade subjects. Teachers are starting to send notes home complaining that "Saúl is coming to school tired and fails to show interest." As for Omar, he is failing every subject except computers. He should be in summer school, but Tamar has been unable to put aside any time to find out whether there is a spot for him. "I should go to his school to find out," she worried in June, "but I can't miss work. I'm afraid I'll lose my job." There are no public phones at the factory, so she cannot call from her job. She asks Víctor to go in her place, but he doesn't bother.

Management has limited patience for the burdens that working mothers face in the Missing Class. Factory jobs don't come with paid vacation, at least for those who are not in a union. (And somehow Tamar keeps losing her hold on that blue-collar job just when she becomes union-eligible.) Getting the kids to the doctor, responding to court dates when her landlord sues for back rent—these occasions have already knocked Tamar off track at work. She misses a day here and there, and the boss gets angry. She gets laid off for a day and is reinstated only because she's a good worker.

Of course, there are plenty of reasons that Tamar is happy to be working, too. The work may be grueling, but "I get out of the routine in the house," she notes. She clearly does not want to rely on Víctor, particularly when it comes to caring for Omar. ("You never know about men," Tamar confides.)[13]

In a culture where work is the signature of responsible adulthood, there is no substitute for it as a source of honor and respect. But Tamar doesn't think in these lofty terms; she just wants to be in control of her resources to some limited degree. She doesn't want to yield to Víctor's opinion that she should not work.

Over the course of the many years of our fieldwork, Tamar had five or six different factory jobs, interspersed with odd jobs, and dry patches when Víctor's salary and SSI payments were the only income coming into the house. Her children's lives were less chaotic when she was nearby and could pay attention to them, when she was not drained by a long day's commute and the physical demands of a factory job. On the other hand, there were more presents under the Christmas tree when Tamar was on the job.

Dropping out of school is not something that happens suddenly.[14] Gradually students begin to pull away, skipping classes more often and racking up detentions. Some just want to be released from a site of failure. Omar had some of those feelings, but when he was fourteen, he also had more grown-up desires to be somewhere other than Mr. Garcia's geography class. He wanted to earn some money. On the job, Omar felt capable rather than confused and stupid, the two emotions that were his constant companions in school. So when the neighborhood florist asked if he'd like to deliver roses during school hours on Valentine's Day, Omar didn't hesitate. The next month, he took time off school to post flyers for a woman who promised to pay him handsomely and then reneged. He was more careful when he was approached by a landlady who wanted some help putting up Room for Rent signs.

Tamar is ambivalent about her son's entrepreneurial spirit. She doesn't want Omar to skip school, but she's elated at the thought that he might be able to buy his own clothes and maybe help out his brothers from time to time. Instead of thinking of him as a chronic source of trouble, Tamar is beginning to see Omar as a provider. "He has a good height," she muses. "He can work anywhere." Perhaps she will be able to resume giving her mother some money if Omar is bringing in another income.

Unfortunately, the authorities at school do not see these pluses. What they see is a kid in academic trouble slipping into a pattern of absences that lead directly to dropping out. Tamar and Omar are summoned to the district headquarters uptown, where a phalanx of special ed teachers, psychologists, and learning specialists assemble in a last-ditch effort to save Omar Guerra.

Ms. Gonzales, Omar's guidance counselor, leans over to Tamar and asks in a low voice whether she knows how important this meeting is. "No, I know nothing about it," Tamar replies, her throat tightening. Tamar rarely hears anything encouraging about her son's school experience, and today brings her another round of depressing news. It seems the specialists want to put Omar in a trade school in Queens, but he has flatly refused; he sits with his eyes cast to the floor, his arms crossed over his chest.

Omar is on the verge of tears. When asked by the assembly what he wants to do in life, he answers that he wants to be an aviation mechanic or a football player. Even Tamar knows these dreams are out of the question. "He is going to mess up everything," she concludes. "He will not accomplish one thing."

In the spring of 2000, Tamar's premonition comes perilously close to the truth. Fifteen-year-old Omar and two other boys are accused of touching two girls—one of them a twelve-year-old foster child—in private places. Omar denies the charge, but later admits that he kissed one of the girls and touched her, though not below the waist. He claims Nolita is his girlfriend and that they met behind the school to make out. Nolita sees the episode differently, claiming that Omar fondled her breasts and rubbed his penis on her.

This is the last straw. Omar is given a month in a juvenile detention center in the Bronx. Later he is released to probation and moved to another middle school, this time in Midtown Manhattan, a long subway ride from his Washington Heights neighborhood.

One month after his release, Omar finds himself in the worst possible trouble. As he tells the story, a girl with a crush on him was put off by his lack of attention and falsely accused him of sexual assault. He never touched her that way, he insists to his mother. He just pushed her away when she stepped on his new Jordan sneakers and told her she was ugly. He admits that he pushed her against the breast but denies that he fondled her.

It is her word against his, but he is the one on probation. "Who's going to believe him?" Tamar cries. "He's a guy. The guy always loses." His lawyer believes that Omar has no chance, given his prior record. He urges the boy to plead guilty. Tamar stands behind her son but loses all confidence when she discovers that the case will be adjudicated by the same judge who put him on probation. At the hearing, the judge is visibly angry with Omar, reminding him of the promises he had made only a few weeks before about staying out of trouble. He is sentenced to eighteen months.

Tamar visits her son as often as she can at an upstate New York detention facility that costs a bundle in bus fares. The confinement does not go down easily for Omar. He has problems obeying orders and controlling his temper. He rails against the authorities for confiscating his possessions. "They think everything is for a gang," he complains to his mother. "And if you're not crazy, you're going to get upset." To him, everything about the place seems designed to drive someone insane. When Tamar tries to reason with him, he snaps at her. "Yo, do you know what it's like in here? You got to get permission to go to the bathroom!"

"He flies off the handle," Tamar laments, "and he gets written up." The authorities, meanwhile, lie to him about when he's scheduled for release. "It's all bullshit," Tamar notes with disgust, "because he's still there."

For a long time, Tamar was in denial about Omar's problems. She defended him vociferously, believed his version of events rather than those of his jailers, and was certain that everyone was against him. She brushed aside reports that even behind bars he was caught with nude pictures, caught lying, caught breaking various rules against contraband. But unlike other parents of juvenile offenders, she took time off her job to attend his evaluation. Tamar came away convinced that it was she who had been mistaken.

She now realizes that Omar has trouble distinguishing between harmful and beneficial courses of action. He has difficulty following instructions. And he needs help. "Before, I was blind," she notes with a sigh. "I didn't accept what people said about Omar." She prays for her oldest son. Maybe it's not too late for him to change.

THE POLICY PARADOX

Children who have not mastered reading by third grade are at great risk of failing in school. This fact has spurred critics of social promotion to call for an increased reliance on standardized testing and holding kids back if they cannot pass. Their arguments have struck a resonant chord among the American public, including the Missing Class. Danielle Wayne made it clear that she approved of the decision to hold her daughter Elesha back when she floundered over those tests because, like many parents, she was convinced her child would do better in the end if she took care of business now. And before she went to work, Danielle took up the role that school boards throughout the country expect parents to fill in the era of No Child Left Behind: that of an auxiliary educational labor force.

But now that Danielle has a full-time job, she can no longer do as much. The neglect shows in Safiya's imperfect speech patterns and in the older children's shoddy grades. If Danielle's kids fall into the "at risk" category—which seems increasingly likely—her absence from their daytime lives will be implicated, particularly because the institutional infrastructure of schools and child care that she can access is too weak to make up for her departure.

The costs of Tamar's absence to her family—with two hours of commuting time added to an eight-hour shift—are not the kind we can quantify easily. Would Omar have ended up a school dropout and convicted sex offender if his mother had been able to watch over him through middle school as she did when he was younger? Missing Class teens like Omar would probably get into trouble more often than middle-class kids, even if their parents were around to supervise them. Omar started to falter academically at a young age; thousands of kids with learning disabilities disappear from the New York City public school system every year.[15] Yet his performance and behavior in school became noticeably worse when Tamar no longer had time to spare. And the same loss of concentration overcame his brother Saúl, who had done well in school—until the time Tamar started her factory job. By fourth grade, he, too, was on a downward spiral.

It would be tempting to focus on the income side of the equation and assume that only good can come from the opportunities the adults in these families have to earn a living. Having more resources stabilizes most families. And lifting a mother like Danielle out of her depression through employment cannot help but be good for her kids. At the same time, it is important to consider the price exacted by those rising earnings—the disappearance of crucial hours at home, which is all the more costly in a context of uneven child care and troubled schools. Neither money nor the satisfaction that comes from having a job will help very much if there is no one around to mind the children.

Nationwide, some 10.5 million low-income children live in families where one or both parents are working. The Annie E. Casey Foundation estimates that there is a gap of twenty to twenty-five-hours per week between parents' work obligations and students' school schedules. The steepest increase in working hours in recent years has happened among families toward the bottom of the income distribution. Missing Class families depend on those paychecks, and in this respect the increasing work hours are helpful. Where this leaves their kids is another matter.[16]

Architects of social policies have tended to focus on a single issue. The policy wonks who designed No Child Left Behind were not the same crowd as the cheerleaders for welfare reform. Critics of social promotion wanted students to master basic skills and needed parents to help with the task, since schools could not manage the burden on their own. Reformers trying to eliminate welfare either by punishing recipients or rewarding workers—or both—were not thinking too much about kids and schools. They simply wanted dependent women to get off the dole and into the labor force. This myopia brought about clashing priorities, making success in either domain impossible for many poor and Missing Class families.

Those of us who want women to be able to stand on their own feet do not like to hear that the children the women leave behind during the workday may be doomed to repeat the lives of their poor mothers. But in a world where high-quality child care is available only to the wealthy or the lucky, a child's prospects can be irreparably damaged if her mother disappears for many hours every day, leaving her in the care of someone who lets drug addicts into the house. What matters more, the mother's shot at present-day security or the next generation's potential for future success? At the moment, we may be addressing the problems of the parents, only to see a "sacrificed generation" emerge, a cohort of children condemned by poor schooling or entanglement in the criminal justice system to a life not unlike the one their parents were running hard to escape.

FIVE

In Sickness and in Health

> While the uninsured are most at risk, researchers estimate
> that about a fifth of insured individuals are underinsured
> and face limits on coverage or substantial financial costs
> if faced with an illness.
> —Kaiser Commission on Medicaid and the Uninsured, 2002

THE HALL FAMILY

Gloria Hall is angry. She is angry at the board of her co-op, who refused to get her a parking space in the building even though her car mirrors have been smashed twice and there are plenty of unused spaces in the lot. Gloria will even get up and agitate about it at the co-op meetings, so much so that her neighbors routinely boo her off the floor.

She's upset at her bank, which charged her huge fees for bounced checks and never told her about them, until she noticed her savings account was a few hundred dollars short. In a fit of fury she closed her account—and then found herself struggling to open a new one, having lost the citizenship papers a new account required.

Come to think of it, Gloria is angry at America. She came here as a teenager from Panama, just one more descendant of slaves hoping for an opportunity up north, but soon enough she had her fill of the word "nigger," the rude stares, and the constant harping about how people from other countries were lazy and degenerate and uncultured—when she knew for a fact that wealthy, powerful America couldn't even care for its own.

She is truly furious with her ex-husband, the father of her three children. When she first met him he was a responsible black man, a supervisor at the factory where she worked, who eventually got hired by a construction company. But after the two were married, Samuel went "off the deep end." He started drinking; he drank so much that he would collapse and get robbed as he stumbled back home. He got hooked on drugs and began hanging out in crack houses.

Samuel went to live with his sister in Jersey and supposedly cleaned up his act, but when he came back to Brooklyn nothing had changed. He became a deadbeat dad, too busy drinking to attend when Mallory, their eldest son, graduated from junior high. Samuel barely noticed when Mallory went off to a boarding school in Massachusetts at the age of thirteen, and he seemed too busy to care when Mallory graduated and joined the army.

Gloria divorced him. Wounded by this turn of events, Samuel found his way into a treatment program, recovered fully, and—wonder of wonders—found a well-paying, white-collar job. Gloria's wrath did not die; he was still a good-for-nothing man who had time for a girl-friend and Saturday overtime at the firm but couldn't manage to pick up the two younger kids for the weekend—his court-mandated weekend—and couldn't be bothered to pay his full share of child support. Yet he had the nerve to tell their sons that Gloria was greedy for asking.

She is fed up, too, with those sons of hers, thirteen-year-old Stephen and nine-year-old Terrell, who expect the world of her—to play catch even though she's sick, to take them to the movies even though she's tired, to pay for a school trip to Spain even though she can barely save a dollar, to make them into men even though she doesn't know how—and yet expect nothing from their father. Is she the only one who notices? He's the one who shuts them up in their rooms with Game Boys while he goes off to his weekend shift at work. He was the one who kept promising to take Terrell fishing but never did. *He* was the one who said he'd accompany Stephen to a play but decided at the last minute he wasn't "properly dressed" and bailed. She is angry that *they* are not angry.

And then eighteen-year-old Mallory goes off to the military and signs an insurance policy that will give the money 50-50 to his father and mother—50-50!—when *she* was the one who raised him, was there for him when his own dad was off giving a bad name to fatherhood everywhere.

But what makes Gloria angriest of all—what sinks her into long bouts of depression and suicidal thinking, pushes her onto the very edge of her sanity—is that she is dying.

She has been diagnosed with thymoma, a rare cancer of the thymus. It started in that small vestigial gland behind her breastbone, then spread to her bloodstream, and then into her diaphragm, requiring the removal of part of her lungs. Gloria went through chemotherapy. The cancer went into remission—only to come back several years later. A few years ago, things reached a point where she felt the need to approach her ex-husband about her health. She needed to make sure he would take care of Terrell and Stephen if she died. Her expectations of Samuel were so low that she wanted him to either commit himself to the arrangement or relinquish his rights as a father so that her own family could take custody when the time came.

After hesitating, Samuel told her he'd take care of the boys. Gloria was not convinced.

Perhaps fate wouldn't seem so spiteful, or her life so awry, if it had not been so good before. Once, she was a unionized city employee. She wasn't rich, but she was far from poor. Her days of pressing and labeling pants on a factory assembly line seemed to be behind her. In fact, when they were married, Samuel wasn't so sure he liked having a wife who made more money than he did. It was one of the reasons for their breakup. In spite of Samuel's objections, Gloria insisted on making her own living. "I don't like to depend on people to take care of me," she says.

So it upsets her to think of how little freedom she has left. Now she must make do on a fixed income from SSI and her ex-husband's alimony. The total comes to about $1,200 a month. Her body, meanwhile, is breaking down. Gloria was always on the heavy side, but now she can barely walk. Her dusky skin is puffy, her rounded face drawn; her eyes register the ache in her body as she moves, carefully, as if measuring each step. Walking two blocks down the street leaves her gasping for breath. Her older sister, Amelia, who is retired and suffers from breast cancer, once had to accompany Gloria to the supermarket. Amelia left her there to shop, but then came back because she feared Gloria wouldn't be able to make it home. "And I was in the same spot where she left me," Gloria says. "So she just took the bags. And I said,

'Oh, man, I can't believe this is happening to me.' . . . I should be the one that's helping her."

At night Gloria cloisters herself in her room and puts on some gospel music. Her stern mask falls away, and her eyes, habitually slit with pain, relax. Gospel does that. "Why you playing the same song over and over?" her son Stephen asks, exasperated. Gloria just ignores him. She feels good when the music is playing. She feels like herself again. She remembers how much she loves her children, how much she wants to be there for them in the years to come.

The frustration dissipates. But following behind, always, is regret. If she does not have that fury to propel her forward, onward, then her memories pull her back—to bad decisions, to failed relationships, to lost friends. The children—where did she go wrong with them? Why are they so unruly and argumentative? "Was it my fault?" she asks herself. "Did I do this right? Did I do that right? Could I have done it better?"

But it's no use. "Sometimes I just think that no matter what I do, it's not enough. It's just not enough."

Much attention has been paid—justifiably so—to the plight of uninsured Americans, who numbered more than forty-six million in 2006, a disproportionate number of them poor or near poor.[1] Recent studies have also examined the predicament of working families saddled with responsibilities for caring for sick children and elderly parents.[2] But what happens when the working caregiver becomes the sick patient? The story of Gloria Hall is the story of many Missing Class Americans who find their lives, in public health expert Jody Heymann's apt phrase, "predictably unpredictable." They may be fortunate enough to have health insurance and decent-paying jobs, but once illness strikes their households, uncertainty and anxiety set in. There is, in the forefront, the frightening prospect of impending death or physical disability. But there is also the psychological trauma of greatly diminished abilities and the fear of no longer being able to provide for loved ones—fear that can express itself in depression, anger, or both, as Gloria Hall has discovered.

Gloria had health insurance from her job as an officer in the city's health department police, where she worked the night shift out of one of their Brooklyn facilities. The job was a good one—public sector, with plenty of benefits and a decent pension if she stayed long enough. With that reliable paycheck, Gloria rose beyond her family's humble beginnings in Panama and said a final good-bye to her days as a low-wage worker in New York. But the job's health coverage, she soon learned, was less than adequate. For one thing, her cancer remained undetected for years because her doctors didn't listen to her and her HMO refused at first to pay for a test.

Gloria had started complaining to her doctor in 1989. "I feel like something is growing in my chest," she told him. One X-ray showed an abnormality. "Maybe you didn't hold your breath," the hospital staff told her. This state of affairs went on, with Gloria insisting there was something wrong and the physicians doubting her. Finally, a physician's assistant told her, "Either you're crazy or something is really physically [wrong with you]. I'm going to set you up for this test." The results of the CAT scan did not look good. Gloria needed an MRI, they said. Yet Gloria's insurer wouldn't pay for it.

Finally, after some wrangling, the MRI was done, and in 1993 Gloria was diagnosed with thymoma. Chemotherapy treatments sent the cancer into remission but damaged her heart.

The next round of problems cropped up when Gloria's doctor told her that her chances would improve if she could see doctors who specialized in this unusual form of cancer and recommended she visit Memorial Sloan-Kettering Cancer Center, a world-class cancer treatment and research center in Manhattan. Her HMO refused to pay for it. "The only time they approve [it] is like when somebody's dying already," Gloria says. "When it's too late, that's when they'll approve." Gloria dropped her HMO and got on Medicaid, the government's health insurance for the poor. Sloan-Kettering accepted Medicaid.

Like many working Americans faced with life-altering illnesses, Gloria was learning the limits of the nation's health-care system. Yes, she was insured, but only weakly so. Unlike many Americans, Gloria was a member of a union. Even so, she lacked the generous health benefits enjoyed by the nation's wealthier workers, who can command such largesse. Her health insurance didn't want to pay for expensive diagnostic tests. It didn't want to pay for a state-of-the-art treatment center. Fortunately for Gloria, she was quickly descending into the ranks of the poor and *publicly* insured. Once she was too sick to work, she began to live on monthly SSI payments of $768 and child support of $500. The low income meant that Gloria now qualified for Medicaid.

After her cancer was diagnosed, Gloria became a regular visitor to the Brooklyn Hospital Center, what she calls her "home away from home," a nonprofit teaching hospital a short distance from her apartment in Fort Greene. She liked her doctor, an Indian man who was a pulmonary specialist. When the doctor learned Gloria didn't have a prescription drug plan, he handed her several dozen samples of heart medication—a costly drug—so she wouldn't go without it. Gloria's other interactions at the hospital, however, left a lot to be desired. Emergency-room doctors had no bedside manners. (It didn't help that many of them had never heard of thymoma, a rare cancer seen mainly in populations from tropical areas; one doctor confessed she didn't even know how to spell it.) The nurses, with some exceptions, tried her patience. It pained Gloria to hear elderly patients crying out in pain, only to be ignored. "Unbelievable," Gloria says. "My sister went there once, and she called and called. Nobody paid any attention. She had to [urinate] on herself." Meanwhile, the hospital technicians, many of them Russian immigrants, were hurried and brusque. Do they dislike black people? she wondered.

What Gloria encountered at Brooklyn Hospital Center will fail to shock anyone familiar with the grim frontlines of America's health-care system, where chronically understaffed hospitals struggle to serve low-income communities. Patients often receive halfhearted bedside attention from physicians and other hospital staff, even when they are—like Gloria—insured. The treatment they are given telegraphs a message: You think you deserve better? Guess what? You don't. True, the care at Brooklyn Hospital Center was better than nothing—it sure beat waiting in the emergency room for hours for someone to treat her—but sometimes, after hours of being shuttled from one surly hospital worker to another, Gloria felt like she was being treated in a destitute Latin American country again, rather than in the world's richest nation.

. . .

The heat is already fierce as Gloria and her friend Leah make their way down Atlantic Avenue past the shopping center. Gloria has brought a wet towel to pat her face as they walk, but the sweat is flowing freely from her pores, pumped out by the unusual exertion of the day. She asks Leah if she can stop by Pathmark to buy some water, and the two duck into the supermarket, taking their time to rest up and soak in the soothing air-conditioned coolness.

After boarding the number 6 train, the pair gets off at the Fifty-first Street stop. The subway steps are a challenge for Gloria: climbing causes her heart to race wildly, as if someone were chasing her. When they reach the top, Gloria looks around blankly, silent and breathless, as if trying to gather her wits.

There are another ten minutes of slow, measured walking—the most that Gloria, in her anemic state, can handle—and then the two are at their destination: Memorial Sloan-Kettering Cancer Center. The doorman recognizes Gloria and asks her if she's visiting the usual office. She says yes. On this trip, she'll have some blood work and X-rays done, and then she'll meet with her doctor.

Gloria and Leah walk into the medical suite. It's an extravagant setup—a huge, softly lit waiting room decorated in muted pastel colors and decked out with comfy chairs. Behind the reception area is a sculpture, a carved wooden panel featuring a running fountain. Soft "smooth jazz" drifts into the room from hidden speakers. In one corner is a well-stocked refreshments area, with coffee and tea of all types, cold drinks, cookies, pretzels, and chips—all complimentary.

Gloria checks in with one of the receptionists, who cheerfully points out the refreshments and entertainment in the room. All the reception staff, in fact, are strikingly professional, ready with immediate, polite answers to any questions. They are a mix of different ethnicities, too: Asian, black, and white. The patients waiting in the room, on the other hand, are almost all white and over fifty.

Gloria begins her long wait. Leah has to head back to Brooklyn to pick up Terrell and take him to his first day of music lessons, and so she leaves. Later that night, the two catch up. The tests went well, Gloria says. Thank God the cancer has not spread to other parts of her body beyond the diaphragm and the small part of the lung where it is now located. But it has grown slightly larger. She and her doctor agree that it would be best if they could avoid more chemotherapy—the last treatment damaged her heart—but that may not be possible. For her part, Gloria is intent on looking into alternative therapies. Somewhere, somehow, she will find the treatment that will save her life.

How did Terrell's music lessons go? Gloria sighs. The lessons were fine, but her older son, Stephen, didn't bother to pick up his little brother when they were over. Terrell waited at the music school for more than two hours for someone to come.

Gloria was born in Panama, the youngest of six in a family descended from Jamaican slaves. Her father, a restaurant owner, was never around. Her mother raised all the children—one son and five daughters, including Gloria—by herself. Life in Panama was hard. People hustled to survive. They ran numbers. They baked bread and fried fish to hawk on the streets. If they had a disability, they had no choice but to beg on the corners. Panama didn't have food stamps, social services, or anything of the kind, Gloria says. People had "to struggle there to eat. Really, really struggle to eat."

For those living with that kind of hardship, America is a beacon that draws them closer. Gloria and her family were enthralled with the idea of going to the United States. First to leave was Veronica, her older sister, who moved to New York and quickly found work. So successful was Veronica that she soon saved up enough money to cover the down payment for a house. But it was 1962. A real estate agent quickly squashed that dream. "Not only are you single," the agent told her, "but you're black, too. There's no way you're going to get a home." Four decades later, Veronica is on the verge of retirement and still renting.

Rhina, Gloria's mother, moved next, finding work at a luxury department store and then a hotel. Gloria followed at the age of sixteen. By then, her entire family was living in New York. It was a blessing to be with her mother again and encouraging to think they would leave poverty behind forever.

But the family's good fortune did not last. Twelve years ago, one of Gloria's older sisters, Zurina, died of a heart attack. She was just thirty-five. Zurina left behind two sons, aged ten and two. The older boy, Jacob, couldn't deal with his mother's death. He never talked about it— never really grieved—and for years he shuttled in and out of institutions. "He flipped out. . . . He just took it the wrong way. Took it hard." Gloria saw Jacob acknowledge his pain only once, on Zurina's birthday. The boy started bawling, wailing that he missed his mother.

Gloria blames the insurance company for her sister's death. Zurina was signed up with an HMO that, according to Gloria, was fixated on cutting costs.[3] "If she had a different kind of insurance, I feel she would still be alive," Gloria says, "because my sister had a heart problem probably all her life, and they never caught it. And she went to the hospital so many times—came home with all the monitors every time—every time—and they took it off. 'Oh, we didn't find anything.' You know, no extensive test was done on her to see that she had a problem then. None."

It wasn't that Gloria and Zurina lacked health insurance. They were covered, but like many in the Missing Class, they weren't covered enough. Managed care meant miserly care. Some HMOs won't pay for the expense of spotting the surreptitious approach of killers like cancer and heart disease. And too many hospitals fall in step with this line of thinking, Gloria alleges. "They don't wanna send you for the test that they know you need because it's too expensive. It's almost as if they're getting like a cut of the HMO money or whatever. . . like they work hand in hand."[4]

For their part, HMOs probably look at the bleak statistics and grimace. The Missing Class tend to be poor insurance risks: the poorer and darker-complexioned the population, the higher the rates of illness.[5] In Gloria's previously poor, persistently black and Hispanic family, a conspicuous number of family members have fallen ill. Gloria and her sister Amelia have cancer. In addition to Zurina, another sister has heart problems. Gloria's two younger sons (and Gloria herself) have asthma; Terrell sometimes has to be rushed to the ER when he has a violent attack. And her mother, Rhina, suffers from bone cancer, recently diagnosed as terminal. "Her mind goes and comes," Gloria says. "Sometimes she don't remember anything."

The declining health of the family matriarch has, in turn, brought to the surface some unsightly rifts between the siblings. With the exception of one sister in Massachusetts, Gloria has never been close to any of them. "Supposedly I'm the youngest one and my mother spoiled me," she says. Now their wrangling over the inheritance has poisoned any remnant of cordiality. One sister wants the family to use Mom's money to pay for another burial plot; Gloria says the cemetery space they already have is enough. Rhina asks Gloria to take her money out of the bank but won't tell the other daughters about it. "That's none of their business," she snaps. Gloria shouldn't share the money with the others, she insists. "Whatever happens, don't give it to them." But that has put Gloria in an awkward position. She doesn't want to be accused of stealing the money. "It's gonna be a big mess before my mother closes her eyes—if she closes them before me."

THE GUERRA FAMILY

> Wendy Agustín, a Dominican mother of five who has lived in New York most of her life, never opens the windows of her cramped, two-bedroom apartment in a drafty six-story building opposite the 126th Street Bus Depot. That is because fumes from the nearly 200 buses that circulate daily through this tiny block, between First and Second Avenues, are making her children sick.
>
> —*New York Times*, November 5, 2006

When her oldest son, Omar, was born, Tamar was twenty years old, a fresh-off-the-plane immigrant cowering in the presence of her abusive boyfriend, Enrique. Six months after the boy was born, the boyfriend was out of Tamar's life for good. Enrique had been a terror, and she was glad to see him go. Her son, however, continued to bear traces of the earlier, unhappy union that had conceived him. His health was erratic and nerve-racking for his young mother. Born with a small stomach, Omar retained little food and vomited constantly.

Tamar took Omar to Columbia University Medical Center, to an outside pediatrician, to anyone with a stethoscope and a willing ear. They all assured Tamar that there was nothing to worry about.

Tamar's mother, Olivia, was, as usual, suspicious. The elderly island-born woman—wary of doctors and city bureaucrats—posed the theory that Omar's physicians weren't paying attention to him because he didn't have health insurance. She urged Tamar to apply for Medicaid.

Before she had Omar, Tamar had worked a succession of off-the-books jobs with low pay and long hours at the Tri-State Region's drabbest factories and clothing stores. She had tried to apply for public assistance but had always been rejected. The authorities didn't believe that she didn't work (true enough) or that she didn't have a husband (her *machista* scoundrel of a boyfriend at the time refused to marry her). After those initial attempts, Tamar gave up. Health insurance was not simply worth the ordeal of wrestling with the city's dreary bureaucracy every week.

But now, with a vomit-reeking baby slung over her shoulder, Tamar changed her mind. She and her mother decided to go to the welfare office and apply for Medicaid the next day. The problem was, what to do with Omar? She couldn't bring him there. He'd throw up and frighten all the caseworkers; plus, there was that awful odor that followed him everywhere.

But there was no time to find a sitter. Tamar brought Omar to the office, and sure enough, he started vomiting—twenty-five times in thirty minutes. The caseworkers were flabbergasted. What kind of mother would bring her sick child into a place of business? A half hour later, the paramedics arrived and drove Tamar, Olivia, and the puking tot to Columbia University Medical Center.

The same doctor who had told Tamar with a straight face that Omar was completely fine was now telling her that her son had to undergo a major operation on his stomach. Tamar berated him angrily. Why didn't he examine Omar properly the first time? Was it because she didn't have insurance?

The operation was successful. Omar's vomiting was cured. And Tamar, while tending to Omar at the hospital, received an unexpected phone call. It was the welfare office. Her application, she was told, was approved. This time there wasn't an official interview or a single document to photocopy—she got her insurance in a bureaucratic flash.

Tamar still wonders why she didn't get insurance the first time she applied. If she had coverage then, perhaps the doctors would have examined Omar with more care, she reasons. "This country has always been like this. When you don't need it, they give it to you, and when you need it, they don't give it to you. When you speak the truth, they don't believe you. When you say five hundred lies, then they believe you." Tamar had pleaded for the government's help with all her honesty and earnestness—and look where it got her.

Welfare, however, would not become a way of life for Tamar and her family. Before long she started working, and Víctor—formerly her boyfriend, *finally* her husband—shouldered the burden of paying more of the bills. The extra income brought new school supplies, fashionable clothes for the kids, and generous Christmas gifts. But soon Tamar learned that money—or at least the money *her* family made—could not buy health.

Urban America can be a dangerous place for the young, as millions of this country's families know well. Central cities harbor a wide range of pollutants and toxins—from smoggy air to pest droppings to more potent poisons. Their crumbling housing stock dates back decades, sometimes a half century or more. Living amid these surroundings puts children at risk for lead poisoning, asthma, and other respiratory conditions. In neighborhoods with less money and fewer allies at City Hall, oftentimes the pollution is worse, the health risks deadlier. But even when the dangers are spread more or less equally across class lines, the resulting illnesses hit Missing Class households—with their lack of public health knowledge, inflexible work schedules, weak or nonexistent coverage, and other impediments to care—especially hard.[6]

Tamar's family has been scarred by environmental hazards of all kinds. Omar, now a teenager, suffered from asthma until the age of five. Nine-year-old Saúl has severe allergies, another condition associated with pollution.[7] He often wakes up painfully congested, and his mother doesn't have the heart to send him to school. He'll get better, she knows, as the day goes on—but if the school calls her at work, she won't be able to head back to Manhattan and take him to the doctor. The problem with working at a factory is, after all, that you work at a factory; the assembly line waits for no one.

As for Manuel, her four-year-old baby, the danger was undetectable at first. When he was born, Tamar's family was living in the same place as it does now, a gloomy railroad apartment in an older Washington

Heights complex of gray stone walls and tiled floors. Their Chinese landlord wasn't fixing the place fast enough to keep the ceiling up, which would fall down in chunks of painted plaster. The real threat, however, was the paint itself. Tamar was unaware of the lead risk posed to her children until Manuel went to the doctor for a routine checkup and had his blood tested. "Before I knew it, the city was here at the house," Tamar says. Tests had revealed a disturbingly high level of lead in Manuel's blood, the health officials said. A level of 8 is considered normal. Less than 10 is acceptable. Manuel's reading was 20.9.

Manuel—the playful rug rat who was fond of Winnie the Pooh—was suddenly the object of intense medical scrutiny. For more than a year, he had to eat iron-rich foods—broccoli, salads, and other kid-unfriendly meals—and take special supplements to counteract the anemia that lead poisoning causes. Tamar did what she was told, but she didn't know much about Manuel's condition, much less about her rights as a parent and renter. "I didn't even know that you could sue someone because of lead," she says. A city health official finally suggested she do just that. One phone call later an inspector arrived to photograph the apartment and meticulously collect paint samples from its walls. They had to act fast, Tamar's lawyer told her, because the landlord might clean up the lead. She laughed. "This landlord won't fix [it] even if they put eighty charges on him." The next day the landlord sent in a building crew. "He came flying—flying!" Tamar recalls. "I said, 'Oh my God, if they hadn't come, [the landlord himself] would have removed the lead.'"

When a serious condition like lead poisoning strikes their children, Missing Class families are often at a loss. They may not be able to find the treatment or testing they need. They may lack knowledge of the medical and legal systems to do what's best for their families. Tamar was fortunate enough to find a lawyer to advise her and a doctor to put Manuel on a course of treatment. Even doing that much pushed her to the limits. "I'm so dizzy from the mess," she says. "I go around and around." Other families are not so lucky. Her husband's relatives also live in the building, and Víctor's niece, Patricia, was also poisoned by lead. In her case, the condition wasn't caught early enough. School-aged but unable to read, Patricia is now stuck in special education classes.

Tamar worries about what long-term damage might have been done to Manuel. As an infant, he wasn't "dumb," but his development may have been stunted. Though he is almost five, Manuel is still in diapers. Tamar gives him laxatives, hoping the diarrhea will force him to use the toilet. She reminds him that all his cousins are using the toilet; she pleads with him to follow her instructions. All her efforts have been to no avail. Manuel insists on soiling his diapers.

Manuel's condition is keeping Tamar in a state of high anxiety. He hasn't relieved himself in two days; at this rate, she frets, his intestines will explode. And how is he going to go to school like this? "I am terrified that he doesn't change. I am afraid he will be classified as special ed." The boy's pediatrician tells her not to worry. Manuel will grow out of his problem by his next birthday, he assures her.

Maybe the doctor is right. Perhaps Manuel's condition is simply a minor blip on the road to adolescence. Yet, for a family like Tamar's—a family no longer on Medicaid and hence without health coverage— even the smallest problem could be a catastrophe in the making. After all, she was told not to worry before, when Omar had his stomach ailment. What if Manuel's condition turns out to be something far graver? She doesn't have the money to pay for anything critical, she points out. "Something big can happen, a serious illness—God forbid, but we're all prone to it. . . . It can happen from one moment to another. We're children of death."

Whenever Tamar or the boys get sick, they pay cash. She goes to the dentist for a root canal; Víctor pays the $200 bill. Manuel has an appointment to monitor his anemia, and Víctor forks over another $35. Tamar visits the doctor to check on her sickle-cell anemia: another hefty fee. She and Víctor used to take the boys to the dentist twice a year, but that's no longer affordable. If something does happen, they'll have to take their chances at Columbia University Medical Center, whose ER the family knows all too well. "There you spend enough time to get well again before they see you," Tamar smirks. "I have gone there with a pain so intense that I had to crawl—and it went away before they called me."

Tamar remembers with longing the sense of security she had when her family was enrolled in an HMO through Medicaid. "If you have a pain in your finger, they send you to a specialist for your finger," Tamar says with awe. "They really take care of you until they make sure you receive appropriate attention. If you say 'I have got a headache,' they don't rest until they have done CAT scans on you." When Tamar graduated to the Missing Class, she and her children lost this safety net.

New York is one of the country's most generous states when it comes to insuring lower-income families. Children who are in families that aren't eligible for Medicaid but fall somewhere below 2.5 times the poverty line can qualify for coverage through Child Health Plus, gaining free or discounted access to examinations, drugs, emergency care, counseling, and other types of care. (In 2001 the state also began offering health insurance to near-poor adults through its Family Health Plus program.) As an immigrant with limited English, Tamar didn't realize at first that she could obtain this kind of coverage. A friend finally recommended that she talk to a local community group that helps Spanish-speaking families gain access to health care.

Now that she knows her options, Tamar is eager to apply. What is stopping her, she says, is work; if she takes a day off, she'll jeopardize her job at the cosmetics factory. Every week they've been laying off another batch of workers. Now is not a good time to be asking for favors, she says. "I'm waiting for the job to be a little slow and they're not firing people, then I'll ask for a day."

AN UNHEALTHY TRINITY

Parents are assembled in the auditorium of I.S. 25 for an informational meeting. The topic of conversation is lead poisoning and asthma, twin afflictions with which families in this neighborhood are all too familiar. Physicians, nonprofit directors, and even lawyers (for lead-poisoning cases) paint an unsettling picture of the severity of the two illnesses endemic to the area.[8]

Lead often gets a lot of the attention, but it isn't the only environmental hazard in the neighborhood. Peggy Shepard, executive director of West Harlem Environmental Action, runs down the list of dangers. In northern Manhattan, she says, a half dozen bus depots befoul the air with emissions.[9] A sewage-treatment facility sits near a local park, exposing children to toxins. Within the neighborhood's decrepit housing, cockroaches thrive, contributing to the asthma epidemic, since insect

waste is one of the allergens linked to asthma, essentially an immune response gone awry. Even killing the roaches brings problems; vigorous
use of pesticides has left residues that cause cancer, Shepard says.

Across the East River, in Sunset Park, Jim Stiles worries about another set of disparities. Stiles came to the city in the early seventies and
worked in the health-care industry over the next few decades, as hospitals began to bring health care to the 'hood. As executive vice president
of Lutheran Medical Center in Sunset Park, he played a key role in the
hospital's push to establish clinics throughout southwest Brooklyn, a
mammoth effort that required crossing a number of cultural and linguistic hurdles: finding doctors who spoke Spanish, nurses who understood Creole, and therapists who appreciated East Asian beliefs about
death and dying.[10] But in spite of Lutheran's efforts to target and tailor
its services, the stratification remains stark in neighborhoods like Sunset Park. There are sizable and persistent racial and ethnic inequalities
in the prevalence of certain diseases, Stiles points out: higher rates of
depression, hypertension, and diabetes among African American and
Hispanic populations.[11]

Meanwhile, the socioeconomic divide in access to health care is
glaring. Middle-class residents come only for in-patient care, while the
Missing Class and the poor crowd the emergency rooms. Once changes
in welfare laws in 1996 started to push rising numbers of families off the
rolls, many lost their Medicaid coverage—some because they weren't
aware they were still eligible, and others because the system had tight-
ened its rules. Hospitals like Lutheran found themselves struggling to
get these families insured. "We spent a huge amount of effort to get
kids onto Medicaid or... Child Health Plus," Stiles says. "We looked
back at it the next year, and there were more uninsured than there were
before.... The kids were falling off from welfare at a greater rate than
we were enrolling them." Many of the parents, meanwhile, were making do without health insurance, public or private. Yes, they might be
working, but at what kind of job? "The new jobs are not giving out
health insurance," he notes.

Farther north, in Fort Greene, the Reverend James Hughes sees the
same problem in his immigrant parish. "It becomes a whole other world
when you don't speak the language," he says. From prenatal care to cancer treatment, foreign-born families not fluent in English stand at a

serious disadvantage when it comes to getting quality care or accurate medical information—not to mention any kind of health insurance. It's no wonder, Hughes says, that many families turn to homespun remedies or even occult practices imported from overseas—*brujería*, voodoo, and the like. Hughes questions, too, whether local hospitals are all that invested in the health of local residents. Is Brooklyn Hospital Center there to serve the interests of the community or to provide a stepping-stone for medical students? "How many physicians have private practices in the area which the average person can have [access] to?" he asks. "How many dental offices are on the corner?" Hughes doesn't blame them, really; he understands the economics at work. "What doctor would be down here if he were not on a personal spiritual mission—if he had the opportunity to be elsewhere?" Among the neighborhood's African American population, too, the same cruel economics are operative: those who live in the housing projects north of Myrtle Avenue wait in the endless purgatory of an emergency room, elbow-to-elbow with the immigrants, while those who live south of the neighborhood's dividing line have, he says, "other possibilities."

It's true that some parts of Fort Greene have felt the Midas touch of gentrification in recent years. But the parts Hughes knows well are still very much in need of care—care of all kinds. The neighborhood is still poisonous in many ways, Hughes says: the "toxic" dumping grounds at the nearby Navy Yard for sure, but also the venomous mentality that arises from the streets—its "psychology of the projects," as he puts it. "A one-percent frustration level will elicit from a person a volcanic reaction," Hughes says. He sees men in their early twenties hunched over, walking with canes, and wonders if their problems are more than physical in origin. Hopelessness stunts a human being in many ways. "I think what we have down here is a spiritual crisis," Hughes says. You can renovate a building, repaint it. But what, he asks, can you do with the souls and hearts of people? What feeds the underlying anger is a feeling of dispossession—an aspiration to power, a desire for material possessions, a hunger for modern society's manifold temptations—and this sickness has become endemic. "Maybe, in some ways, we're even just dealing with spiritual evil that's embedded itself in a society—not just in a specific neighborhood, but in the society as a whole."

Hopelessness is not the mainstay of the near poor. They *do* have resources—never enough, to be sure, and conspicuously less than others, but nothing like the abject desperation of the truly disadvantaged. What they lack is the financial wherewithal to do what more affluent families from Brooklyn or Washington Heights have done: get out. They stay put, largely because they have no choice. Even though they are not living in poverty, the Missing Class is exposed to the same foul air, the same unequal care, and the same street rage.

THE HALL FAMILY

Gloria is on the verge of a nervous breakdown. Her sons, Stephen and Terrell, will not give her any rest. Every afternoon when they get home from school, the fighting begins. Stephen, the middle schooler, thinks that his younger brother is a crybaby. To mend Terrell's ways, Stephen shoves him for no apparent reason. Calls him names. If he doesn't start balling, Terrell fights back. Gloria has to step in and break up the argument. Terrell, she reminds his brother, was born with a heart condition. "Don't stress him out," she says. "You never know what might happen."

"Oh, you baby him too much," Stephen grumbles. "That's why he's a sissy." Stephen complains that his mother always takes Terrell's side.

It's the same tired story week after week. Stephen, the wannabe gangsta, belittles Terrell for his R & B tastes. Terrell retaliates by taking his brother's electric toothbrush and throwing it behind the toilet. "I'm the one who has to go and replace it." Gloria sighs.

Their behavior was much better when she was healthier. "I wouldn't say they were afraid of me, but they respected me more when I could discipline them," she says. "Now they don't have that respect.... They know I can't do anything." The two boys seem to understand that they have the upper hand in dealing with her, and as Gloria sees it, they take full advantage of it.

It would help, of course, if her ex-husband would pitch in once in a while. Samuel, the office manager at a Manhattan law firm, has no patience for disobedient kids. He's supposed to have the boys two weekends every month, but usually he doesn't want to be bothered. When he does come by, sometimes he'll take one boy and not the other, complaining that the two together are too much trouble. "This is the worst weekend I ever had!" he bellows when the boys act up. He's taken to leaving them by themselves while he finishes up work. He doesn't seem to care that they'll grow up without fond memories of the times they have spent with their father. "I keep telling him these kids are not gonna remember nothing," Gloria says.

Samuel's laissez-faire attitude is unfair to her, too. "You know, when he's stressed out he can go home and relax and whatever," Gloria gripes. "I can't relax in here. My kids are really getting to the point now that they fight so much that I just don't know what to do with them. They go to bed fighting. They get up fighting.

"It's just driving me crazy. Too much, too much, too much."

The boys resent the fact that she's sick. They ask why she doesn't go to work like other parents, and why she can't buy them more of the luxuries of male adolescence: video games, trendy clothes and sneakers, the latest electronic accessories. The other day Stephen said that she wasn't a "regular mom." Regular moms play with their kids, even if they don't like the games. Even if they are busy and tired. Gloria knows Stephen is right. "I have to try to meet him halfway before I lose him the whole way." It's not like she hasn't tried, she insists. She watches movies with her sons. She'll play educational computer games with them. She'll even go to the park and play catch. The last time she did that, Gloria was exhausted from her chemotherapy. "I had to lay down and play catch with them," she says. "I couldn't chase the ball." Last summer she took her sons fishing. In spite of Terrell's pleas over the last three years, their father has yet to do that.

Gloria worries about how little her young sons seem to like each other. To be honest, the two boys appear to be anything but brothers. Stephen is the bookish one, shy in public but belligerent at home, the kid who was bullied incessantly by the oldest brother, Mallory, and now takes it out on Terrell. "No matter how old you get, I'll always be able to kick your ass," Stephen once boasted to his younger brother. ("Why would you want to tell your brother that?" Gloria asked, incredulous.) Stephen works out and takes pride in his body; he belittles Terrell for being effeminate and overweight. Terrell is, without a doubt, obese— he's filling out into a husky size, forcing his mother to shell out extra cash for every new pair of pants—and he's clearly more sensitive than

Stephen, to the point of bursting into tears at any criticism. With Stephen's puberty in full swing, the contrast has grown even starker. "Now he's like the king in here," Gloria says of her middle son. "But he's still the same thirteen-year-old he was before he started getting a little hair on his thing, you know?"

The differences between the brothers play out constantly in the Hall household. Late one night, Gloria was in the kitchen and touched the burning-hot surface of the oven. She cried out in pain. Terrell, who was sleeping, woke up screaming. "Screaming and crying and carrying on," Gloria says. "And the other one is standing there laughing." One recent morning, she woke up coughing violently. She stumbled over to the bathroom and threw up. "Who do you think came to the bathroom to ask me, 'Mommy, are you OK? Can I get your medicine?'" Terrell ran and brought over her asthma pump, while his brother just sat.

With his dad out of the picture, Stephen has taken it upon himself to serve in the capacity of father to his younger brother—albeit a most stern and authoritarian father figure. "Stephen likes to bully Terrell around," Gloria says. "And he speaks with such authority—like he's the parent, you know? And I tell him all the time, 'I'm right here. If something happens, come to me.'"

But Stephen doesn't listen. "You're not there, Mommy, you're not there," he complains. "You're always siding with Terrell."

Feuding between siblings is a normal, albeit irritating, aspect of family life. But Gloria's patience has already been frayed by the daily indignities and anxieties of her illness. When her sons come home from school, she's no longer in the mood to negotiate. She and Stephen inevitably start fighting. "He's very argumentative," she says, "and I don't like that. I don't like that at all." Sometimes she'll try to avoid confrontation by not saying anything to him. Then Stephen complains that the two can't have a conversation. "Every time I try to have a conversation with this boy, it turns out into a verbal confrontation, you know? It's no good."

Stephen has been seeing a counselor at school, but it's been a mixed experience in Gloria's view. She's sick of how Stephen parrots the counselor. "I don't know what he's saying to him. But I know he come home a lot of times and say, 'Oh, my counselor say so.'"

"Your counselor don't live in here," she tells her son. "He doesn't run my home. He can try to help you out—but not help you out to make my life miserable."

Gloria fears that without a father to help tame their rowdiness, her sons will turn out like so many other young men in their neighborhood —hooligans who look for "easy money" on the streets rather than go to school, slackers who mooch off the mother of their kids rather than raise a family. Stephen is already a fan of the most noxious rap music, the kind that features ex-cons droning on and on about "mothers on welfare and this got shot and I'm not your baby's daddy"—negativity that she can't bear to hear her son repeat. The fact is, the streets are tough enough for boys like Stephen and Terrell. "They are like an endangered species," she says, "because they're male and they're black and that's all the police see." In the face of all these bad influences and dangers, Gloria tries her best to instill in her children a respect for education.

Her oldest son, Mallory, a serviceman stationed in Japan, has come to this belated conclusion. He gave up a full scholarship to the University of Massachusetts to join the military, but now he regrets the choice. "Mommy, I should have listened to you," he writes in his letters home. Mallory used to be a troublemaker, too. What was to blame for the oldest son's "outrageous" behavior: his teenage hormones, his derelict father, or the fact that he once got shot at school at age eleven? In any case, she won't accept any more excuses from her younger boys. "Every day I tell them I don't care if you can't watch the television, I don't care if you can't do the dishes, but make sure your priority is your schoolwork. If the house is falling down with mess, leave it, do your homework first." Gloria vows that as long as they continue to go to school, she will support them; otherwise, they're out the door.

Fortunately, Stephen seems to be heeding his mother's advice. He spends his summers tearing through library books as fast as his mom can take them out. His voracious reading has paid off; Stephen now attends a magnet school for talented kids. His standardized scores have hit the ninety-seventh percentile in all areas—high enough that Johns Hopkins University stuffs the family's mailbox with glossy applications for its programs geared to kid geniuses. Terrell, on the other hand, doesn't care much for books. He tells his mother flat-out that he doesn't want to read. When she forces him, he sits down and cries. "I have to stay on top of him," she says.

Through all of Gloria's troubles, the one steady rock has been her church. Every Sunday she finds solace among her brothers and sisters in Christ. "That's like my little family," Gloria says. When Gloria misses a service, someone inevitably calls her to see how she's doing.

For individuals battling serious illness, having friends and family to turn to is crucial. Their long-term prospects of recovery often hinge upon their ability to cope with their deteriorating health. The presence and nurturing care of loved ones can help reinforce the belief that things will improve.[12]

Even though Gloria is a relatively new member of her church, the congregation has accepted her warmly. "I could call somebody no matter what time, no matter what my problem is," Gloria says. One friend, Brother Chikae, has become especially close. He's an attentive listener and an exceedingly patient man. When she's in a bad mood and snaps at him, Chikae doesn't flinch. "You can't run away from me," he told her after one argument. "You're like my daughter. As a matter of fact, you *are* my daughter."

Gloria thrives in the affectionate embrace of her Church of God congregation. At the same time, she doesn't tell her fellow churchgoers everything. "I talk to them about some things, not everything," she says. One thing she doesn't mention is her financial problems. She doesn't want to feel like a charity case, she says. The pastor respects her right to privacy. If anyone tells him a secret, he keeps it—even from his wife. "If he feel like it's something he's gotta share with his wife, he'll say, you know, 'Sis, if you don't mind, I would like to share this with my wife.' And if you tell him 'No,' he won't even tell her. That's the type of person that he is."

The atmosphere was different at her last church. There, the pastor was hands-off. "He didn't care what you did as long as you was there Sunday morning with your little change to put in the box," Gloria says. "I was in the hospital a couple of times, [and] I saw that pastor one time." All that mattered to him was money; he would even exhort his congregation to bring in their winnings from the lottery or Atlantic City and stuff the collection box. That's another difference: at her new church, gambling is frowned upon. The pastor there won't accept gifts from suspect sources, poker chips included. "You don't play church," he says.

Gambling happens to be one of Gloria's weaknesses. Now that she's in her forties, she has no urge to party anymore, but she continues to play Bingo. It's a way of relieving stress after being cooped up with the kids most nights and weekends. She doesn't see why it's wrong. The Bible says Jesus threw the money changers out of the synagogue, she points out. "He didn't throw them out of anyplace else. I'm not gambling in the synagogue. You know what I mean?" Her friends in Christ, however, don't agree with her biblical exegesis. One friend said to her, "Listen, anytime you look to another source for something instead of looking to God, it is wrong.

"Pray about it," he told her. "Pray about it and, you know, the desire will leave you."

These days, though, Gloria has plenty of other things to pray about. Cancer has forced her to reevaluate her life. She's only recently started to acknowledge that she has clinical depression and has had it since she was a little girl. "I haven't really dealt with it," she says. "But I realize what it is."

What she still needs to learn is how to make peace—with others and with herself. "You go to Sunday school," she tells Stephen, "and they teach you about the Bible. And you know what the prayers say. 'Forgive.' You may not be able to forget it, but you have to learn how to forgive. That's number one."

She has the same message for her other son. "You're going to get more upset than this in life," she tells Terrell after one of his frequent outbursts. "What are you going to do then? Are you going to be like the people that work in the post office? You know, they get upset and they shoot up the place? You have to control your anger. You have to learn to enjoy yourself." It's a truth that's easy to repeat but hard to practice.

THE GUERRA FAMILY

> It doesn't matter if you are poor, rich or middle class. Plastic surgery
> is something we want.
>   —Brazilian woman quoted by Knight Ridder
>   Newspapers, April 29, 2001

It's another day on the job for Tamar: a full eight hours in the mammoth warehouse in New Jersey, lifting Pierre Cardin perfume bottles off a conveyor belt and fitting them into boxes, working valiantly not to drop anything or leave a single hair on a bottle top. At times Tamar is a speed demon on the assembly line, plucking and placing bottles like a woman possessed. "I try to do my work fast, not because I want to suck up but because I do not want to fall asleep," she says with a laugh.

Sometimes, though, her mind drifts. She obsesses over her weekly paycheck and all the things she'll be able to afford someday. One day she completely lost her concentration. Her Mexican coworker asked her what the problem was.

"I have to save up for the liposuction," Tamar said.

Tamar is on the heavy side and has long regretted it. But now her weight has peaked—at slightly over two hundred pounds—and her size makes her feel terrible. Whenever she sees a fat person on the street, her self-image worsens: the person reminds her of her own weight problem or seems to portend how morbidly obese she'll eventually become. She prefers, in fact, to see only thin people.

Tamar struggles with her smoking; she struggles with her inability to exercise regularly. (Her once-fat, now-thin husband, Víctor, on the other hand, works out daily.) Tamar works at the factory in part because she knows that's the only way she'll ever be able to obtain slimness: by paying for surgery. Víctor doesn't make enough money; he can't help her. "I'm going to help *me*," she declares. "I have to have an operation."

Tamar doesn't even know how much the procedure costs. She just knows she needs it. "Before you know it, it will be December again, and then I don't have any money," she says.

So she continues to grab the endless procession of perfume bottles. All the while a pleasing thought trickles through her brain: "You're going to see how pretty I'm going to look when I take off all this fat."

. . .

Liposuction isn't an option in most health plans. But many Americans—even those without means—desire it, especially now that obesity has become epidemic among poor and rich alike.[13] Why risk such an invasive procedure? To Tamar, liposuction seems an easy solution to a problem that is certainly physiological—obesity contributes to heart disease and diabetes—but in her case is also psychological: the idea that she's fat and needs to be beautiful. Now that she's part of the Missing Class, now that she's covering the household bills with her own paychecks, Tamar feels she deserves a little something for herself. A woman in a two-income household can dream such dreams, even though for many the expense may seem barely sustainable and hardly justifiable.

Thinking about how nice it would be to look pretty also helps to take Tamar's mind off some of the less appetizing medical problems in her family. In spite of her doctor's past assurances to the contrary, Manuel, now seven years old, continues to refuse to use the toilet. "He thinks shitting is disgusting." Tamar sighs. "Then he walks around smelling like shit, and he doesn't understand that." Tamar is terrified about what will happen to Manuel if his unhealthy habit continues. She knows of a boy who had to be operated on—and a section of his intestines removed—because he was just like Manuel. Will the same thing happen to her baby boy? "He has to get something, yes, because that can't be normal," she says. "You can't be like that with your body."

In the summer of 2001, as her weight pushed 210 pounds, Tamar decided she couldn't wait any longer on the liposuction. In search of something affordable, she headed back to the Dominican Republic and found a place that charged $3,500 for the procedure and two days of hospital rest. Tamar signed up. The operation was scheduled for July 4. "If I die, I'll die on a historic day," she thought.

Complications set in right after she came out of the operating room. A lifetime of smoking had clogged up her lungs, and the shock of surgery induced a dangerous level of congestion. Her Dominican doctor gave her an IV with a drug that was supposed to quell the blockage. The medication burned in her veins. Tamar started screaming in pain —it was worse than having a child, she wailed. "I thought I wasn't going to live to tell about it," she recalls.

But Tamar survived. She was kept four days at the clinic, and she stayed another two months on the island before flying back home. The additional treatment pushed up the cost of the procedure to a whopping $5,000. Fortunately, Víctor came to the rescue. She had already put aside her income tax refund to pay for the operation; now Víctor got a friend in the Dominican Republic to drop by the hospital with the additional money in U.S. dollar bills. (The Dominican clinic would accept only cold American cash.) Víctor told her that the money came from yet another of his (secretive) revenue streams: a house that he rented on the island.

The surgery was a success—of sorts. Tamar lost thirty pounds—the net weight of fat sucked from her back and stomach—and after she got home she started dieting and lost another ten pounds. However, almost a year after the surgery, she continues to suffer from intense back pain. And she now sports a set of gruesome scars, a testimony to her postoperation ordeal. With her clothes on, she looks fabulous: her stomach is remarkably flat, if strangely so, given that a disproportionate amount of fat still clings to her hips and other parts of her body. But underneath her underwear is a two-inch-wide scalpel incision traversing from one hip to another; the unsightly scar tissue is much darker than the rest of her.

Still, Tamar is happy about the surgery. If anything, it made her realize how harmful her smoking was. "If I had not done that, I wouldn't have found out that the cigarettes were killing me," she says. Tamar has been trying heroically to quit since she got back. Her doctor gave her four nicotine patches, but she's saving them up for particularly rough stretches. Instead, she takes walks to blunt her cravings. "I haven't smoked as much as I did before, and I try to control it," she says. "Little by little, I know that I'm going to make it." When she's calm, she can go three or four days without a puff.

The problem is, Tamar is rarely calm these days. Omar's incarceration upstate and the uncertainty over his release are sapping away her last reserves of sanity. She's depressed and at times breaks into tears. She's also put on some of the weight she lost. "You know when I eat a lot?" she says. "When I go to [visit Omar]. . . . As soon as I have to go there, I get so hungry."

Like many American women, Tamar finds herself caught in a vicious cycle of stress and self-loathing, which revolves dangerously around her weight problem. When she's feeling anxious, she overeats and gains weight. Her disgust with her body image, in turn, makes her even more depressed. In this unhealthy state of mind, Tamar finds herself vulnerable to morbid thoughts. She snaps at anyone who mentions cancer in her presence. "I always think I'm going to die of cancer," she says. She torments herself with the thought that she won't live much longer because of her smoking. She fixates on the possibility that her kids will become orphans.

The next time she sees Omar, she is frank with her oldest son. "I'm not going to last a long time," she tells him.

Omar starts to cry. "Mami, why do you say that?" he asks. Tamar has never told him about her near-death experience in the Dominican Republic.

"I have this feeling that my end is near," she says. "So stop all your craziness and getting into problems. Because anyone who comes to see you—I pay their transportation." It was true: for all the cousins and aunts who have visited Omar over the last few months, Tamar has footed the bill.

"When I die, nobody is going to come see you."

THE HALL FAMILY

> For her part, Janusz is already planning to bring up the subject of her eventual death with the three grown children she has with her husband, Steve. A friend showed her a letter from a parent to a child that talks about children being a form of immortality. It will make a good starting point, she said.
>
> —*Minneapolis Star-Tribune*, February 19, 2001

In 2000 Gloria's mother died of cancer. In May of that year, Gloria's doctors told her that her own cancer was terminal. One doctor wanted her admitted to a hospice. She refused. Instead, with the Medicaid she now received, Gloria hired a home health aide to come to her Brooklyn apartment and tend to her during the day.

A year later, Gloria is still hanging on, tenaciously. During her last trip to Sloan-Kettering, which was supposed to be for a routine checkup and treatment, Gloria was on her way upstairs to another floor when her condition suddenly took a turn for the worse. She ended up staying at the hospital and was later diagnosed with diabetes. Ugly black marks appeared all over her body. When she got out of the hospital in May 2001, Gloria could no longer walk and needed a wheelchair. At home ten months later, she can barely get up from her bed. The bureau on the other side of the room is crowded with dozens of prescription bottles.

She has begun to approach family and friends with the news that she is dying. Though he knows her condition, Samuel still refuses to step up and take custody of the boys, complaining that he is very stressed himself. He has, however, started giving them allowances, which have taken some of the financial burden off her. Gloria's sisters, on the other hand, have turned out to be extremely supportive. Once, when she was pulling herself through a bout of especially intense pain in her stomach and back, one of her sisters slept on the floor beside her bed through the night, to make sure Gloria would make it to the next day.

Since hearing the bleak prognosis, members of her church have rallied in support of her with encouraging words, thoughtful cards, and even small gifts of money. But other friends have stopped calling or paying visits. "I guess they figured I don't have nothing to say, you know." One friend admitted that she didn't know what to tell Gloria and that's why she didn't call. "I mean, what were you saying before?" Gloria says with bitterness. "I'm in a wheelchair; that doesn't change me as a person."

As disappointed as she has been by the lack of devotion of friends, Gloria has found herself surprised and moved by the thoughtfulness of strangers. Shopping at Pathmark one day, she suddenly doubled up in pain. She had to make her way, slowly, to the bench in front of the store. While she sat there, catching her breath and strength, several people stopped to ask her if she was OK. She was shocked. She hadn't expected such kindness, especially in a big city like New York.

Speaking of kindness, Gloria finally moved to the top of the waiting list for the parking space that she had been clamoring for insistently, for so many years, at her apartment building. But as luck would have it, the building's board granted her the space when she was sick in the hospital. Because she didn't claim it, the spot was passed on to someone else. Now Gloria is back on the waiting list.

Gloria has yet to tell her sons that she's dying. It's hard for her these days to connect with the boys, she admits. "I tried, but nobody wants to talk." Sometimes she manages to have a good conversation with Stephen, but whenever his younger brother is around, the harassment inevitably ensues. Stephen is getting "wild," she notes. Now a strapping, weight-lifting sixteen-year-old, he slams things down and punches the wall whenever he doesn't get his way. He speaks in a noticeably more direct and assertive voice to his mother—telling her what he wants to do, rather than asking, and ignoring her requests to put on a coat or quit picking on his brother. By now, she's learned not to bother trying to change his belligerent ways. "He's a big boy now," Gloria says. "If he don't know better than by now—that's what he wants, that's what he wants."

In any case, these days Gloria can't even put up the pretense of being an attentive parent. Terrell will ask her to go in-line skating with him, but she just doesn't have the strength anymore. He gets upset anyway. Though normally happy-go-lucky, her youngest son has in recent years developed an explosive temper. "He has become much, much more aggressive," she says. Both boys are in therapy, but it doesn't seem to have pacified them. In the past few months, as Gloria's health has grown worse, the fighting between the brothers has intensified.

They should know better, she points out. They're both intelligent boys. Stephen is attending a high school in Midwood, a Jewish neighborhood where the streets are paved smooth and the academics are superb. He seems to be surviving there. Terrell has become a whiz on the Internet. He tells her he wants to become a veterinarian when he grows up. They have so many talents, these sons of hers.

And yet they have such *anger*. It is the hostility of siblings who know each other too well. The rage of young men who want more than what their surroundings can offer them. The resentment of sons who know, in the darkest corners of their hearts, that their mother is dying.

Nevertheless, Gloria has faith in them. "My goal is for them to succeed in life where I failed," she says. With any luck, they will learn something from the lessons of her own life, while she still has the strength to teach them. "When you think the children are not looking and they're not listening, they are. *They are.*"

SIX

Romance without Finance Is a Nuisance

Congress [has] earmarked $750 million over five years for programs to promote "healthy marriages" and "responsible fatherhood."... In what amounts to a large experiment, the grants should extend the reach of marriage education to tens of thousands of low-income couples, many in communities where stable cohabiting relationships, let alone lasting marriages, are rare.

—*New York Times*, July 20, 2006

THE LINARES FAMILY

Tomás Linares is trying to quit smoking. A father of two adult daughters, he's nearing the half-century mark, and the last few decades of nicotine and tar have jaundiced his once-attractive looks. His Boricua complexion has become wan, almost sickly, as if the tropical sun of his youthful days in Puerto Rico had slipped behind a gray haze of chain-smoking. When he stops to think about it, Tomás is scared about his health. Plus, a pack a day, or $90 a month, adds up. These days he can't afford to splurge on anything. He works seven days at week at two jobs, both of them as an attendant for people with severe mental disabilities. The childlike residents in his care push and scratch each other. Tomás throws his hefty frame between the contenders and makes peace, sometimes forcibly. Most of the time, though, the job kills with boredom. Tomás recently watched *Stuart Little*, that family-friendly film about a talking mouse, for the third time.

So when Sunday night rolls around, he'd like nothing better than a cigarette, but he checks himself. Instead, he gets into his car for a drive across the Verrazano-Narrows Bridge to Staten Island, where his girlfriend lives. Amanda is also intent on quitting cigarettes, or so she says.

Halfway there, just as he clears the bridge, Amanda calls him on his cell phone. She has a sudden hankering for a smoke. Can he pick up some cigarettes on the way in?

Tomás is tired and more than a tad annoyed. Why is she asking him now? Why is she even *asking* for a cigarette? He's had a long week. He just wants to get there and relax. "Wait until I get to the house," he tells Amanda. There's a store across the street.

"Forget about it," Amanda answers, clearly ticked off.

"Wait till I get to the house and I buy the cigarettes."

"*Forget about it.*" She hangs up. Tomás doesn't stop.

When he pulls up in front of his girlfriend's house, Amanda comes out to meet him, and the fireworks begin. Once again, she's upset with his inattentiveness. He's always stuck at work, or visiting his mother, or checking up on his daughters. He never has time for *her*.

Tonight Tomás isn't in the mood to play games with Amanda. Before he even reaches the front door, he changes his mind about staying over. "You gonna keep that attitude, I ain't gonna [come in]," he tells her. There's no way that he's going to ruin his weekend relaxation time by letting her temper infect him.

Tomás gets back in the car and drives off.

They don't talk for a week. Finally, on Monday Amanda calls him, asking for a ride. She's often in Manhattan and always needs someone to chauffeur her back to Staten Island. This time Tomás refuses. He's on the way to his mother's house. Predictably, Amanda is irate—again.

It's a miracle that Tomás puts up with her, he tells himself later. What does he do to deserve the abuse? He's a supportive partner. He makes the twenty-five-minute trip across the bridge to see Amanda weekly, sometimes more often. Whenever he stops by, he gets on his knees and starts cleaning because he can't stand the mess that Amanda, her daughter, and granddaughter pile up on the floor of their small, three-bedroom house. Tomás does more than this. He also helps pay for Amanda's mortgage—$150 every fifteen days. Why does he do it? Out of love. Or duty. Or foolishness.

Recently, he's been thinking of breaking off that arrangement. "Every time, I give it to her—even if we fight, or she don't call me," he says. "But now we're getting in the stage that it's, like, shaky. And I'm not going to give it to her no more then."

·   ·   ·

Balancing the needs of the heart with the demands of the pocketbook is always a tricky business, but this is perhaps even more the case for those who have a lot—the superrich, with their cautious prenuptials—or those who have little. Among the Missing Class, the luxury of seeing a potential partner as *just* a soul mate—rather than another wage earner —does not exist. Money is the constant calculus underlying decisions to join and separate incomes, merge and split households.

Romantic desires inevitably exact a financial price. As social scientists have long argued, poor women have good reason to reject un-jobbed or McJobbed men as not worth the cost of a long-term commitment—if such desires are even mutually held—because they have children to feed and household bills to pay. (This rationale has been used, among other things, to explain growing rates of out-of-wedlock childbirth: men with low or no wages can father children but simply aren't marriage material.)[1] But what does this mean for the men with good wages who have become so hard to find? If they do not yet make enough money to graze in whiter, more affluent pastures—if they cannot yet afford the middle-class admission price of storybook love —then they find themselves dating within their neighborhoods and pairing up with low-income women, frequently with children from previous relationships, who can never let desire blind them to the fact that they must consider the finances alongside the romance.

In Tomás's case, this means that every one of his relationships is freighted with concerns, spoken or unspoken, about the money he can bring to the table. The payments to Amanda started from the very beginning, when Tomás began to date her. She was living in Brooklyn at the time, just across the street from his apartment. Amanda's husband had recently died of a liver condition, possibly related to drug use. She was on welfare and wasn't working, so he gave her money—$50 here and there. The payments became regular. He gave her money to get the fingerprints she needed to apply for a job at the city's Board of Education. She got the job and started saving up. When Amanda bought the house three years into their relationship, the two made an agreement that he'd chip in.

Before Amanda, Tomás was dating another island girl, Julia. Tomás bought her a plane ticket to Puerto Rico every summer so that she could visit her family. For middle-class couples, gifts to a loved one express the extravagant thoughtfulness of giving things she *could* buy for herself but won't. For the Missing Class, they entail the things she'd *like* to buy for herself but can't. In either case, they are the gestures that demonstrate love and attachment.

Why does Tomás choose to spend his money in this way? There are plenty of reasons not to, he admits. At times he feels like he's playing the part of the love fool. His relationship with Julia, in particular, left a bitter aftertaste. Those trips to Puerto Rico to see family? Julia was actually seeing another man there. After he learned the truth, Tomás broke things off. He hadn't been very serious with Julia, but the betrayal still stung. "I guess with time I got more disgusted, you know, thinking this and that," he says. "I said, 'I ain't gonna be silly with this one then.'"

More to the point is the fact that Tomás does not have much money to spare for the women in his life. Before taxes, he makes $500 every other week at his day job, and his part-time job on the weekends pulls in another few hundred—on a good week, as much as $310. After the money he gives to Amanda and his daughters, plus the meals he buys for his mom a few times every week, there's not much left over for Tomás. Recently he had problems with his car; it was vibrating and swerving to the right. Tomás went to a garage but didn't have enough money to pay for all the necessary parts. Nagging health problems add to Tomás's list of expenses. He's on pills for arthritis, and his doctor just prescribed him a $385 piece of padding for his foot condition. Tomás feels that's too expensive and is scouting for cheaper options.

As a single man not sheltering any dependents, Tomás's $20,000 yearly earnings place him well above the poverty line. A quick glance at his lifestyle, wardrobe, or accommodations, however, makes clear he's not yet middle class.[2] And that may be the point. Tomás doesn't make enough money, or boast a sufficiently prestigious job, to woo women in Park Slope or Williamsburg, much less in tony Manhattan. So he dates women like Amanda—women from his class, culture, and community —who desperately need his money. Of course, the transaction is not one-way. Tomás receives what is for him a valuable return on his investment: company. His daughters are grown up. In his late forties, he is still mildly, but not dramatically, attractive; tall but slouch-shouldered, he suffers from a back ailing from age. In other words, Tomás's time as a competitive bachelor is running out.

He met Amanda five years ago, as his relationship with Julia was hacking its last breath. "You wanna go to the movies? You wanna go eat?" he asked her after divining that the widow was now accepting suitors. Amanda said yes, and the two started going out. Many monthly payments later, Tomás and Amanda are "intimate," as he puts it. She wants to go further. In fact, she has pestered him about buying an engagement ring. ("Yeah, when I get the money!" he tells her.) She's given him an ultimatum for the summer. "That's what she say." He sighs. "I'm taking it like a joke, but... I don't know." He has serious misgivings about her and their future. "The way it's going now—with her like this, with her attitude—it would be worse then."

It would also spell the end of his devoted ministrations to his elderly mother and two daughters. Marrying Amanda would undoubtedly corrode the bond with his family, the only company (besides Amanda) he keeps these days and the only recipients of his loyalty. Then, if he and Amanda divorced—which, on a bad night heading over the bridge, seems to Tomás quite probable—he would wind up with nothing: single again and alienated from his family. This is a risk that this only son and divorcé father is not yet prepared to take.

In Puerto Rico the Linares family lived in a small wooden house on top of a hill, in a poverty-stricken neighborhood in the northwestern coastal town of Aguadilla. There was electricity but no indoor toilet. The neighborhood houses were stacked one next to the other, with the railroad tracks on the south side. Tomás walked fifteen to twenty minutes to get to school. He worked in the local bazaar cleaning sacks. "It was very poor," he says. "Like Mexico, you know." Still, there was a sense of community in Aguadilla that Tomás has since grown to miss. "Everyone was poor, but everyone ate. Everyone was united in those times.... Everyone helped everyone else." If Tomás's family didn't have food, he'd go over to a neighbor's house, and the woman would give him coffee and cookies and sometimes even cook him a meal.

Tomás's mother divorced his father when Tomás was six. Alicia headed to New York in search of paying work, leaving her mother, Maritza, to raise Tomás and his older brother, Adrián. When Tomás was fifteen, the family finally moved to New York and reunited with Alicia. By then, his grandmother was sick with cancer. The family hoped America's much-vaunted health care system could save her. She died two years later.

Maritza's death devastated the family, especially Adrián, who had been close to her. Ten years later Adrián got into a car accident and broke his leg. He started taking Valium for the pain. One day, in a fit of depression, he took the whole bottle and overdosed. "I think it was because he was thinking about my grandmother," Tomás says of his brother's suicide. "He always had that in mind. When she died, it seems that that affected his mind and he wanted to die." Adrián was twenty-six.

With poverty, divorce, and death as the backdrop to his youth, it may not be surprising to hear what happened next to Tomás, a young, small-town immigrant plopped into a vast urban ocean teeming with crime. He soon got caught up in the sixties-style debauchery of Sunset Park's rebel youth, abusing his body with a cocktail combination of alcohol, marijuana, cocaine, and even heroin. ("I never injected it into my veins," Tomás stresses.) Along the way he married an Italian American woman, Sara. Tomás was twenty-three; she was eighteen. There was no party. A friendly minister rounded up some witnesses and married the couple for free, and Tomás borrowed the $5 fee for the marriage certificate from a friend.

The marriage lasted about two years. Still in his twenties, Tomás insisted on acting the part: going out every night, smoking pot, and drinking until he stumbled back home at any godforsaken hour. Even after his daughters were born, he was spending his money—his family's money—on liquor and other late-night activities. "I wasn't thinking about marriage," he remembers with a trace of shame. "I thought I was still single." Sara wouldn't put up with his nonsense. "Where's the money?" she'd demand. They argued relentlessly, violently—she'd even brandish a knife. "We used to get into little fight," Tomás says in his distinctly peppery immigrant English. "Not really bad fight, but little fights." Then he discovered love letters and gifts of perfume from a man Sara was seeing in the army. "So we fought more."

Sara left him. She moved in with her mom and asked for a divorce. "I guess she did the right thing," Tomás says. "This guy drinking, come whenever he feel like it—I don't blame her." The divorce ended up costing $400—more than his marriage, he muses.

Tomás is still single after all these years. By now, his idea of romance has been crusted over with a half lifetime of cynicism. Instead of looking forward to another wedding, he reminisces about a youth of carefree love, stocked with movies and restaurants, parties and dancing, girls and more girls. The dreams of wealth and passion he had at nineteen didn't come to pass. But for all his unfulfilled ambition, Tomás is proud of the fact that he's remade himself into a new man—a species apart from the ne'er-do-well who married Sara more than two decades ago. He has a job. He has a car. He has no life, he avows, but he knows what it means to be a responsible father and grandfather. That wilderness of drugs and desperation is beyond him now, rooted out and replaced with something else: family.

Weeds, though, have a habit of springing up anew. As Tomás's personal history suggests, some members of the Missing Class were previously poor—at best, working poor—and struggled in their youth. Take a snapshot of them in their thirties and forties, and they have achieved stability and some degree of success. But still they bear the marks of that former destitution—not just psychologically but also in the flesh-and-blood record of their children, who spent their formative years in poverty and display symptoms of their tough upbringing. It's not just a matter of interrupted or uninspired educations or dubious prospects for economic success. There's also the challenge of learning the fundamentals of love and parenthood, having grown up in neighborhoods where solid marriages that last a lifetime are relatively rare. Research shows that the higher the levels of unemployment, poverty, and welfare in a community, the more likely marriages are to break up.[3] While the Missing Class no longer resides in places that are quite so poor, they live close enough, and oftentimes they or their children have grown up in or around broken families.

Even when these marriages fail, though, many ex-spouses step up to their duties as parents. Tomás and Sara don't talk anymore—"What I'm gonna speak to her?" he gripes—but he has been a fixture in the lives of his two daughters, who were just toddlers when their parents separated. In fact, Tomás hands out cash to the older daughter, Yula— $50 here, $50 there—whenever she insists she's broke, which these days is often. That's money that could go toward repairing his car—or, for that matter, saving up for Amanda's engagement ring—but instead is dropped back into the cash-hungry maw of his biological family. Twenty-four, unemployed, and living in Sara's basement, Yula hasn't bothered to go on welfare, even though she has a three-year-old son. She's been waiting for months to hear about a position at the law office where her mother works. "She better get a job because every time I'm broke" she's asking for money, Tomás grouses. Of course, his ex-wife doesn't understand this; whenever Sara sees him, she'll start up with her "remarks." "Why don't you help your daughter?" she'll pointedly ask, as if he were some kind of deadbeat. ("I need somebody to help me," Tomás complains.) He used to give money to his other daughter, twenty-three-year-old Ella, too—$80 for books, $30 for a week's worth of lunch—but now that she has a supervisor's job at the Gap, she's been able to fend for herself.

Parents aren't just wells of cash for their children, of course; they're also potential conscripts for babysitting duties. On Yula's insistence, Tomás heads over to his ex-wife's place at least once a week and dutifully watches over his grandson—from 3 to 10 P.M., at times—in spite of the many sufferings the sugar-crazed toddler inflicts upon him. David is a terror. He wails uncontrollably until he is put back in his crib. He yells and sticks his fingers in his mouth. He throws up what he just ate. Tomás has taken to inserting a video into the VCR and praying the boy will quiet down. "He's not a well-behaved kid," Tomás acknowledges. "Sometimes you have to be stern with him."

But Tomás takes the frustration in stride. He's glad to be helping out his daughters. He's proud that he's not like other dads, who procreate and disappear. "Some people, they don't care or they don't have no feeling," he says. "I don't understand that, because this is your own blood."

As a reliable parent and doting grandparent, Tomás is almost unrecognizable to those who knew him in his salad days. He has tried his best to distance himself from that previous lifestyle. He still smokes and drinks—in fact, as recently as 1997 he was arrested for drunk driving as he left a bar—but Tomás has, for the most part, cleaned up. At times friends from his past will call asking to hang out, but Tomás can't be bothered. They are unemployed men in their late forties who live with their mothers, he points out. Spending any time with them would just be a waste. "I have no friends, you know."

If Tomás has made amends for past sins, his older daughter seems determined to repeat them. Growing up, Yula took a page from Tomás's years as a hell-raiser in Sunset Park. She stayed out late at night, cut classes, drank, and hung out with "too many" boys. She's had about six abortions. Ever since David was born, Yula's behavior has improved, but she still manages to disappoint her father. What upsets him most is Yula's refusal to marry David's father. The boyfriend, an Ecuadorian immigrant by the name of Arturo, works irregularly as a street vendor and makes little money. Yula, too, recently quit a good job at Nine West, after her supervisor accused her of stealing. She denies it, but Tomás has his suspicions. When she was living with his mother several years ago, Yula stole $50. When she got kicked out and moved in with Tomás, a blank money order happened to disappear.

Ella is Tomás's clear favorite, adored for her hard work in school and her consideration for others, but even she has recently given her family reasons to fret. Ella and her boyfriend have become more serious. Tomás's mother, Alicia, doesn't approve, and Tomás has his doubts, too. With her full-time job and her full-time boyfriend, "she ain't got no time for nobody," Tomás notes. Alicia slipped into another one of her moody spells a couple of days earlier because ex-wife Sara called her house asking where Ella was. (Tomás was at his girlfriend's house on Staten Island at the time.) His ex-wife never calls his mom, so Tomás knew right away things were serious. Not calling home, making her mother worry—what had gotten into that girl?

Ella and the boyfriend have even talked about marriage, an idea that alarms her dad. "I only seen him like twice, you know?" he says. "For maybe five minutes. 'Hello, how are you'—and that was it. . . . From the way she said, he come from a good family." Though vexed by romantic problems of his own, Tomás tries to give his daughter useful counsel. Don't follow him around like a puppy, he tells her, because that'll only puff up a man's already swollen ego. Leave him alone for a while, so he misses you and needs you. If you're with him all the time, staying over his place, why should he marry you? "She's smart," Tomás says of his younger daughter. "She uses protection. She didn't tell me that; my mom did."

He hopes Ella will avoid the mistakes he made. There's no reason to rush into a commitment as binding as marriage. "She gotta understand the person real good. You could be a boyfriend and girlfriend for five, six years, and when you get married it's a different story. Then it start showing up. 'I don't like this. I don't like that.' Every little thing becomes a fight." Tomás knows from experience.

THE RUSHING FAMILY

> Even though single women of all ethnic groups bemoan the lack of available men, it's not just an empty lament for blacks. Whereas white, Hispanic and Asian men in their 20s significantly outnumber their women, there are just 89 black men for every 100 black women.
> —*Chicago Sun-Times*, December 7, 2005

Valerie Rushing has been looking for Mr. Right for a long time. Finally, at the age of thirty-three, she thinks she may have a shot at finding him. Her well-paid job cleaning trains for the Long Island Rail Road recently qualified her for a loan to get laser surgery on her eyes. The Coke-bottle glasses she once had to wear are now history. Her newly restored vision seems to call for a new look, so she goes shopping: new gold earrings, new gold chains, new pants.

Now, all Valerie needs is to meet a man worthy of her time. She rejects outright the ones she considers cheap. When she goes out she wants her date to pick her up in a car. "I am not riding nobody's bus. This is supposed to be a date. This ain't me traveling." Valerie wants to be taken to fine restaurants, escorted to trendy dance clubs, pampered, and appreciated. Recently, a hapless suitor suggested the two of them go to her place and hang out. "It don't work like that—no," she told him. "You ain't got nowhere for us to go, then we don't go nowhere. You're not coming in here and sitting in my house and scope out what I got. That ain't a date. That's you coming over visiting my house."

Valerie wasn't always so focused on the bottom line. Her first serious relationship was dazzling, intense, and ultimately tragic. She met Edward in her apartment building, where they both lived at the time. Their romance lasted for nine years; Edward is the father of Valerie's only child. But with time, the two drifted apart. Valerie found out Edward was sleeping with other women. Devastated, she retaliated by cheating on him. "I've been hurt one time, and I said I'll never be hurt again," she remembers bitterly. In the wake of that disaster, Valerie became ruthlessly no-nonsense, even cynical, about her relationships.

The next time around, Valerie turned out to be the unfaithful one. Perhaps it was payback for what Edward did to her, but Valerie recognizes she was to blame. "I did all the cheating." (She and her boyfriend split up but remain friends.)

Valerie has been unattached for four years now. She's no longer sure she wants to be committed to anyone. If Mr. Right doesn't bump into her anytime soon, she declares, "I'm gonna find somebody I could geese."

"Geesing," Valerie explains, is taking a lover for what he's worth—cash only, please.

I'm just gonna have to start sucking people outta their money. Any means necessary. I don't care. I'm not saying, you know, you sleep with everybody you meet or whatever, but . . . I might tell him, "You wanna go out, I need a babysitter. I need an outfit. My rent is due. I need such-and-such money."

He gonna get what he can get outta me and move on to the next one. So I'm gonna play the same game. That's the way it is now.

If you gonna eat at my table this week, next week I want some money for some food. 'Cause that means if you eat at my table this week, then you gonna expect it next week, and then maybe the week after that. It cost to eat. You know what I'm saying? So that's the way it goes: you eat this week, you pay for it next week. . . .

Men were playing the field and leaving the women home feeling pitiful. But now it's like the women are leaving them home and going to have their fun also. Ain't nobody waiting for nobody no more. If it happens to be, it'll be. . . . But why sit home and wait when you could be out there doing something? He might be fooling around, and you sitting home.... Women are not putting up with what men were doing to us no more....

Finance without romance is a nuisance, and don't nobody wanna be with a nuisance. Women need money now.... A little extra ain't gonna hurt. And I ain't saying I ain't never gonna settle down and meet Mr. Right, but for now I gotta get what I can get. And I hate to be like that, but you know, I'm tired of being Miss Victim.

The men Valerie meets nowadays always disappoint, either with their miserly ways or with their antiquated views. The last two men she dated told her she was too independent. As a single mother fortunate enough to have a steady paycheck, Valerie won't accept any man's dictating what she eats or wears or thinks. Sure, she'd love to have a partner to rely on. "When you want somebody to cuddle up with and you ain't got him, you be like, 'Damn!' You know?" she says. "But then you think about it —yeah, well, you ain't gotta hear the nagging. You can go where you wanna go. You ain't gotta answer to nobody, you know? So those are the pluses."

It's not just the lackluster personalities of the men she dates, however, that lead her to be so particular. She is looking for more than a warm body in her bed; she wants a man who can help support the household. "Just because I have a job," Valerie points out, doesn't mean she has it easy. "It's like the more you make, the more bills you create."

Valerie is a single mother who supports two children—her daughter, Akeelah, and her niece's son, Johnny, whom she adopted after both his mother *and* grandmother proved to be irresponsible. Aunt Valerie is tired of paying rent, tired of living in a tiny basement apartment; she longs to buy her own house. She wants a taste of the good life, whether that means fine leather jackets or laser surgery for her badly nearsighted eyes. With all these bills to cover, Valerie pays attention to the salaries of her suitors. She's willing to entertain any options for extra income, including those bearing gifts of flowers and chocolate. But marriage? Not under consideration.

Sociologists Kathryn Edin and Maria Kefalas have written about the reasons that poor women become so selective in their choice of marriage partners. "The failed past relationships of those young women living in impoverished communities, along with the pervasive distrust of men, make marriage seem risky," they write.[4] "They mitigate this risk by holding marriage to a high standard both in economic and in relational terms—so high that many will never marry at all." A related logic applies to Missing Class women like Valerie. It's true that another income would allow them to do more for their children, not to mention themselves. "If I had somebody staying, it would be a lot easier on the bills," Valerie points out. But she insists she is not desperate. She has a union job and full benefits. Things could be better, but then again, if the wrong man came into the picture, they could also get a lot worse. She has something to lose—her financial stability—and she's not about to risk it on an unknown quantity.

That may explain Valerie's ambivalence about her latest lover. Charlie is a southern gentleman—quite a bit older, too—who treats her with great courtesy and charm. For Christmas he bought her a leather coat. The other weekend he took her out to Atlantic City and paid the way. "I didn't have to buy anything," Valerie says. "I didn't have to pay my own money for gambling." They spent one afternoon shopping for clothes, hit the casino, then strolled the boardwalk, taking in the sights and enjoying each other's company, like a young couple in love. "He's forty-six," she notes. "But that's all right. He's a nice guy."

He's also a man of means. An electrician for the Long Island Rail Road, Charlie works two jobs with lots of overtime. He earns three times as much as Valerie's salary of $30,000, and he's made it known to her that he's willing to help out financially. Yet, in spite of all the goods that Charlie brings to the table—his plump paycheck, his selfless, almost paternal generosity, his gallant attempts at courtship—Valerie is not convinced that Charlie is marriage material. "Knowing me, I think I ain't never gonna find Mr. Right because I'm a picky person," she confesses. Though it's been several months since she and Charlie started dating, she's not willing to call him her boyfriend or make any pronouncement of exclusivity. He's still just a "friend." In the meantime, the two of them are keeping their relationship a secret from their coworkers: "We're on the down low, for now."

As women like Valerie search for a partner into their thirties, they worry about the example they provide to their children, who are themselves struggling with questions about love. Policing a teenage daughter's hormones is enough trouble. Akeelah is fifteen years old and has started hanging out with boys. She and her "friends" will sit on the front stoop and talk for hours. Valerie won't let any male visitors into the apartment unless there's a grown-up around—namely, her. They can sit in the living room while she's there, maybe even head to Akeelah's bedroom to play video games. "But if it's just you and him, no," Valerie tells her daughter. "You ain't committed to nobody but me."

As for her younger charge, Johnny, fortunately he's too young right now to worry about girls as anything but convenient targets for teasing. What does worry Valerie, though, is the bad influences that seem to surround the boy. He was born of a dysfunctional relationship, and though his mother and father split up soon after his birth, Johnny has continued to endure the consequences. When he was still an infant, his mother, Yamika, left him at his father's place, and the father's new girlfriend, frazzled by his incessant crying, lashed out. She broke his leg and cracked a few of his ribs. Remarkably, when Yamika discovered that her baby was hurt, she brushed off his injuries, dismissing them as a sprained ankle. Yamika's refusal to rush him to the hospital got her in trouble with the courts, who asked Valerie to take custody of the baby.

Valerie would love Johnny to have another adult in his life, but unfortunately his own mother can't be relied upon to be there for him. So Valerie finds herself helping him with his homework and playing the part of the disciplinarian. This summer, with Valerie unable to provide for his academic enrichment, he's taken to spending his days eating and playing. "He has his Super Nintendo, he has cartoons and cable TV, so he should be content," she says.

FAMILY LOYALTY

The Center for Family Life opened its doors in 1978, on a block situated between the neighborhood's drug-ridden park and the roaring Gowanus Expressway. Two nuns from the Sisters of the Good Shepherd, Sister Mary Paul Janchill and Sister Geraldine Tobia, founded the community center as a bulwark for Sunset Park's beleaguered families. The neighborhood was in steep decline, Janchill recalls. "Sunset Park was not considered a very safe place to raise children, and politically and racially and ethnically, there was a lot of tension." By then, the Irish and Italians and other white ethnic groups that had once called this neighborhood their home had already fled to the tree-shrouded quiet of New Jersey and Staten Island. The Puerto Rican families who replaced them were leaving in droves too, their patience exhausted by crime and drugs. When these longtime residents began to leave, the community's remaining foundations buckled. For the unfortunate families who couldn't afford to pick up and go, the neighborhood became a ghost of its former self, its factories shuttered, its storefronts abandoned, and its long avenues of houses reduced to cracked and lifeless shells.

Sunset Park was thriving in one way: youth gangs flourished in the absence of a real community, fighting and killing their way to the top of the hill. Gang members from different Latin American countries or even different enclaves in Puerto Rico waged a quasi-nationalistic war over turf. Anyone who got in the way was hurt. When the center opened up shop, the staff would leave work every day to find the tires of their cars slashed. "Day after day after day," Janchill says. "Until we got to say, 'Look, if your mother gets sick, we would need this car to go get the help.'"

The two sisters believed they could help turn Sunset Park around. Their center focused on the neighborhood's families, providing child care, after-school and summer programs, job training, housing rehabilitation, and, most important, family counseling. Joblessness and poverty had fractured relationships. The deep frustration of men who could find no work fed the viciousness of domestic violence. Mothers and fathers alike, meanwhile, found themselves increasingly at odds with their own children, who sought solace and solidarity in gang life. The psychological wounds that these families bore were manifold and spanned generations, but few services were available at the time to help them, Janchill says. "The mental health system sees individuals. They don't work with the families." So, the center began offering free and confidential counseling, emphasizing group sessions, home visits, and accessible and continuous care. By 2000 it was working with 450 families in the neighborhood.

Neighborhood institutions like the Center for Family Life provide a crucial support system for many Missing Class households, who do not qualify for the dwindling government-provided benefits for the truly poor. Near-poor Americans struggle mightily to pull themselves up the economic ladder, and yet their hourly wages place them in a no-man's-land between dependence and independence: above the income thresholds for public day care, Medicaid, and welfare but lacking the financial wherewithal to buy their own child care, their own counseling, and their own portion of middle-class stability. That's where organizations like the Center for Family Life come in. Though underfunded and overwhelmed, these scrappy nonprofits weave a small safety net for families living beyond the ken of most policymakers.

"It is not enough," Janchill concedes. She is an elderly woman, her wispy brown hair peeking out from beneath a nun's habit, her body bowed down by eight decades of doing God's will, yet her voice is firm and articulate, with a grandmother's gentleness.[5] "It's not enough because they need many other things. . . . They need supports in the rearing of their children. . . . Jobs, money, housing, education—the whole list. But the other list is very important, too. . . . They need opportunities for companionship, enjoyment, appreciation of the arts. Enlargement beyond this neighborhood. In a word, they need whatever *everybody* needs."

Sunset Park has never gotten all that it needs, but it has been able to carry on over the years with a few reasons for hope. During those dreary years in the sixties and seventies, many businesses closed up shop and disappeared. Not the hospital, though. "[Lutheran Medical Center] had almost given up remaining here," Janchill notes. "They were in an antiquated facility much too small for their needs, and there were many who encouraged them to leave the community and relocate elsewhere." But the hospital chose—"courageously," she says—to stay put in Sunset Park. The medical center headed over to the waterfront, where it bought up old factory buildings and refashioned them into a modern medical center, which opened in 1969. More than three decades later, Lutheran Medical Center remains a dominant employer and has steadily expanded its array of family-friendly treatment centers.

Things in Sunset Park really started to change, however, in the late 1990s, when the national economic boom helped lift many of the neighborhood's families into the workforce and into the Missing Class. While rising levels of investment have improved life in Sunset Park, money alone, Janchill insists, cannot sustain these families. Now as before, what the community could use is a focus on human relationships: reconciling couples, fostering honesty and trust, and giving parents the strength to nurture their children. "When husband and wife are hurting each other or getting hurt," Janchill points out, "it affects them so deeply in their functioning—individually and as parents. And unfortunately we see a lot of that."

The needs of Sunset Park's families have changed in recent years, she adds. In the last two decades, tides of global migration have deposited clusters of newcomers—one after another—on Sunset Park's blocks. Large numbers of Chinese have moved in and bought up homes and storefronts on Seventh and Eighth Avenues, converting a once-deserted swath of Sunset Park into a thriving Chinatown, the city's third-largest. Contingents of Arabs, Guyanese, and other groups have set up shop as well. In their wake have come even tinier cohorts from other Asian and Latin American ethnicities. Their work ethic is astounding. "They work in factories for long hours and in restaurants long hours," Janchill says. "Many of them work for very low to modest wages." Within the Chinese community, fathers head off to New Jersey to toil slavish workdays, bunking up at night and returning once every two weeks to see their families in Sunset Park. Fractured and handicapped in this fashion, immigrant families face serious problems adjusting to the new circumstances of their lives in America. "It's very hard for them to parent children in a new culture and in a very competitive climate," Janchill says.

The advantage that these families have, of course, is their strong social networks—their ability to rely on grandmothers to watch over children, aunts to share apartments, so that the family as a whole can survive and prosper.[6] But even tight-knit families fray under the pressure of close-quartered housing—the only accommodations available to many Missing Class families, now that rents are rising and government subsidies no longer dull their sting. "We've had families who are living in one room—a whole family living in one room. You can imagine what it's like to do homework." What's more, not all families enjoy the luxury of having able elders watch over the kids. The immigrant newcomers are "desperate" for child care, Janchill notes. They can't afford the day care that's available, and for the centers in their price range, the waiting lists are, bewilderingly, in the hundreds—part of the price of having more employed families in the neighborhood.

It's a problem in near-poor neighborhoods across the city and around the country: child care that costs too much, capacity that isn't there to support the demand. The immigrant parents who come to Sunset Park would rather care for their own children, but their Missing Class status—as wage earners, as renters, as family members with assorted obligations—means they have no choice but to seek help. Janchill remembers the case of one Chinese woman who came to apply for child care for her school-age child. "Somebody told her there's a long waiting list." A wry smile unfolds from between the sister's reddened cheeks. "So she sat down, and she said, 'I'll wait.'"

THE LINARES FAMILY

> About a million American children watch a mother or a father get remarried every year. . . . Don't think you're off the hook just because the kids are grown and no longer living at home. . . . "Where will we go for Thanksgiving?" becomes an issue. And money and inheritance comes into play.
>
> —*Washington Post*, December 7, 1999

Every day, it's the same routine. Arrive at 9 A.M., leave at 3 P.M. Then head to the night job—on some days, 4 to 10. Weekends, too. "The same routine," Tomás writes in his journal in September. "Nothing different," he writes a month later.

Once in a while there's trouble in the residential facility for the developmentally disabled where he works. "They're like babies. . . . There are some that don't stand still." One person will be quietly eating, and then another will come up and bop him over the head. Sometimes, when the natives get "wild," three or four people on staff will have to hold down each troublemaker.

On most days he's also driving his charges around the borough: to the boardwalk on Coney Island, to the pier on Sheepshead Bay, to any of the many Brooklyn parks. Tomás often volunteers to drive—it's a mammoth van, equipped with a lift, and he's one of the few who know how to operate it—but recently he's gotten tired of the responsibility. "I hate to get lost," he says. "It's too dangerous. . . . Something happen, forget it."

But even though he complains a lot, Tomás seems to like his job, or at least certain aspects of it. He's a people person at heart, and he gets along with most of the residents, who reciprocate the affection. One Sunday in January he spends the afternoon watching *Singing in the Rain* with the residents. One of them, an elderly man who's befriended Tomás over the years, holds his hand as the movie plays. ("I like him, he's so funny," Tomás says of his friend.) But the movie is making Tomás sleepy, and before it ends, at 4 P.M., he's dozing off. "After it get quiet my head was going—thunk!" Tomás says, dropping his chin.

Working every day of every week is taking its toll on him. The hours drag, and Tomás feels spent at the end of his shift. But he hardly uses his sick days or personal days, and he hasn't taken a meaningful vacation since July. There's nowhere to go. "I ain't got no money," he says. "Have a couple of beers over here, and lay down over there." Tomás hardly reads, but the TV in his apartment is on at all hours—from the time he gets home, through his seven hours of sleep, until he wakes up in the morning. Most days, the background chatter and canned laugh track are his sole companions.

Tomás hangs out sometimes with his girlfriend, Amanda, but most nights he's at his mother's place instead, eating Mom's cooking and keeping an old woman company. One night after Christmas he brings a friend over to Alicia's Sunset Park apartment. It's only five minutes away from Tomás's own place. The three of them sit at the kitchen table, where Alicia is serving her chicken soup and fried *plátanos*. The TV is on, as always, but Alicia loves to talk. The conversation turns to the latest news: the world's most famous Puerto Rican, Jennifer Lopez, was arrested today along with her rapper boyfriend, Sean Combs, in connection with a nightclub shooting. Lopez deserved to get arrested, Alicia clucks. She hung out with trash. Her parents must be heartbroken. She was making the entire Puerto Rican community look bad.

For longtime residents like Alicia, the waves of new immigrants and investment moving into Sunset Park bring to mind the precarious situation of old-timers like them. Once a Puerto Rican bastion, Sunset Park is being overrun by Mexicans, she claims, and her feelings of insecurity drive her to combative, even bigoted, conclusions. As this sexagenarian sees it, the Mexicans are the reason that the streets have become dangerous, thanks to their penchant for assaulting and mugging people. You have to be careful walking around at night, she says; even complete strangers are being harassed. Alicia doesn't like to go out herself—her hearing is giving her trouble these days—but sometimes she has to. Whenever she does, she makes sure to cross the street to avoid the Mexicans.

Tomás brings up the fact that his mother lost the keys to her apartment the other day. She called up Tomás at work to get another set. Alicia admits that she's starting to forget things. She's sixty-eight years old and has had two mild strokes. The last one occurred several months ago; for some time afterward her mouth was twisted. And that's not her only problem. Her feet hurt. She has diabetes, hepatitis, and asthma. She wolfs down pills for her multiple conditions every day.

And she's a lonely woman, Alicia adds. "In a few years," she says, turning to Tomás, "you'll understand what I'm talking about."

As his mother's only remaining son, Tomás is devoted to Alicia and feels obligated to spend as much time as he can with her. It's as if he's making up for his former life of debauchery and all the suffering he inflicted on his mom. Tomás intends to stay by his mother's side in Sunset Park. "I think I will die here," he says.

This kind of filial loyalty does not apply to Tomás's father. Alano still lives in Aguadilla, where he works as a cab driver and lottery vendor, but Tomás doesn't keep in touch with him. He has never bothered to return to the old neighborhood, in fact. (He's heard it's become so infested with drugs and gangs that even the police can't set foot there.) Alano, on the other hand, has shown interest in seeing his son. "He called me once," Tomás says. Alano told him he had prostate cancer. "He called me so I would go and see him." Tomás has yet to go.

For Christmas the week before, Tomás's aunt gave him a framed picture of his grandmother. It was a black-and-white photograph of the woman who had raised Tomás until the age of seventeen. He decided not to show the photo to his mother. She would cry.

· · ·

Although they do their best to start meaningful, long-term relationships, single men like Tomás find themselves pulled in the opposite direction by the demands of family. Whereas middle-class families with
more resources can turn to other solutions—senior residences that are
full of activities and like-aged company, day care to watch over the kids,
and even psychiatrists to offer a willing ear for troubles—members of
the Missing Class typically can't afford them. And so they find themselves struggling to fill in as babysitters, confidants, and helpers for
family members they will not, or cannot, rebuff.

Tomás and his girlfriend, Amanda, have felt the tension from the
very beginnings of their relationship, but things have gotten only worse
since she moved a borough away. She wants him to be near her at all
times, but "I got things to do," Tomás points out. His mother cooks for
him most nights. (Tomás has used the stove only twice in his life.)
Tomás, in turn, buys food for his mom and drops in regularly to check
on her. That's the reason he can't get married, he adds; he can't leave his
mother by herself. "She's bored, depressed. I got to go stay with her at
night because she's lonely and sick." After all, he points out, his mother
is the only person in his life he can really rely upon. On a more pragmatic level, it's also true that Alicia has considerable savings—part
of which she keeps in a trunk, part of which she's transferred to a
certificate of deposit in Tomás's name—and she's made it clear that
when she dies, Tomás will get the money.

Alicia leads a somewhat unconventional life compared with other
elderly Hispanic women in that she lives alone, without a spouse or relatives.[7] But she is similar to many of her peers in that she can depend on
the help of family, namely her son. Many American adults provide
financial support, care, or other kinds of assistance to one or more of
their elderly parents. Like Tomás, these caregivers tend to be older—
aged thirty or more—and live either in the same house or nearby.[8]

Though he good-naturedly shoulders the burden of providing his
mother with much-needed companionship, Tomás concedes that at
times he feels resentment. His mom could "get around" if she really
wanted to, he says, but she'll hardly set foot outside the apartment. Instead, she'll talk for hours on the phone. "I'm fifty years old," he says. "I
can't be babysitting all the time over there."

A somewhat less necessary burden that Tomás has taken on recently is providing free lodging for his "nephew." Guillermo, his cousin's son, had been the live-in boyfriend of a Dominican divorcée, but the woman and her ex-husband decided to reconcile, leaving Guillermo without a place to sleep. Guillermo then moved in with Alicia, but he brought too much clutter and disarray into Alicia's traditional Puerto Rican home, so, as usual, the problem was foisted upon the most obliging family member, Tomás. While he waits for renovations to be completed in his basement apartment ten blocks away, Guillermo is staying for almost free at Tomás's apartment. He is a counselor for people with HIV/AIDS, so presumably Guillermo makes a decent wage. Yet, in the two or three months since he moved in, Guillermo has ponied up a measly $20 toward a phone bill (he's on the modem often) and an insulting $50 toward Tomás's rent. "[He] should have given me at least $100, right?" says Tomás. "But I don't say nothing." He's family, and Tomás feels obligated to lend a hand. "I'll help him. He didn't have no place than the street."

All these family responsibilities inevitably get in the way of Tomás's love life. It's not just the time Tomás must spend listening to his mother or watching over his grandkid. It's also that his family seems to resent Amanda as an intruder who is stealing Tomás away from them. This is a common issue in many poor households, as Carol Stack documented more than thirty years ago in her classic book *All Our Kin*.[9] The ailing mother or the broke daughter fears the loss of a family member who can provide needed help, and so she does what she can to break the couple apart. Gainfully employed Missing Class workers like Tomás face even more pressure: he is the golden goose that his blood relations need to keep at hand. They dislike Amanda intensely and make no bones about their opposition to his relationship with her as it is now, much less in marriage.

Alicia, for instance, complains loudly that whenever Amanda calls, the woman doesn't bother with pleasantries. There's no "How are you" or "How's everything" or even "Hello." The conversation goes like this: "Linares there?" "No." "Thank you."

"My mother didn't like that, and she told me," Tomás says. She also brought up the fact that Amanda has never bothered to invite Alicia to any family gatherings—not even a "little" dinner at her house.

His daughter Ella has issued the same complaint: your girlfriend has zero people skills. One day Amanda dropped by the Gap to shop. She knew that Ella worked there. She saw Ella in the store but didn't say a word. "And Ella got upset, you know?" Tomás says. "She could have said 'Hi' or something, but she didn't. . . . I don't understand that."

The hostility that his family shows to Amanda grates on Tomás's heart. Now that Amanda has given her engagement-or-else ultimatum, he is contemplating the prospect of another marriage and yet dreading his family's reaction. He knows his mother will be upset.

It's not just the pressure from his family, though, that makes Tomás keep his distance. At times, she exasperates him with her secrecy. When they started going out, Amanda didn't want anyone in the neighborhood to know it. She seemed to think that a widow who dated would be frowned upon. So she made Tomás pick her up two or three blocks away from her Brooklyn apartment. What's more, she never once invited Tomás into *that* apartment. "Maybe everything was on the floor," Tomás quips.

Now, after five years together, Amanda has yet to tell her adult son, a pastor in training, that she's seeing Tomás. "The son thinks she's only my friend—just like that—and I just help her, you know?" What really galls him, though, is that Amanda still insists he not call her his girlfriend. Yet she's already thinking of marriage.

Tomás, for his part, is not ready to rush in. "We have to understand one another, the way we are," he tells Amanda. "Before we make a mistake and get divorced right away. I'm not like when I was young.

"Now I got more experience."

Tomás and Amanda have split up. "She wanted me to be with her all the time," Tomás says when we next see him, two years later. "I had to see my daughters and I had to be with my mother." In any case, he didn't have the money to buy her an engagement ring. Tomás tried to get Amanda to see his point of view, but she dumped him anyway. "We can still be friends," she said. Tomás said fine, but in his mind that was the end. "I never went back."

As for his daughters, Ella has gotten a master's degree in psychology. She's making $45,000 a year working in the personnel department of a Brooklyn hospital. "Everyone knows her, everyone likes her," Tomás says. Meanwhile, she's still "crazy" about marrying her boy-friend, a half–Puerto Rican, half-Chinese man who works as a security guard, but for now they're waiting—the boyfriend's father has lung cancer, and he'll have to take care of his mother if he dies. Yula isn't married yet, either, but at least she's in a stable relationship now. She and the father of her son broke up. Arturo had found a well-paid job polishing metal, but he was giving Yula nothing and all but ignoring her. An image of the youthful Tomás, he would go out with his friends and come home in the early-morning hours. He neglected his own son; David, a "slow" child, was already stuck in special classes. Yula and Ar-turo argued bitterly until she finally told him to leave. Now Yula has a new boyfriend, whom she found on the Internet. This one helps out at home. He washes the dishes and does the laundry; he takes her out to the movies and even—much like the older Tomás—pays her rent. The two are expecting a baby.

Tomás's mother has moved on, too. After she had another small stroke, her third one, Alicia decided to swap her unheated apartment on Forty-second Street for senior citizen housing next to Lutheran Med-ical Center. Tomás has visited her there and likes the variety of services the building provides. "She's got an elevator, a social worker, a home at-tendant that visits her twice a week," he says. "If she needs anything, she rings for the security officer."

Not much has changed for Tomás. He's living the same monastic life of long stretches of work punctuated by television and sleep. On ac-count of his poor health, he's cut back on alcohol—"I can't even drink beer anymore," he notes glumly—but he has yet to give up on the ciga-rettes. He still needs them to get through the stress of each workday. The litany is familiar: "I have to take one guy to the bathroom twenty thousand times. I have to tell another guy to sit down. He sits and the guy next to him stands up. Another is moving back and forth, another is rocking, another is making noise"—he buzzes his lips—"you under-stand?" At our last interview, Tomás looks especially run-down, having caught a bug that even antibiotics can't seem to shake. Maybe the pres-sure is getting to him. "Sometimes I leave work feeling exhausted, with my mind wasted," he concedes. The red welt on his nose, though, hap-pens to be from his grandson.

THE RUSHING FAMILY

In the Rushing clan, the sins of the mother have been visited upon the daughter—and the mother's sister, to boot. Stephanie, Yamika's too-stoned-to-care mother, saw to that. Growing up in the shadow of Stephanie's addiction, Yamika was mentally abused and physically neglected. She did not travel her mother's path to crack, but she did follow her footsteps in another way: she had a son when she was only sixteen. An immature, self-absorbed teenager, Yamika seemed oblivious to Johnny and to the rest of the world. She would land a job and then not show up for work. In time, Yamika's carelessness endangered little Johnny's life. Then just six months old, Johnny was summarily handed over to his aunt Valerie to raise. Valerie kept the boy and treated him as her own. Johnny called her "mom" and thought of Valerie's daughter, his cousin Akeelah, as his sister.

Recently, after drifting at a distance for several years, Yamika entered her son's life again. As Valerie sees it, that's the reason that Johnny's behavior has started to slip. "Last year about this time, he wasn't seeing her and he was doing good," she says. "Now she's coming over maybe twice a week, three times a week. And she let him get away with everything, so he feels he can do that now." Yamika is wholly unreliable. She promises Valerie she'll come on Thursday but shows up on Tuesday. She tells Johnny that she'll give him things and fails to follow through. Bitterly disappointed, Johnny avenges himself by acting out in class. "When he's in school, it's like he don't want to take no orders," Valerie says. "He's hitting kids." What's more, now that his mom has come back into his life, Johnny has started to call her mom, and Valerie auntie. Valerie says she doesn't mind. Yamika *is* his mom, after all, and she wants him to bond with her. But whenever Yamika goes back on her promises, he runs crying to Valerie. "When she don't come around, it's like, 'Mom, Mom, Mom.'"

Matters come to a head in the fall, when Yamika asks to move into Valerie's apartment. She was staying with her mother and her mother's boyfriend, but the boyfriend threw them both out. Next she stayed with a friend, but then the friend's boyfriend got out of prison and moved in. Yamika is without a place to stay again. Valerie can't let her niece live on the streets.

As part of the bargain, Yamika is supposed to bring in some income
—either by getting a job or by going on welfare—so that she can pay a
modest rent of $25 a week. She is also supposed to look after Johnny, in-
cluding picking him up from school. True to form, Yamika flakes out.
She doesn't get a job. She procrastinates on applying for welfare for two
months, until Valerie makes threats and Yamika finally seeks out the
benefits. She pays rent, but only in useless dribbles of $5 or $10. As for
mothering her only son, Yamika is with Johnny all the time now, but if
Valerie wants the homework done, she has to be the taskmaster. Yamika
has more important things to do, like nattering on the phone for hours
on end. "She's a phone freak," Valerie complains. The calls come at random times and from random places. Once, she wonders aloud if the
man on the line asking for her niece is calling from prison.

Valerie is not pleased by what her niece has dragged into the home.
It isn't just the phone calls or the fact that "every Tom, Dick, and Edward" in the neighborhood has suddenly figured out her address and
stops by. Yamika's constant presence is also having an effect on Johnny's
behavior, and not for the better. Fed up, Valerie tells Yamika she'll have
to leave in another two months.

The situation with Johnny and his mother upsets Valerie no end,
but she insists on soldiering on. "I ain't got no choice 'cause I ain't com-
mitting suicide or nothing," she says. "I'm not going nutty." Instead,
she's learning to adapt. She refuses to tolerate a presumptuous house-
guest anymore. She's reconsidering her generosity to other family
members, too. Her brothers stop by her place every weekend to drink
beer and listen to music. But with the long hours she works, oftentimes
on double eight-hour shifts, Valerie no longer has the patience to deal
with visitors. She gets home, and there are people chatting in the living
room. It's just too much.

So Valerie is contemplating moving: to Long Island. When people
in her family are in trouble, she's the one they call on. If she lives far
away, it'll be harder for them to drop by her house, she reasons, or otherwise intrude in her life.

That would leave more time for romance, too. She's been getting
other offers for dates, she notes, but hasn't been able to fit them into her
schedule. "I've been dead out there."

． ． ．

In spite of their best efforts, poverty has a way of creeping back into the lives of members of the Missing Class in the form of relatives who can no longer manage and must lean on more fortunate kin. A single mom like Valerie may, with enough luck and pluck, be able to secure a promising future for herself and her children. But her extended family always seems to be trailing right behind her with their dramas, burdens, and importunate requests. And who can say no? Certainly not Valerie, who has long borne the responsibility for Johnny and shoved her own interests—among them, dinners with eligible bachelors—off her list of priorities.

Because of the obligations posed by their extended families, the well-being of the Missing Class workers cannot be assessed merely by looking at their incomes. These men and women are part of larger constellations of need—financial, emotional, and legal. As the reliable hubs that keep these networks intact, people like Tomás and Valerie are frequently the targets of requests—appropriate or not—for their money, time, and home space. More often than not, they want to help. They do their best to be generous. At times, though, the problems they are asked to tackle are simply overwhelming and threaten to drag down benefactor and supplicant alike. Tomás cannot build a new life with Amanda in part because the needy members of his old households—his mother and two daughters—keep entreating him to step in and save them. Valerie's visions of love and romance are complicated by her need to be a dependable parent to her daughter and adopted son.

It should be no surprise that when those family obligations diminish, members of the Missing Class feel an intense, and telling, relief. The next time we see Valerie, in 2002, she's a changed woman. She smiles more freely now, with a much cheerier disposition to match, and the contentment shows in the twenty pounds she's put on in two years. Her secret, Valerie says, is that she's won her freedom. Johnny is no longer living with her; neither is his mom. Yamika ended up having another child, and when that happened, Valerie demanded she take the boy, too. Johnny wanted to live with his mother, anyway, and Yamika finally seemed ready to be a better parent, having shed some of her apathy and immaturity. "She's cleaned up her act a lot," Valerie says.

For her part, Valerie is glad that Johnny is back with his mom. At the end of his stay with Valerie, he was becoming impossible. "He didn't want to do no work in school," she says. "He was acting out, maybe because his mother was having another baby. He wanted to be with her." Every other day she'd get reports from Johnny's school that he didn't want to sit down, that he didn't want to do homework. Johnny is back with his mom now, but apparently he's still misbehaving. "Now *she's* feeling it," Valerie says.

Valerie declares that she'll never take custody of any child ever again. "I had no choice," she says. "I did it because that was my nephew. I didn't want to see him in the system." But raising Johnny was a real burden for her, she notes. "Now that I see what I can do with my own time by myself, I don't want to start over again."

The other big change is that Valerie has moved. The apartment is just a block away from her old place, but it is spacious and snug. In her new home she's finally been inspired to decorate, adding a sofa, putting up framed pictures and plaques, and stocking the coffee table and shelves with ornaments. The new place costs a few hundred dollars more in rent every month—a jump from $636 at the old place to $945 at the current one. Valerie is getting help from her "friend" Charlie. He pays half the rent but doesn't live there.

Valerie insists that even without Charlie's help, she'd be able to make the rent. "If I don't want to be bothered with him, then I say, 'Look, you and me are breaking up' or whatever. . . . It's not like he's—I mean, he is a necessity, but he's not the main necessity." Still, she admits that she leans on Charlie quite a bit, not just financially but emotionally. Whenever she needs to "get my yells out," she goes to him. "He will let me yell at him. I don't beat up on him, but I do yell at him."

SEVEN

On the Edge
Plunging Out of the Missing Class

The late 1990s and the early part of this decade were very good times, relatively speaking, to be poor in America.[1] Many of the families we have encountered in this book so far started out at the bottom of the heap a decade ago, but thanks to tight labor markets and soaring wages, they worked their way into the Missing Class. Rita Gervais started thinking about buying a house. Julia Coronado and her new husband could afford vacations in the Dominican Republic. Valerie Rushing was making a handsome salary and no longer had to "geese" men she didn't like. For the first time in years, Danielle Wayne was toiling contentedly at a stable job, no longer stuck in the role of the depressed, welfare-dependent mother who had to will herself out of bed to take care of her kids.

In a thousand ways—large and small—good economic times improved the lives of parents in the Missing Class. There was no magic to this turn of events. These parents worked furiously in pursuit of their families' economic security, trading time with their kids for bread on the table and the luxury of being one step ahead of the bill collectors.

Not every child prospered, however. Tamar's son Omar found his way into the criminal justice system, in part because his mother was spending so many hours commuting to her factory job that she could no longer supervise him. For many other children, though, the trade-offs were worthwhile. Steady incomes placed a more reliable foundation underneath them. Yes, their parents were gone most of the day. But they no longer had rodents creeping into their kitchens through holes in the floor. Their families were no longer clinging to the roller coaster of public assistance, their benefits disappearing without warning. For the first time in their lives, Missing Class kids were able to stay in the same schools, live in the same apartments, and know that from one year to the next, the longitude and latitude of their lives would not change much.

Yet for all the success stories, there was still a significant number of near-poor families who saw their earnings erode. Missing Class households are vulnerable to downward mobility when they lack buffers: a surplus of earners, savings accounts, and homes they own and can borrow against.[2] While they live better than the truly poor, the difference between Missing Class monthly expenses and household earnings is rarely large enough to sock away for a rainy-day fund. An abrupt layoff; a marriage that collapses, leaving one wage earner to manage what used to require two; illness that strikes suddenly, even when the family is insured—these are the trip wires that can swiftly drag families back down below the poverty line. Their hold on the good life is precarious, and they know it.

The economic boom aside, income insecurity, measured as the risk of being poor, has actually been growing over the last decade. The odds of falling into a temporary spell of poverty doubled in the 1990s for all Americans except those seventy and older. In the 1980s about 13 percent of Americans in their forties spent at least one year below the poverty line. By the 1990s 36 percent found themselves in these straits.[3] Unions have wilted, and the value of the minimum wage has eroded over time, leaving more of us vulnerable.

We might imagine that this is less of a problem for Missing Class families. After all, they are starting out fairly close to the bottom of the wage distribution; surely there is nowhere to go but up from there. There is some truth to this assumption. As American University economist Tom Hertz has shown, households at the bottom of the income ladder do see more upward movement than declining fortunes. Even so, a significant number of them experience losses, and that proportion is even greater among their slightly better-off brethren, the near poor. When Missing Class families falter, poverty cannot be far behind.[4]

The labor market will probably become even more inhospitable for poor and Missing Class workers in the years to come, as wages for high school graduates continue to stagnate and highly skilled jobs (for example, engineering and computer systems design) grow in number. Already, African Americans and workers with only high school degrees have unemployment rates that are about double those of whites and workers with bachelor's degrees, respectively. Although the national unemployment rate was fairly healthy in 2006—at 4.6 percent—the long-term prospects for workers who lack the skills this economy increasingly demands are, at best, unpredictable. Many are being shunted to the margins of the labor market because their poor access to education or limited English prevents them from properly competing.[5]

When weak economic growth or bad luck pushes Missing Class families down the income ladder, some land in familiar territory. Sadly, these particular individuals rose up from poverty only to revisit it. With a sickening feeling of déjà vu, they face bills they cannot easily pay, the awkwardness of having to turn to family and friends for help, and the disappointment of children—particularly teens—who do not take kindly to the constraints of poverty and continue to ask for things their parents can no longer provide. Once the pressures become intolerable, these parents press their teenagers into the labor market. At first the kids earn money to help pay for "extras"—stylish blue jeans and athletic shoes—but in time they are expected to contribute to the household coffers. This might seem nothing out of the ordinary to survivors of the Great Depression, who were counted upon to work in order to help their families. But it is far from the current middle-class model of a protected childhood.

This much of the story is well known to readers who are familiar with the voluminous writings of sociologists and journalists on life among America's poor.[6] Perhaps less understood is the way that this free fall robs hardworking people of their privacy, their dignity, and the freedom to manage their lives as adults. Dropping out of the Missing Class means reengaging with an enemy from the past: the public bureaucracy.

THE RAMOS FAMILY

Fewer of those eligible for welfare are signing up for it. In 2002 . . . about 48% of people who were eligible for welfare signed up, according to the Urban Institute. That was down from 79% in 1996. Analysts say the

decline in the "take-up rate" is tied to a greater stigma in obtaining
welfare, more paperwork required to receive benefits and a culture
of work instilled in people by welfare officers. One fear is this new
framework could end up discouraging needy people from seeking
help for themselves and their children.

—Wall Street Journal, August 26–27, 2006

Back in 1989, the word on the street in Santo Domingo was that the
only way to make serious money was to find a way out. The island economy was in shambles. Dominicans were leaving in droves, looking for
any means to cross to the U.S. mainland. Many started their journey in
Puerto Rico, working as domestic servants for more fortunate families
and biding their time until the moment arose to set out for New York.

Ricardo Ramos was pretty handy with power tools. He knew a
thing or two about construction; he could repair electrical circuits,
plaster walls, and fix floorboards. Marisol, Ricardo's wife, urged him to
head to America. Many of her girlfriends' husbands had made the journey and were doing well enough to send money home. Ricardo was
willing to try his luck, but he had heard that *la migra,* the immigration
police, was on the lookout for Dominicans arriving in New York without papers. He thought he'd take a more obscure route, so he set out for
Panama. From there Ricardo made his way to Mexico and then slipped
across the border into Texas.

That's where his luck ran out. Ricardo was picked up by the border
patrol and detained for three days. His compadre Felix bailed him out
by paying some fines, but not before Ricardo had acquired an immigration violation on his record. It seemed unimportant at the time, and
even less important by the time he made it to New York and began
looking for a place to live. He barely noticed the deportation notice
that arrived at Felix's home three days after their arrival in Washington
Heights. Ricardo was preoccupied with finding a place of his own and
figuring out how to spirit Marisol into the country.

For her part, Marisol was playing a waiting game. In 1982 she and
her sister Beatriz had applied for green cards through their older sister,
Angela, a legal resident of New York. Married and with a daughter
of her own, Angela was lonely for her family. Family reunification had
become a priority in the American immigration system after 1965,

so Marisol and Beatriz had only to wait until Angela's petition was granted. In 1990 the long wait came to an end. The sisters packed their bags, said their good-byes to their mother, and boarded a plane bound for Manhattan.

What Marisol and Beatriz found when they arrived was a disappointment, though they tried not to show it. All their Dominican neighbors had rattled on about how rich America was, how much easier it was to live in New York than in Santo Domingo. They weren't lying exactly, but the truth was a bit more complicated. Marisol soon learned that Ricardo's options for work were more limited than she had expected. An illegal immigrant who could not speak English, he was confined to the Dominican enclave of Washington Heights, where he was indeed able to find work, but not the kind that paid enough to live well. The best the couple could manage was a studio apartment for $575 a month. Beatriz slept in the hallway.

Slowly, Ricardo and Marisol found their way. Relying on their connections to family and friends in the neighborhood, they landed jobs in firms where their immigration status didn't matter much and English wasn't necessary. Ricardo was hired by a money-wiring service that sends cash and ships packages to families waiting back home for American dollars, clothing, and medicines. Marisol babysat for mothers working in the factories. She harvested job prospects for her sister from these women, and within a few weeks, Beatriz was toiling at a sweatshop, too. Between the three of them, they made enough to pay the rent on the studio, with money to spare. Though none of them was on the tax rolls, they would have qualified for membership in the Missing Class if anyone had bothered to count.

Even so, their home life was not what they had hoped for. For one thing, the apartment was a shoebox. "It was so small that you had to turn sideways to pass each other," Marisol remembers. "To watch TV, you had to get into bed." Beatriz tried to give the couple some space, but with only one room, they grated on each other's nerves. To make matters worse, despite Marisol's ambitions to study English and work, she became pregnant. She stuck with her child-care jobs, hoping to continue earning money as long as possible, but the pregnancy entered a troubled phase, and in the fourth month, it ended.

Shortly thereafter, Marisol became pregnant again, and this time Ricardo insisted she stay home to protect her (and the baby's) health. The family resolved to survive on Ricardo's wages and the contributions Beatriz offered from her factory earnings. Little Elena was born a premature infant in 1991. Ricardo paid for the delivery in cash, since they had no health insurance, but at last—after a frightening interlude in the hospital's intensive-care unit for underweight, underdeveloped babies—they had a healthy daughter to raise.

Now there were four of them living in the studio apartment. A crying baby, no space, and the loss of Marisol's earning power proved a recipe for claustrophobia and insomnia. In the midst of this turmoil, Ricardo received another deportation notice but paid it little mind. "I am in New York, and nobody is going to get me out," Marisol remembers him saying. As for her, she was too frazzled by the demands of caring for a newborn to worry about *la migra.* So many of her relatives had found ways to "get their papers" that she figured Ricardo would, too. Neither of them contemplated hiring a lawyer; the cost was out of the question.

Meanwhile, a solution to the housing crisis materialized. Marisol and Ricardo heard about a landlord who was letting tenants move into his ramshackle apartment building for a minuscule rent in exchange for doing the necessary rehab themselves. For $400 a month, they could put their hands on a one-bedroom flat. Marisol was ecstatic—until she saw her new home. "These apartments were semidestroyed," she recalls. "There were mice, cockroaches, and dirt all over." The refrigerator didn't work. Neither did the stove. Marisol grew frightened. How could she raise her child *here?* "I don't want to go in there," she told Ricardo. "No, no, no!"

Ricardo reassured his wife that they could fix the place. They threw out all of the old appliances, and Ricardo and his cousin got to work rebuilding the bathroom and kitchen. For two months, Marisol cooked on a hot plate. "It was a tiny stove, and we didn't have a refrigerator. So we bought things to consume every day." Slowly the apartment began to take on a habitable shape.

When the next threatening envelope from the government arrived, it began to dawn on them that Ricardo was in real danger of being thrown out of the country. This time, they panicked. Ricardo needed to get papers somehow. Reluctantly, the couple filed for divorce so that he could arrange to marry an American citizen and apply for a permanent visa. It was a business arrangement and nothing more. Ricardo and Marisol continued to live together as husband and wife.

A U.S. citizen can "import" a prospective spouse into the country as long as his (or her) intended is outside the country at the time of application. Hearing this, Ricardo got his "fiancée" to apply for a visa on his behalf. After months of waiting, he received word that he had been granted an interview with U.S. authorities in Santo Domingo. Wasting no time, Ricardo kissed Marisol on the check, snuggled Elena for a moment, and said a quick good-bye. "I'll be home tomorrow," he reassured Marisol as he headed off to the airport. The next day, he turned up on time for his appointment in Santo Domingo. Ricardo was nervous that the authorities would discover his marriage plans were a sham, but they never got that far. A routine check uncovered his arrest in Texas and the pending deportation order. The immigration official informed Ricardo that he would never be admitted into the United States again. Case closed.

Waiting at home in New York, Marisol was confused and anxious. She was sure that Ricardo would get his green card and be home on the next plane. But when she didn't hear from him, she grew alarmed. Not only did she have no idea where Ricardo was, but she had just realized that the nausea she was feeling in the morning wasn't from the flu —Marisol was expecting once again. When Ricardo finally called to explain what had happened, she started shrieking. *"How am I gonna manage? I've got Elena here! I'm gonna have another!"* Marisol collapsed on the couch and then called her sisters, sobbing that her husband was in trouble.

Back in the Dominican Republic, Ricardo alternated between outrage and fear. He had been through an illegal crossing before and knew its dangers. But how else was he going to get back to his family? Out of options, he decided to engage a smuggler to take him across the waters. Only a few miles out to sea, they were caught. Ricardo spent three days in a crowded and squalid Dominican jail.

Had Marisol and Ricardo realized that they had legal options in dealing with the immigration service, the situation might not have been so grim. But like many immigrants, they were flummoxed by the bureaucracy, preoccupied with trying to provide for their families, and reliant on advice from people who had only a partial understanding of how the system worked. The consequences of their hasty decisions were irreparable. With the loss of Ricardo, the household's top wage earner, Marisol was ejected from the Missing Class overnight. No longer was there any cushion of income to blunt the rough edges of life in the big city; Marisol had slid from two-income stability into impoverished single parenthood.

Saddled with one infant and another one on the way, Marisol had no choice but to apply for public assistance.

Marisol grew to dread her visits to the Dyckman Job Center in Washington Heights. There, the city's welfare bureaucrats spend most of their day explaining to desperate people across the counter that they are not eligible for assistance. Looking to dampen the appeal of illegal immigration, lawmakers in 1996 restricted access to welfare, Medicaid, and a host of other benefits that often make the difference between survival and desperation for foreign-born families. Since then, illegal immigrants and lawful residents alike routinely face caseworkers who can do nothing for them.

Normally a mild and fairly upbeat person, Marisol puts on a dark scowl when she talks about her first foray into the Dyckman Center. She was no illegal alien. All of her papers were in order. But by that time, even legal residents were being denied public assistance. Her caseworker insisted she had to be a U.S. citizen to qualify.

"How will we manage?" Marisol pleaded. She was already short on this month's rent.

"You can make do with the $80 you earn from babysitting."

"But I'm pregnant!"

"Well, who told you to do that?" the caseworker retorted.

It wasn't right of this woman to make things so difficult for someone in need. "The money isn't coming out of your purse!" Marisol pointed out. She demanded to see a supervisor, who turned out to be even more aloof and abrasive. "I did not ask you to get pregnant so the government would pay for your child's maintenance," the woman said, apparently reading from the same script.

Marisol insisted that she wasn't after permanent assistance—just some help with her rent so that she wouldn't lose her apartment. "Right now nobody is going to hire me with such an advanced pregnancy," she reasoned.

A month and several bouts of crying and begging later, Marisol's case was finally opened. The whole episode infuriated her. "People in need are treated as if they have abused the system," she says.

So began Marisol's "administered life." Accustomed to the independence and privacy of her former existence, she struggled to overcome her discomfort about explaining intimate aspects of her life to strangers—a de facto requirement for her government aid check. She had to produce receipts from her landlord showing that she had paid the rent, utility bills attesting to the cost of lights and heat, doctors' bills to prove that she had been under their care. The bureaucracy was maddening. Ordered to appear at the Dyckman Center at 9 A.M., Marisol sometimes would wait for hours, with nothing to eat. One day her caseworker took so long to see her that she nearly gave birth in the waiting room, seized with the labor pains announcing Belkis, her second daughter. On another occasion the caseworker kept her waiting for four hours and then had the nerve to tell Marisol the meeting had to be rescheduled because she needed to grab lunch and was booked for the rest of the day. Marisol pulled her short, stocky frame up to the reception desk and slammed the folder with all her paperwork down, demanding at the top of her lungs to be seen. The caseworker reluctantly agreed.

Black caseworkers questioned Marisol about her love life and Ricardo's whereabouts. She detected a tone of racial hostility, a suspicion shared by many of her Latina friends with welfare experience. The welfare bureaucrats never believed her; they cross-examined her as if she were a criminal; they demanded her presence at audit hearings. Since most of the mailboxes in Marisol's building were broken, she failed to receive notices announcing her hearings. Her benefits would be cut off, and Marisol would have to beseech the judge at her fair hearing to reinstate them, producing once again bills, letters from her landlord—the paper trail of her life. Terrified that she might end up in a homeless shelter, Marisol did everything she could to satisfy the bureaucratic machine.

When the benefits were coming, Marisol received $280 a month in food stamps, Medicaid coverage for her daughters, and a Jiggets rent subsidy of $143, which, together with her babysitting earnings, were supposed to cover a month's expenses.[7] It was never enough. Only through the (hidden) charity of her sisters was she able to manage.[8]

Eventually, the work requirements imposed by welfare reform caught up with Marisol, and she was ordered out into the labor market. Her first stop was a nursing home on Manhattan's Upper East Side, where she served tea and coffee to elderly patients. Marisol enjoyed the job. She felt useful and looked forward to leaving her neighborhood for a new environment every day. Her sisters helped look after Elena and Belkis; Marisol reciprocated by taking care of their kids in her off-hours.

What she didn't like very much were the ugly looks coming from her coworkers. Marisol thought she could read their minds: "There comes another [Latina] wanting to take my job." Convinced they were going to lose their jobs to the city's conscripted labor force, the regulars did what they could to force the competition out. Marisol stuck with it but soon realized the job was a dead end. Working off her benefits was not putting any extra money in her pocketbook.

She asked the welfare authorities to send her to school while she continued working at the nursing home. Hunter College accepted her into their English as a Second Language program for two months. Although not well educated, Marisol is a willing student, and she took to the course with enthusiasm. She studied sentence structures, practiced irregular verbs, and acted out conversations in role-playing groups. "I tuned my ear," she says proudly. Soon after, Marisol passed the first-level exam. Her teachers were so pleased that they asked that she be assigned to assist new students.

Emboldened by this success, Marisol signed up for a computer class. Though she expected computer skills to open doors in the labor market, she was disappointed to discover that the class didn't progress beyond teaching her to use the keyboard and push the mouse around.

Still, with this limited training and Marisol's command of the alphabet, she was able to qualify for her first white-collar job.

After five years on public assistance, Marisol landed a clerical position working for an association of doctors who run a pediatric clinic in Midtown. It's not exactly exciting work. She spends her days climbing footstools to reach files and walking paperwork to the offices that must stamp each piece of paper. She enjoys a bit of light banter with her coworkers, the most she can manage with her limited English, but she is alone with her thoughts for much of the day. "What I do is so simple that anybody could do it," she admits. "The person who helps the secretary is nobody. My job is not important."

Marisol is not proud of her station and wishes she knew enough English to compete for better opportunities. At the same time, the doctors give her two weeks of paid vacation every year and five personal days, benefits that are rare in low-wage jobs. Marisol appreciates this flexibility, which allows her to attend parent-teacher conferences and stay home with her daughters when they are ill. She will lean on her sisters for help when necessary, but she doesn't want to depend on them. Self-sufficiency is still important to Marisol, even though her annual income—several thousand dollars below the poverty line for a family of three—now qualifies her as poor.

Marisol's salary is less than $6 an hour, and she always manages to fall just short of full-time hours. She knows she could earn more in a factory. In fact, one year the doctors' association didn't have any more work for her, so she was forced to join her Dominican countrywomen at the factory gates. She was paid nearly $2 an hour more for packing flowers than she was for filing. It was a relief when the doctors called her back, though, for the higher wage came with no vacation, no sick days, and a far less forgiving work regime. One missed day got workers fired in the factory. Doctors are more lenient.

In spite of her low wages, Marisol is doing better financially than she was before she went to work. Her earnings are low enough that she continues to qualify for food stamps, Medicaid, and housing allowances, albeit on a more limited scale than in her welfare days. And then there's her tax rebate. One of the happiest days of the year is the annual arrival of her Earned Income Tax Credit check—a government subsidy targeted at low-wage workers. Marisol squirrels away that springtime windfall to pay for her daughters' school uniforms and summer child care.[9]

While the most fortunate members of the Missing Class earn enough on their own to clear the poverty line by a wide margin, the least advantaged avoid penury only when they can keep a second wage earner in their orbit. Those lucky enough to enjoy secure employment—people like Julia Coronado, Tomás Linares, and Valerie Rushing—fall into the first camp. Those who can turn to a spouse for another income stream, as Tamar Guerra does with her husband, Víctor, fall into the second. Marisol Ramos, however, has neither a well-paying job nor a spouse nearby anymore—and this scarcity of household resources has pushed her out of the Missing Class.

Elena is now nine years old; Belkis is six. Their dad calls them frequently, and they see his picture on the mantle in the living room, but he is far from a regular presence in their lives. At least this is the official story. Unofficially, it seems fairly clear that Ricardo is around, at least from time to time. His is the male voice we hear on the other end of the phone when trying to reach Marisol for a get-together.

The girls are too young to keep secrets very well. When asked where they have left their Rollerblades or why they don't have their library books, they explain, "We left the skates in Papi's car" or "Papi didn't take us to the library." Marisol borrows liberally from her patient sisters, but the outgoing expenses do not square with the official income flowing into the household. This gap provides another hint of Ricardo's continued attachment to his family, but his presence is illegal and furtive. Furthermore, whatever contributions he is making are clearly not sufficient to pull the family above the poverty line. Marisol and her daughters are perpetually in financial trouble. They have fallen out of the Missing Class and may stay there until the girls are old enough to bring home wages of their own.

Though she has become a U.S. citizen, Marisol is often exploited in ways we associate with illegal immigrants.[10] She is largely unaware of her rights and feels, perhaps correctly, that she has very few options before her. With the exception of her stint at the flower factory, she has been working for the doctors' association for almost six years but has seen only the paltriest of wage increases: from $5.15 an hour in 1998 to $5.98 in 2002. Her supervisor continues to load on piles of work that never seem to shrink. The doctors give her more benefits than other employers might, but they do not hesitate to dock her pay if she exceeds her allotment of vacation, which happens regularly, since Marisol must take time off whenever her daughters are ill or she is summoned to their school. These penalties leave Marisol feeling unappreciated, for she knows she works hard.

One Monday at work, some papers cascaded out of the files one of her coworkers was handling, and one of them landed in Marisol's left eye. Her face swelled up like a balloon and her eye was crimson, spilling tears all night long. The next morning she went to an eye clinic near her home, where she waited five hours to be seen. The damage to her eye was not too serious, but she needed medication. Her eye doctor told her to return on Wednesday so that he could check for infection.

Marisol's boss balked. She complained that Marisol had already missed two days of work and had used up her sick leave. Marisol protested, "My vision is not clear yet!" But it didn't matter to her supervisor. "Tears were dropping from my eyes," Marisol recalls, "but she was pressuring me."

Marisol was initially unaware that she had any right to a workmen's compensation claim. A friend at work told her that she shouldn't have to give up her salary for the days she missed because the accident happened at work and wasn't her fault. Marisol asked belatedly how to go about filing a claim. Her employer ignored her, deliberately it seemed; the woman who had caused the accident professed that she had no memory of it.

"So now they want to make me look like a liar," Marisol frets. "I didn't want to create alarm [when it happened]. Now I know. Next time I am going to cry loud!" She eventually decided to give up on her claim.

Marisol has lost out on other entitlements because she didn't know her rights. Belkis suffered from lead contamination before she reached her first birthday. An active toddler, even at that age she had a habit of leaning on the bedroom window where the paint flaked and floated into the air. When Belkis started vomiting in the night, Marisol took her to the doctor, who diagnosed lead poisoning. She later asked around and discovered that many of the children in her building had similar problems. Nevertheless, Marisol didn't bother to sue her landlord. She had no idea how to go about it.

Through the years, Marisol has suffered through countless battles with her landlord over the condition of her apartment. Things are better now, but she remembers with disgust how decrepit the building once was:

> The entrance was always covered with garbage; the mice walked across your path. The windows on the courtyard side could not be opened because of the bad odors coming from the outside. Flies, mice, and cockroaches used to come in abundance. Maintenance was a real problem.... The electricity failed often because this building has old wiring.... The fuses went off constantly; even the bulbs exploded. The plumbing used to break often, too.

Marisol got nowhere when she pressed her landlord for help. Neither did her neighbors. Then one day, a pipe on the fifth floor burst. Water started rushing into Marisol's fourth-floor apartment, rising to the seats of her kitchen chairs. The entire apartment had to be evacuated. "I had done some shopping that day, but it got ruined," Marisol recalls. She ended up throwing out her new clothes.

Marisol and her neighbors could no longer stomach their landlord's myriad offenses. Together, they approached the Northern Manhattan Improvement Corporation, a nonprofit organization that represents low-income tenants. Northern Manhattan filed a lawsuit on their behalf. A judge determined that the building was dangerous and assigned a city official, a "7A administrator," to oversee it.[11]

Their victory in court meant a great deal to Marisol. It was the first time in her life that she could remember not feeling alone with her troubles. And for once, a bureaucrat—the 7A man—was fighting on her side. Long-postponed renovations and maintenance were at last completed: a new boiler installed, apartments painted, backyard swept of garbage, vermin exterminated. What's more, Marisol finally had a mailbox, which meant no more treks to the post office to pick up her welfare notices.

Several years have passed since the court case, and Marisol is still having trouble with her landlord. In recent months he's raised rents in an attempt to root out the poor black and Hispanic tenants who organized themselves and stirred up so much trouble. (Outside court one day, the man brazenly confessed that he now wanted to rent only to "white Americans.") Marisol and others have taken to sending him money orders via certified mail so that he won't try to return their rent. Fortunately, Northern Manhattan's lawyers are still representing the tenants and keeping them a step ahead of the landlord's tricks.

Few families who fall out of the Missing Class are able to rely on advocacy organizations like Northern Manhattan. Instead, they must somehow prevail on their own in their struggles to secure and protect the benefits they are entitled to. It is an exhausting endeavor, one that most hoped to leave behind for good in their more successful days. Returning to this battleground of impersonal bureaucracy underscores the indignity of their newfound poverty. It reminds people like Marisol that what they want more than anything is to enjoy the freedom that most Americans take for granted: to manage their own affairs without having to explain them to strangers.

A MINISTRY ON A HILL

It's a foggy January morning, and the streets of north-central Brooklyn are still. Men huddle on the corners, shivering in front of boarded-up warehouses like a hushed picket line. The buildings around them were once alive with the yells and whistles of factory workers, the frenzied industry of a workingman's district. Now the factories are shuttered, the stream of workers replaced by hooded men on the corners, hands stuffed in their pockets.

Along the border of Clinton Hill and Bedford-Stuyvesant, several blocks south of the Pratt Institute, Mt. Sinai Baptist Church remains one of the few places that welcome street-corner men. Inside, the furnishings are modest. Aged walls are covered with posters, announcements, and decorations celebrating figures from African American history. An elderly black man is speaking on the phone, scolding a representative from the company that supplies juice for the church's free meals. The shipment is going to be too early, he complains. The men who are supposed to help him carry the boxes of fruit drinks into the basement won't be here yet.

Fifteen minutes later, the delivery arrives, as do the helpers. The men start unloading the boxes from the truck outside. As they carry the boxes inside, the pastor walks in, dressed in a suit. He asks the elderly man if the work is going all right and then heads to the back of the room, up a small staircase, into his office.

Behind the desk is a neat arrangement of certificates and awards—a Drew University doctoral degree among them—that announce Curtis L. Whitney's station in life. Pastor Whitney has preached at Mt. Sinai for over two decades. He has watched the changes that have come to Clinton Hill and Bed-Stuy over the years. The factories were gone before Whitney arrived, he says, and a long fallow period followed. Many of his parishioners headed south. But nowadays business and construction seem to be returning to these street corners, following on the heels of newly transplanted Asian and Latino families. Bodegas—nowhere to be found when Whitney first arrived—now stand on almost every corner. Just across the street, a boarded-up hotel was bought by private developers and is being converted into new homes.

Nevertheless, the community is still fragmented, Whitney says. The existing barbershops, beauty parlors, and other small businesses are sprinkled across the neighborhood, so it's hard for locals to find the products and services they need. It is a problem many poor and previously poor neighborhoods face: the big chains find the consumer base unappetizing and won't risk the investment, so as a result there's a dearth of grocery stores with plentiful fresh produce and department stores with decent kitchenware and clothing. Meanwhile, the crime on the street, though improved, persists. Whitney's congregation is a member of Central Brooklyn Churches, an association that has met with the local Seventh-ninth Precinct to complain about the loitering and prostitution.

Pastor Whitney has also noticed a marked increase in the number of people requesting food through Mt. Sinai's pantry program. The church used to serve food once a month; now it offers lunch every Wednesday, with at least a hundred people showing up, the vast majority of them men.

Churches like Mt. Sinai are finding themselves struggling to meet the increased demand for food and services. (Nationally, the nation's largest network of food providers—America's Second Harvest—served 25 million people in 2005, up 9 percent from 2001.)[12] Whitney is troubled by the desperation but pleased that churches like his are once again taking up the call to service, evoking that earlier, godlier time when clergy served as stewards of the nation's schools and universities, attendants to its orphaned children and elderly, and providers for its hungry.

Mt. Sinai is planning to expand its family counseling services, the pastor notes. "Family life now, as I see it, is splintered," he says. Two-parent households are busy working; single parents are overwhelmed. People in general are harried, insecure, and apprehensive "because everything is in such a flux." The need is spiritual, and to address it, Mt. Sinai must become a "city on a hill"—a community to comfort and uplift souls before they topple to the bottom of that hill. In other words, Whitney believes in preventive care for the soul, a kind of nurturing that consoles and fortifies not just those who have fallen astray but those who have yet to fall.

"Basically...what we are doing now—we're doing the bottom of the hill ministry," Whitney remarks. To remain relevant, the pastor says, churches will have to change the ways they minister. They will have to remember the power they wield to change lives—all lives. Through God's love, every valley shall be exalted, and every mountain and hill shall be made low. Even Clinton Hill.

THE GUERRA FAMILY

> Out of ignorance, confusion or an effort to save money, immigrants turn to unqualified people and outright charlatans, often set up as notaries or paralegals, for help getting green cards, and work and travel permits. They find out too late that their "lawyers" haven't filed anything or have submitted falsified and error-ridden documents.
> —*St. Petersburg Times*, October 16, 2005

When he was five years old, Omar Guerra was diagnosed with attention deficit hyperactivity disorder. The boy could not sit still; if he saw people sitting down, he'd slap or kick their feet as he zoomed by. "He could not be quiet. He was unbearable," his mother remembers.

Even after he was diagnosed, Omar didn't receive treatment for two years. Tamar didn't have health insurance. She'd take him to the hospital when the situation got out of hand. Finally, the government sent her papers to apply for benefits through the SSI program. This would mean that Omar would be considered disabled and his family would receive regular government stipends. Tamar, however, ignored their letters. Then they threatened her with legal action. "I got scared and I finally went," she says. The SSI checks started to roll in. Five hundred dollars a month made a huge difference for the household, even beyond the costs of Omar's health care.

By the time he was twelve, Omar was having problems focusing on his schoolwork. His psychiatrist prescribed Ritalin. Omar started taking the medication in the morning and after school, ten milligrams a pop. The drug made him sluggish, almost mindless. But it seemed to work. He slowed down and found it easier to concentrate. Omar took Ritalin for about a year and then stopped in January 1999.

A month later, while Tamar was traveling in the Dominican Republic, Omar forged his mom's signature to transfer himself out of special education. After he pulled that stunt, the government grew suspicious. Why was he still receiving benefits for a long-term illness if he was no longer classified as special needs? Two months after Omar started regular classes, the benefits—$500 a month in SSI payments—were discontinued.

At first, Tamar wasn't too worried. She was secretly glad that Omar was no longer classified as special education—although she was furious with the ploy he used to extricate himself—and was willing to find a job to make up for the lost income. Within a few months, Tamar started work at the bottling factory in New Jersey.

In early September the bomb dropped: a letter from the Social Security Administration informed Tamar that her son was overpaid $9,817 in SSI benefits, which she now had to pay back. Her first bill was for $999.99, to be paid by September 8.

She called up her caseworker. Were they *crazy?* she asked. There was no way she could afford to pay that much money every month, even if she sold drugs. Tamar had a total of $15 in the bank. "Go get it," she taunted the caseworker.

Eventually, Tamar persuaded the government to lower her bill to

$100 every month. Even that was too much for her. Where would she get the extra money?

Part of the problem, Tamar now realizes, is that she didn't keep on top of things. In February she was supposed to attend a fair hearing to discuss Omar's SSI case, but she missed it because of that trip she took to the Dominican Republic—the same one that had given Omar the opportunity to write his own ticket out of special ed. Afterward, Tamar received a letter asking her to send the government documents from the school and Omar's pediatrician charting his progress. The problem was, now that Omar had been moved into regular classes, she couldn't get a letter from special education. All the documents she could present said that Omar was doing well and was psychologically healthy.

The four-figure bill now stares back at her, frightfully, from her kitchen table. But there is something funny about the math. Omar left special education just six months ago. Six payments of $500 should add up to $3,000, not $9,817. She is being charged too much, a friend insists.

But Tamar doesn't want to fight the powers that be. She is an immigrant with only passable English skills. She is in a vulnerable situation —a green-card holder hoping for citizenship, a working mother with three sons, a former welfare recipient who belongs to the Missing Class thanks to her husband's decent, but illegal, income—and she doesn't want to stir up any trouble. So, faced with the assured arguments of her surly caseworkers, Tamar shrinks from the fight.

"It is their word against mine," she says. "They have all the papers and records in order. How can I challenge their position? I cannot. That case—I am not going to win it."

A friend pleads with her. At least she should ask for a fair hearing. She could hire a lawyer, gather all the records that clearly state Omar was receiving counseling—and thus warranted benefits—when he was in special education. But Tamar is not to be swayed. She remembers too many cases of friends and acquaintances who tried to buck the system, only to be beaten down for their insolence. Tamar's brother-in-law, too, ran into problems with an SSI overpayment; he even obtained a lawyer to fight it but lost anyway. "All the people I know that have gotten extra money, they have never won the case," Tamar says. How will she succeed where they failed? And if she challenges the case and loses, she will have to pay a lump sum for all the months she missed payments because of the legal challenge, she notes. That would *really* destroy her family.

"I am going to pay it because I do not like owing money," Tamar declares. But she'll never open an SSI case again. When she didn't really need the benefit, the government was clamoring for her to take it. But "when you are in so many problems, they come and demand so much money," she says with spite.

Tamar racks her brain to think of ways to pay off her debt, on a payment plan that will take her eight years to complete. "Look, do you know the things that I need for here?" she says. "For me to send $100..." Every week she brings home a check of $187. Out of that, she spends $20 on van rides back and forth from the New Jersey plant; compared with other transportation options, that is cheap, even if some days she spends the one-hour ride sitting on a milk carton because all the seats are taken. Another $40 comes out of her paycheck every week and goes to her elderly mom. That leaves $127 to pay the bills and buy things for the kids. "If I had a job of $250 a week—a permanent job—I could send a hundred to the Social Security."

The financial nightmare she's going through has made Tamar ill with worry. "I am dying," she says. "I suffer from lack of money. That's my malady."

Early in the morning, Tamar leaves her apartment and heads to the corner of 158th and Broadway. She's supposed to meet Salvador—a friend of Víctor's—but cannot find the man anywhere. So Tamar walks down Broadway and peeks into several bodegas. She heads into the subway and searches around the turnstiles. Finally, she spots Salvador walking down the street. Tamar flags him down.

This wizened Puerto Rican of indeterminate age is what we might call the neighborhood "fixer," a resident legal expert—minus the esquire. Some call him the "poor people's legal aid." He is the person whom Spanish-speaking immigrants in Tamar's neighborhood turn to when they need to deal with the city's bureaucracies and courts but don't have the money to pay for a lawyer. In Tamar's case, she's decided to seek his help with her SSI bill, having (finally) come around to the idea that she has only her pride to lose if she isn't successful.

For a man esteemed for his professional expertise, Salvador is an underwhelming presence. Though well dressed, he is missing several front teeth. He speaks broken, halting English—worse than Tamar's. But what Salvador lacks in polish he makes up for in pluck. "He knows how to work the system," Tamar says. "And he makes a living doing that." According to Tamar, every day Salvador accompanies two or three neighborhood people to their appointments and butts heads with the city bureaucrats on their behalf. He acts as an interpreter and lay adviser. For his pains, he receives payments—in Tamar and Víctor's case, just $20, though Tamar thinks others pay him more.

Salvador was a crucial help to Víctor when he had immigration problems two years ago. On a trip back from the Dominican Republic, Víctor was detained by immigration because a prior arrest showed up on the computer. (The 1996 immigration reform law mandated detention and deportation for even legal residents with earlier criminal offenses.)[13] "I've never been in jail," Víctor protested, but the authorities took away his green card and Social Security card anyway and prepared to deport him. As it turned out, Víctor had been detained for several hours many years ago—according to Tamar, because of a case of mistaken identity. "He was standing on a corner talking bullshit, and they took him," she says. "But it was in error because he never sold drugs or none of that. . . . He didn't remember that because he was in only for [a few] hours."

Tamar was devastated. What if Víctor was deported? As exasperating as Víctor was at times, she genuinely loved him. And the family needed him as a father and provider.

She agonized over her husband's prospects in court. A Legal Aid attorney would be assigned to him, but they were useless. Víctor's friends and family all begged him to hire his own defense lawyer. Víctor refused. "I did nothing wrong," he insisted. "Why do I have to get a lawyer?" Instead, he called Salvador.

Much has been written about the underground economy in low-income neighborhoods.[14] The drug trade gets the lion's share of attention because it is so destructive. Yet by far the largest part of the irregular economy in immigrant neighborhoods derives from the shadow world of unlicensed specialists (craftsmen, babysitters, hair braiders, and the like) who do not exist in any official sense but in vital ways make community life possible. Víctor has never had the income to hire the licensed, legitimate version of any of these occupations, least of all a lawyer. Yet for $20 he can recruit a "fixer" who will attend to the needs that arise at the intersection of life and the bureaucracy.

Of course, neither Tamar nor Víctor would be the wiser if their fixer turned out to be a fraud. They would know if he had been unsuccessful but wouldn't be able to tell whether the failure was due to his lack of skill, bad luck, or a malicious judge who just wouldn't listen. A license is supposed to protect consumers against charlatans, but for many in Tamar's neighborhood, certified professionals just aren't practical.

Salvador accompanied Víctor to his meetings with the Legal Aid attorney. The little Puerto Rican man started peppering the attorney with questions. "[Salvador] got so nasty with the lawyer," Tamar says. "He would tell Víctor, 'Let's look for this or that.'" Salvador anticipated whatever documents the attorney needed before she asked for them. Víctor arrived prepared for every meeting. The case was eventually dismissed, and the government returned Víctor's green card. Víctor credited Salvador for the happy resolution of his legal troubles. "He's not a lawyer, but he knows the laws very well," Tamar says of Salvador.

Tamar had a firsthand taste of Salvador's expertise on another occasion, when the couple was trying to fight their landlord's claims that they owed rent. She went to court with Salvador, where he demanded that a court clerk hand over a printout of rental payments made to the landlord as part of Tamar's welfare benefits. At first the clerk refused, saying they'd have to go to the welfare office. Salvador would not be deterred. "You're going to give it to her," he told the clerk. "Otherwise, let me speak to your supervisor or your boss because you have to give me that. That won't even take you three minutes." He went on and on. The clerk finally relented. "Let me see," she said.

"No, not 'Let's see,'" Salvador said. "I'm going to come back for it now. I'm going to wait for you outside." Tamar was laughing; Salvador's persistence was almost comical. But sure enough, the clerk handed over the paperwork within minutes. Back at home, Tamar told Víctor what had happened. If she hadn't brought Salvador, the woman would not have helped her, she said. "I told you, Tamar," Víctor said. "That's why I bring him every time."

Now Salvador is coming again to the rescue. Tamar and the "fixer" walk into the Social Security office in downtown Manhattan. When their number is called, they head to the window booth, and Salvador starts to make his case. Tamar shouldn't have to pay this money back to SSI because she didn't know it wasn't hers by right, he explains. The money was sent to her by mistake, but that wasn't her fault. Salvador is gesturing with authority and brandishing pieces of paper under the glass barrier.

This time, however, Salvador's magic seems to have run out. He struggles with his English. He is trying to tell the attendant that he and Tamar are there to discuss the overpayment and that Tamar wants a waiver. But the only communication he is capable of is pointing energetically at the letter and mumbling, brokenly, "discuss this." The attendant finally guesses what Salvador wants, and Salvador excitedly nods his assent. Then why is she here, instead of the office in Queens, the attendant asks? "Lady in Jamaica was really nasty," Salvador responds. "She didn't want to help."

The attendant forwards Tamar's case to a caseworker. The caseworker, a white woman around the age of thirty, calls Tamar and Salvador to her desk. Salvador again indicates the purpose of their visit with a barely comprehensible imperative: "discuss this." The caseworker eyes the bill and asks if he is referring to the $9,817 that Tamar owes for an SSI overpayment. Salvador, the harried interpreter, confirms this. The caseworker calls her supervisor, a stern African American woman. When she arrives, another man shows up—Salvador's friend, who tagged along and is apparently looking for somewhere to sit. The caseworker is clearly peeved at the accumulating hangers-on. Salvador urges his friend to wait outside.

The supervisor starts throwing questions at Tamar. When did Omar leave special ed? Why didn't she go to the office on 182nd Street? What happened at the fair hearing she was supposed to attend in February? Salvador can barely keep up. His responses in English careen from one sentence fragment to the next, almost at random, utterly confused in their delivery. At times he introduces new issues that are unrelated to the ones on the table. When Tamar speaks up, in Spanish, he's unable to translate her words accurately to the caseworker and supervisor. What's more, his strategy for challenging the SSI bill seems clearly ill founded. He keeps insisting, in scattershot English, that Tamar doesn't have to pay the money because she never received the letter stating the case was closed. The caseworker and supervisor stare at him, dumbfounded.

Finally, the supervisor has enough. She goes behind closed doors with the caseworker to discuss Tamar's situation privately. Tamar is nervous. Did they say anything they shouldn't have said?

When the supervisor returns, she tells Tamar that the caseworker will help her to fill out a waiver form. She'll need proof of her household income, the woman adds.

Tamar gets to work on the forms. The caseworker is visibly frustrated with her and her strange companion; apparently she believes that Tamar has swindled SSI. The caseworker reminds them, pointedly, that to complete the paperwork they'll need the documents that the supervisor specified earlier. Don't worry, Salvador says, we have all that information. "If you had it, you would have brought it with you," the caseworker snaps.

The government wants Tamar to repay all the SSI benefits she received since October 1997, when Omar was deemed ineligible by an SSI-appointed doctor. Yet Omar was still taking medication as late as January 1999 for his ADHD. How could he be considered ineligible when he was under psychiatric care? The caseworker shrugs her shoulders. Why, she asked, did Tamar agree to a payment plan of $100 a month if she couldn't pay? Tamar responds—with Salvador translating—that she had a job back then, which she lost at the end of September. The cosmetics factory had finally let her go.

"I never lied to SSI," Tamar pleads in Spanish. "When Omar did not need the program, I let SSI know this."

Tamar's waiver is denied. She'll have to find some way of paying back her $9,817 debt.

Tamar is actually one of the more fortunate members of the Missing Class. She may be in debt, she may lack health insurance, but she has Víctor. She is not alone with the financial burdens of raising a family and is unlikely to face a precipitous descent from near poverty to the real thing. Even though she has no idea how much money Víctor earns and has to use the cash he has given her for the electricity bill to pay for Omar's shoes instead, at least that money is there. Víctor doesn't question her too closely and rarely refuses her entreaties. In this, Tamar is better off than Marisol, who—at best—can expect sporadic help from her husband.

Yet for both families, sinking to the borderline between Missing Class and poor means becoming entangled, once again, in the tentacles of the state: the constant surveillance and interference of caseworkers, judges, and school administrators. The more they earn, the further they can pull away from poverty and the insistent tug of rules, regulations, and intrusive bureaucrats. But when they falter, the financial squeeze is accompanied by not only an infantilizing process of oversight and evaluation but also the nagging sense that they are not in control of their own lives. Much of the time, they are running to stay one step ahead of the government ax man who will cut their stipends, take away their housing, or deny their partners the right to stay with their families. Some of these families may be lucky enough to be able to find competent fixers and advocacy organizations that can counsel and assist them. But many are alone with their troubles. Exhausted by the daily burdens and anxieties of life on the edge, cowed by the government authorities who dictate their existence, they lack the energy or courage to fight for their rights.

EIGHT

Missing Class Mobility

The tensions that beset families in the Missing Class are all too real. Yet none of them would trade places with the poor, particularly those who once lived through this kind of absolute privation. Some—like Julia Coronado—now rest comfortably in what we might call the lower middle class. She has enough job experience and skills that she could withstand a substantial shock (divorce, for example) and still keep herself afloat. Julia would not find it easy to manage alone—perhaps she would have to depend on her mother again—but she is not likely to return to welfare. Rita Gervais is already managing on her own. She is a home owner in New Jersey now, and unless her child-care business goes bust, she probably won't see poverty in her lifetime.

Marisol and her daughters may not be so lucky. The Ramos family was skating the lower edge of the Missing Class back when Ricardo was still living with them. Now a single mother able to work only part-time, Marisol is boxed into the end of the labor market that is poorly rewarded and boasts few prospects for upward movement. As long as civil servants are needed to turn the wheels of the welfare bureaucracy, Danielle Wayne will manage. But it's anyone's guess what will happen to her family if she ever loses that job.

As for the children of these industrious workers, their fortunes may diverge from those of their parents in unexpected ways. With Víctor a steady source of (secret) support, Tamar Guerra retains a reasonable foothold in the Missing Class. Yet her son Omar, an academic failure now ensnared in the criminal justice system, will probably not achieve even his mother's modest standard of living after he is released. Mass incarceration has dramatically changed the lot of young men, especially young minority men, looking for work. In today's economy, they are locked out of most remunerative lines of legal work.[1]

Safiya Wayne was just a toddler when she was attending her grandmother's home day care, watching wide-eyed as marijuana smoke drifted through the apartment. She entered kindergarten a couple of years later, and unlike her older siblings, who grew up with a stay-at-home mom, Safiya did not know her colors or numbers. Danielle has tried to help her youngest child with her reading, just as she helped her older children, but these days she comes home from work exhausted. She no longer has the energy to attend to the letters from the Board of Education that remind her that it is her responsibility to read to her child if Safiya is going to pass the next battery of standardized tests.

The Missing Class work hard to survive and prosper in today's fiercely competitive economy, and they deserve respect for what they have accomplished. These fifty-seven million Americans—that forgotten but vital segment of American society whose incomes place them between 100 and 200 percent of the poverty line—sorely need our nation's attention. If we can protect these family's gains and ensure that the next generation walks even farther down the path to financial security, we will see this country make genuine strides at eradicating poverty for good. If these families plummet, we will all be the poorer for it, for the lesson to succeeding generations will be that extraordinary effort may come to nothing.

Most policy debates focus not on the near poor but on those who are in desperate poverty. Yet as we have shown, the dilemmas of these two groups are different. The Missing Class does not live in neighborhoods mired in concentrated poverty; it lives in gentrifying enclaves that have seen both improvement and dispossession in recent years. At times they feel like outsiders in their own communities, yet they readily admit that they now live in safer, more prosperous places. Most are not floundering in the labor market with no skills but have instead become repositories of work experience, even if those track records are newly minted.

Yet Missing Class families still need supports like state-provided child health benefits, tuition assistance for further schooling, and expert help navigating bureaucracies that seem structured to make efficient service a rarity. Their kids are not attending private schools but rely on public institutions. In neighborhoods that have gone up-

scale, some fortunate schools have become crucibles of educational mobility, but there are still too many kids like Rasheea attending classes
that cannot provide the stimulation they crave.

An overwhelming majority of Americans believe in self-sufficiency.
The Missing Class practice it. Yet few of us have the luxury of rugged
individualism absent the public investments the nation makes—in education, housing, health care, and employment training—that make it
feasible. Here we will consider what steps our nation can take to support the upward ascent of the Missing Class and ensure that we see
more kids like Rasheea and fewer like Omar in the years to come.

A caveat at the outset: we do not discuss policies to reform our nation's troubled health-care system—which would require a separate
book—though clearly the forty-six million Americans who are uninsured and the sixteen million Americans who are *under*insured require
our nation's immediate attention. We leave that to others and turn our
attention to issues that are less often discussed.[2]

EQUITY FOR ALL

Home Ownership

Whether they are middle class or not, most American families tend to
live at the edge of their paychecks. What savings they have come largely
from the increasing value of their homes. Forty-four percent of all U.S.
wealth comes from housing equity. More affluent families may also
have access to stocks and bonds and retirement accounts, which are
generally invested in the same markets.

By far the most important mechanism for cementing a family's hold
on the American Dream is access to equity. Home ownership not only
provides a means of accumulating resources but is a backstop in countless ways. Home owners can borrow against the value of their houses
to make college more affordable for their kids or pull their families
through a spell of unemployment or serious illness. When they grow
old, they may downsize their housing and use the difference to finance
a more comfortable retirement. These assets are passed down to succeeding generations, creating a cushion of wealth that takes some of the
pressure off young people. The federal tax code permits home owners
to deduct the cost of mortgage interest from their income taxes, which

means they have more disposable income than renters do.[3] In a society with a flimsier safety net—compared, for example, with our European counterparts—these kinds of private assets are indispensable.

While seven out of ten American households owned their own homes in 2006, the patterns of disadvantage in education and the labor market, coupled with lending policies that favor the majority, translate into uneven access to this vital source of wealth. The poor and Missing Class have significantly lower rates of home ownership than more affluent Americans.[4] Nonwhites are less likely to own a home, and the homes they do own are worth far less than those of whites with comparable incomes. They are more likely to live in neighborhoods that see a slower increase in housing value over time.[5]

Scholars who have studied the "wealth gap" that divides minorities from their white counterparts have been quick to point out that more than money is at stake here.[6] Home ownership helps to ensure access to good schools, public libraries, open spaces, and other amenities that are tied to the local tax base. Families who rent are more likely to live in poorer communities that lack these advantages. Their children will grow up in far less favorable settings. Home owners invest more of their time and energy in the condition of their properties and exert more social pressure on the behavior of their neighbors. Apartment tenants, on the other hand, tend to have less control over the upkeep of their homes and the selection of their neighbors. When these residents find themselves in the midst of a drug war or victims of gang violence, there is little they can do to shield themselves or their kids. In all of these ways, lower-income families who rent—particularly those in public housing —start from way behind the "square one" they deserve.

We need to do more to ensure that low-income families, especially minorities, can cash in on the housing boom that has been so important in underwriting the prosperity of the American middle class. The Bush administration has given some thought to enlarging its "ownership society" by facilitating low-income home ownership. It has, for example, proposed that the Federal Housing Administration develop a "zero down payment" program, which would enable first-time home buyers with good credit to receive 100 percent financing of their home purchase and closing costs. Buyers with weaker credit histories could access mortgages at higher initial rates that would decline over time provided payments were timely.[7] In 2006 the administration also sponsored the American Dream Downpayment Initiative, which sets aside $100 million to assist first-time home buyers in low-income households.

Other housing policies worthy of support include the Homeownership Voucher Program, initiated by the Clinton administration to enable recipients of Section 8 housing vouchers to use them toward owner-occupied homes instead. Over five years, it has helped five thousand families who were previously living in public housing or receiving rental vouchers to become home owners. The 2006 federal budget proposes tripling this amount. Another promising initiative is the federal government's Family Self-Sufficiency Program, which enables families in public housing to set aside money in an escrow account that might otherwise go to rent increases when a family's income rises.[8]

Katherine Newman became a convert to the idea of low-income housing ownership after living next door to Savo Island Cooperative Homes, a housing complex in south Berkeley, California, in the early 1980s. Her neighbors were means-tested, low-income buyers who promised to resell their homes back to the city at a fair market rate when they moved on, clearing the way for new home owners. Down payments were limited to 5 percent at a time when the open market required 20 percent, and mortgage rates were well below market. Savo Island residents lived in attractive townhouses where they set "house rules" governing common areas, vetted potential new owners, and kicked out troublemakers. Progressive mayors in Vermont, Kentucky, and elsewhere have invested in this idea and done their part to increase the access of low-income families to the one asset most likely to improve their financial health.

The strategy is not without risks—poor home buyers tend to be "overleveraged" and at greater risk of foreclosure.[9] They are often victimized by lenders who charge them exorbitant interest rates or contractors who entice them to use their houses as collateral for repair costs. John and Sondra Floyd lost their home this way. The Floyds and many other Missing Class families know very little about the fine print of contracts. We should support the work of nonprofit organizations like Isles, Inc., in Trenton, New Jersey, which offers consumer-counseling programs to teach first-time home buyers from poor backgrounds about the warning signs of foreclosure and the actions they can take to protect themselves if they get into trouble.

What else could we do to increase access to home ownership? Clamping down on subprime lending—high-risk loans at steep interest rates—is a good first step. In 2002 subprime lending topped $210 billion, reflecting the desire of millions of low-income families to get into the housing market. Banks and mortgage companies that charge buyers from poor neighborhoods higher rates for mortgages should be regulated more carefully, and alternative sources of financing outside the subprime market should be promoted. This can be done. In Philadelphia, for example, the mayor's office, the Greater Philadelphia Urban Affairs Coalition, and eight major banks got together to create loan products for low-income consumers with weak credit histories. They are attempting to "crowd out higher-priced lenders" and identify more socially responsible mortgage providers.[10]

Communities could also consider establishing a mildly progressive form of real estate taxation. Rather than setting the rates according to property values—which increase over time and may outstrip the ability of a low-income household to pay—they might consider introducing an income qualification to real estate taxes or a rebate system that, like the Earned Income Tax Credit, refunds to the resident a portion of the tax bill. Progressive cities like Newton, Massachusetts, already do this for their elderly residents. Why not extend the same support to low-income families raising our next generation of Americans?

Housing repairs are often a big problem for low-income home owners. The neighborhoods where they can afford to live are often run-down to begin with. If low-income owners qualified for real estate tax rebates for the improvements they have made to their properties, rather than tax increases that will make those homes less affordable, that would make a positive difference. Moreover, rehabilitation on a large scale opens opportunities for construction jobs, parts supply, and other employment possibilities. Why not extend those prospects to young men in poor and Missing Class neighborhoods who need work? Community leaders in Brooklyn stressed to us that contracting jobs ought to go to the unemployed in the area, who could be taught to do carpentry, electrical work, and plumbing. Young men like Omar and Royce could earn a good living while improving the housing in their neighborhoods.

In the Savo Island neighborhood, a tool-lending library full of power saws, rototillers, and cement mixers was established to make it possible for do-it-yourself carpenters and young entrepreneurs to do renovation work without investing in prohibitively costly equipment. Perhaps we can find public funds or a latter-day Andrew Carnegie to establish thousands of libraries of this kind; they may be as helpful as the sort that holds books.

One out of every five home owners refinanced his or her mortgage in 2002. Nearly a third did so in order to pay down other debts, mainly credit cards. But what happens when the mortgage payments themselves become too much to bear? "Defaults on loans in 2000 amount to approximately one million households losing their homes to foreclosure, during the height of an unprecedented economic expansion," according to *Shelterforce*, a publication of the National Housing Institute. The downturn that followed made matters worse, with delinquencies and foreclosures rising steadily.[11] Poor and Missing Class households are especially vulnerable to sinking into this kind of debt because of their greater exposure to layoffs and their low cash savings. We need to focus not only on getting these families into their own homes but also on making sure they're able to keep them. One step, as discussed earlier, would be to help them to avoid subprime lending and secure credit on better terms, so that the weight of their interest payments doesn't drag them into bankruptcy.

Of course, other kinds of debt, such as credit-card debt, also push households into delinquency. We need to do more to protect them from arbitrary charges, exorbitant rates, and other dubious practices that are becoming increasingly common among credit card companies and other financial institutions. Unfortunately, certain provisions of the bankruptcy reforms that Congress recently passed merely serve to raise profit margins for big business at the expense of many American families: the new legislation entitles credit card companies to go after debtors more aggressively and force them into bankruptcy under more draconian terms.[12]

Savings Accounts

Is it realistic to think that low-income families can save money? For an answer, we can turn to the work of Princeton sociologist Daniel Schneider and Harvard Business School professor Peter Tufano, who have come up with an innovative asset-building strategy for the less affluent.[13] According to Schneider and Tufano, only 71 percent of American families in the lowest-income quintile have checking or savings accounts. The near poor, our Missing Class, are often unbanked as well: 89 percent have such accounts. (The percentage among more affluent Americans is nearly 100.) Both groups tend to be "asset poor," meaning they could not survive for three months on their savings, but they are not at absolute zero. Can this cushion, modest as it is, be set aside to create a buffer against emergencies and a source of retirement support?

The answer for the truly poor is "rarely." But those in the Missing Class are, by definition, not poor. They are better off than those below the poverty line and may respond to encouragement. Wealthier Americans have long been provided with incentives to save. In 2003 the federal government forked over some $335 billion in savings incentives ranging from tax deductions for mortgage interest and property taxes, tax forgiveness for retirement savings through 401K and IRA plans, and generous tax exemptions for capital gains.[14] Unfortunately, we tend to sway in the opposite direction for less affluent families. Asset tests that limit access to public programs like Medicaid actively discourage low-income families from accumulating cash in bank accounts or buying cars lest they lose access to needed programs. Changes in regulations have actually made the situation worse. Congress raised the minimum holding period for savings bonds from six months to one year, which makes it harder for families who are facing economic ups and downs to lock up their money.

The financial service industry does not tend to the needs of these consumers. Banks and brokerages rarely open branches in low-income neighborhoods. Services that connect with clients over the Web bypass people who are not computer savvy. The small balances that poor and Missing Class families can maintain simply do not attract the attention of a profit-driven industry. Indeed, many banks seem to be doing all they can to barricade the doors: setting prohibitive minimum-balance policies, charging outrageous fees for a variety of services that were once free or low cost, and using credit-scoring tools that screen out clients of modest means. As Schneider and Tufano point out, "It is not uncommon for banks to deny consumers with poor credit records the right to open even a savings account."[15]

What, then, might be done to reverse the pattern of neglect and encourage savings among the Missing Class? Schneider and Tufano offer some suggestions. First, they remind us that in 1999 President Bill Clinton proposed a Universal Savings Account that would have matched contributions to retirement savings for adults with incomes between $5,000 and $100,000. "Low-income account holders were slated to receive an annual automatic contribution from the government worth several hundred dollars and...a refundable tax credit that matched personal or employer 401(k) contributions."[16] This legislation did not pass in its original form, but a revised version called the Saver's Credit was signed into law by President George W. Bush in 2001. It gives a tax credit to low-income taxpayers—married filers with incomes under $50,000, singles under $25,000—who contribute to personal retirement accounts; the credit increases in value as income declines.[17] Unfortunately, the Saver's Credit is not refundable, which means low-income families often forgo the federal contribution if they don't owe any tax to begin with. Making this tax credit refundable would encourage many more of them to save.

The Saver's Credit is aimed at retirement savings, but what of the many years before the end of a working life? Individual development accounts (IDAs), a savings concept that emerged in the early 1990s, offer a similar matching program for low-income depositors. IDAs were intended to encourage low-income families to save toward home ownership, small business development, and higher education. Qualified savers deposit money into an account, and their contributions are matched, mainly by private foundations. In 2003 there were 250 IDA programs in the country, with more than twenty thousand savers enrolled.[18] Evaluations of these programs show mixed results, but the most encouraging assessment was of a program that randomly assigned savers to an IDA matching program, with a control group that did not get this benefit (when evaluating policies, social scientists generally place greater stock in the results of randomized experiments like these). The results were very positive: home ownership rates were more than 6 percent higher for the IDA group, with African Americans particularly responsive. IDA holders were also more likely to have sought more education.[19]

This good news spurred advocates to propose expanding the program and making matched accounts of this kind available to the millions of low-income families who could benefit, with the matching funds to come from financial institutions that would, in turn, get a tax break for their contributions. Unfortunately, the proposal has gone the way of many good ideas: into legislative oblivion.

In 2004 leaders of both parties proposed the creation of Kids Investment and Development Savings (KIDS) accounts. All children—not just those in low-income families—would be provided with the first $500 deposit. More funds could be placed into the KIDS accounts by family, friends, employers, and eventually children themselves. For children in families making less than the national median income ($46,000 in 2005), the government would match contributions up to $500 per year. This money could be used to pay higher education costs at any time but would be available for other asset-building purposes (home ownership or retirement) only after the age of eighteen. While the legislation has yet to pass muster in Congress, the United Kingdom began making use of this idea in 2002, when it funded accounts at birth for all children and supplemented those from low-income households.[20]

The KIDS accounts proposed in Congress enjoy a political advantage in that they are universal in their coverage but redistributive in their consequences. Federal programs structured in this fashion have been the most popular and durable of all social policies because they provide something for everyone while heaping the most generous benefits on those who need them most.[21] IDA programs, on the other hand, tend to be means tested and apply only to certain populations. Whether universal or targeted, though, these savings programs share a common feature: they match public resources (that is, tax dollars) with private ones. They are not "handouts," but rewards for self-disciplined behavior.

TO MARKET, TO MARKET

On the other side of the equation from equity and assets lies the territory of costs. In many localities, the marketplace punishes those who can least afford it: low-income consumers. The products they buy and the services they use are more expensive than those that wealthier consumers can choose from. Stores that service poor neighborhoods have markups that are much higher than those in suburbs, largely because the costs of doing business are higher, given security problems, rents, lack of credit, and lower volume.

The Brookings Institution has given some thought to low-priced market alternatives—in everything from banking services to automobile purchases—that could lessen the load of the Missing Class. Among other things, they recommend that policymakers promote business ventures in underserved locations, use licensing and zoning authority to push out predatory businesses that overcharge their customers, and educate consumers so that they can avoid the sharks. Brookings points to many examples of communities that have used these tactics successfully. For example, the city of San Francisco partnered with the Federal Reserve Bank and twenty participating banks and credit unions to develop banking services expressly for less affluent families. New York State's banking department works with local governments and banks to identify underserved neighborhoods and then designates them as "banking development districts," meaning that banks that move in can receive deposits of state funds.[22]

Credit Where Credit Is Due has made it its mission to help families get access to banking services and loans at affordable rates. In 1997 the organization opened a credit union, Neighborhood Trust Federal Credit Union, in Washington Heights, offering checking and savings accounts without big bank fees. Today Neighborhood Trust has more than four thousand members and has given out $6 million in loans.[23] According to Mark Levine, the organization's cofounder, about half of the customers have never owned a bank account before—in fact, it's not uncommon to see someone walk in with a coffee jar full of cash. Almost all of their employees come from the community; some are former welfare recipients. The average loan that Neighborhood Trust hands out is only a few thousand dollars, and some are as small as $500. "There is a lot of need in that range," says Levine. "The single largest demand is actually from entrepreneurs who are starting home-based businesses." One woman who bakes Dominican cakes out of her home borrowed $2,000 from the credit union to buy a commercial refrigerator. Others have taken out loans of several thousand dollars to cover the apartment renovations and other upfront costs required of home day-care businesses.

The idea for Credit Where Credit Is Due took root during Levine's years as a math and science teacher at a Bronx junior high school. Back then, Levine used to talk with friends who taught in the community and lamented the fact that families there didn't have bank accounts and couldn't get loans. While studying at Harvard's Kennedy School of Government, Levine joined a group of finance-minded do-gooders— many of them teachers like Levine—who decided to bring banking to the people. "We ran [the organization] out of my apartment," Levine remembers. Nowadays their credit union is housed in what used to be a branch of Chemical Bank. But their work goes beyond opening checking accounts and offering loans. It's also about teaching people to make sound financial choices. In workshops organized by the credit union, families can learn the basics of balancing a checkbook, writing a budget, or starting a business. Classes are offered in both English and Spanish.

Next to housing, cars are probably the most expensive item in most families' consumer baskets. Low-income households are notoriously vulnerable to bad deals. California's Car Buyer's Bill of Rights takes aim at the problem, requiring automobile dealers and loan providers to itemize their monthly installment bills and disclose any additions to them. It also gives buyers a forty-eight-hour period in which they can return the car for a modest fee. In the Baltimore area, a nonprofit called Vehicles for Change repairs donated cars and sells them to lower-income households, along with auto loans and warranties. According to the Brookings Institution, "The program has carefully carved out a market niche to appeal to lower income drivers looking for responsible car dealers who will not overcharge."[24] Of course, before you can buy a car, you need to be able to afford the insurance policy. California has found a promising way of making auto insurance more affordable for low-income drivers. Insurers in some of the state's highest-priced counties are now required to offer low-cost liability insurance to all qualified drivers with household incomes below a certain threshold ($50,000 for a family of four).[25] This is a more aggressive approach than others discussed here because the government is forcing the industry to offer products tailored to the low-income market rather than just providing incentives and waiting to see who jumps.

What about the daily costs of feeding a family? Here, too, residents of low-income neighborhoods often end up paying vastly more per item than the most affluent households. Family-owned bodegas—a ubiquitous sight in neighborhoods like Sunset Park—face higher costs in doing business and cannot benefit from the economies of scale that the chain stores in the suburbs rely on to slash prices. They pass the costs down to their customers, who, in turn, have few other options for comparison shopping.

To address this problem, a Pennsylvania coalition of nonprofit and public agencies has cobbled together $80 million in financing to bring grocery stores to underserved areas throughout the state. So far, the Fresh Food Financing Initiative has committed $22 million in grants and loans to twenty-two stores, including startups in some of Philadelphia's poorest neighborhoods, and expects to create more than 2,500 new jobs.[26] These supermarkets will provide more options to consumers in low-income areas. Of course, there is a downside here: employees working for mom-and-pop bodegas are going to lose their jobs. Furthermore, while the owners of these small stores may be local merchants, the big grocers are often not as tightly bound to the community. These tradeoffs are complex, but if we are focusing for the moment on the need to reduce the cost side of the ledger for the Missing Class, attracting bigger stores with lower prices is important.

As the examples described here show, there are many ways that state authorities and local partners can protect low-income consumers from overcharging without having to dramatically alter the contours of the market. By creating the right business incentives and not tolerating any price gouging, we can help lower the cost of living and free up much-needed cash so that the Missing Class can attend to other needs.

EMPLOYMENT

Danielle Wayne is a proud member of the Missing Class because she finally landed a civil service job with good wages and a host of benefits. Tomás Linares works around the clock at two modestly paid jobs to pull together an income package that will cover his bills. Julia Coronado is riding high because she is an essential employee in the health-care industry, for which she is well compensated despite not having a bachelor's degree. Clearly, employment is key, and the better paid it is, the more likely it is that a worker will retain a foothold in the Missing Class or—in the best circumstances—move up. One obvious way to help would be to increase the benefit amounts and income thresholds of the Earned Income Tax Credit, especially for single male workers (like Tomás) and workers without children who are all but ignored by current policies.

What else can be done to increase the upward mobility of these workers, to place them in jobs that demand more skills and pay more money? When Katherine Newman started studying the working poor, she examined the importance of career ladders—pathways of promotions within a firm leading up from entry level—in improving the job prospects of low-wage workers. In her book *No Shame in My Game*, she pointed to model programs such as the one at Cape Cod Hospital in Massachusetts, which partnered with health care unions to offer education and training on-site, during work hours, for employees who wanted to gain new credentials and move up from, for example, nurse's aide to radiology technician.

Career-ladder programs provide a steady progression of more demanding jobs and manage the transitions between them for workers willing to train for them. They are a "win-win" situation for both sides of the labor-management divide. Management benefits because it is investing in the very skills that it needs to recruit and harvests workers who are already known and proven as good bets. Workers benefit because they can complete the training while on the job, rather than struggling to go to school during their off-hours, when they need to be attending to their families. At the end of the day, they can look forward to the better pay and more prestigious assignments that are waiting for them.

Could career ladders spread? Northeastern University's Joan Fitz-gerald thinks the idea has some potential. In her book *Moving Up in the New Economy*, Fitzgerald points out that establishing career ladders is not easy and works best in industries that have shortages of qualified workers and therefore an incentive for employers to invest in training.[27] As the Cape Cod Hospital program suggests, health care is precisely one of those sectors. There is a growing—even alarming—shortage of nurses, a large population of baby boomers who will soon need contin-uous care, and no significant capacity in junior colleges to train this much-needed workforce.

Not surprisingly, enlightened self-interest is motivating firms in this industry to grow their own workforce. Cooperative Home Care Associates (CHCA) in New York's South Bronx offers courses that com-bine classroom learning and on-the-job training and qualify its gradu-ates for entry-level jobs as home health aides, positions that come with full insurance benefits, paid vacation, sick pay, and annual dividends from the profits of the worker-owned company. One-third of the coop-erative's administrators were formerly home health aides. The Parapro-fessional Healthcare Institute, a nonprofit organization that helped to establish CHCA, has now spread the model to Philadelphia and Man-chester, New Hampshire.[28] At Apple Health Care, a for-profit chain of nursing homes in Connecticut, workers are paid to attend three train-ing courses, which meet for two hours a week over eight weeks. When the training is over, they qualify for jobs that are significantly better than entry-level ones. Why would Apple invest in such a program? Re-duced turnover. Apple estimates that the program dropped its turnover rate from 50 to 60 percent a year to 30 percent, which both improved patient care and broadened its workers' employment prospects.[29] As companies like Apple are learning, career ladders are a proven strategy for cultivating a reliable and loyal workforce.

Career ladders can also extend outside the firm, linking up with ed-ucational institutions that bestow the necessary credentials. AFSCME 1199C, a health care workers' union, has brokered deals with various hospitals and nursing homes whereby management contributes 1.5 per-cent of gross payroll to pay for training. With these employer contri-butions, the union was able to establish the Breslin Learning Center, the nation's only union-run school of practical nursing, which turns out scores of new nurse's aides and licensed practical nurses every year. As part of its Ladders in Nursing Careers initiative, the Robert Wood Johnson Foundation gave grants to nine hospital associations to hasten the advancement of "low-rung employees." Licensed practical nurses in the program attended nursing school, working part-time for full pay while studying full-time to become registered nurses. In return, they had to sign an agreement to stay on another eighteen months for every year they spent in school. The completion rate was a favorable 60 percent.[30]

Fitzgerald details similar programs in the fields of child care, education, biotechnology, and manufacturing. In case after case, a prudent investment by management, foundations, and government creates opportunities for workers to move up to economic security—and off government benefits financed by taxpayers. If federal and state tax laws would reward employers who invest in the training and promotion of their workers, we would all be the better for it.

Programs of this kind apply primarily to adult workers. What about the young people in Missing Class families? Are there policies to help them build upon the platform of income and assets their parents have already constructed? Next to education, to which we turn in the following section, there is no greater credential than work experience and the references that come with it. It can be harder than many of us realize to create a track record that pays off if you come from a family with few contacts in the labor market.

Middle-class youth have been flocking to public service programs like AmeriCorps and Teach for America clearly for idealistic reasons—as a way to make a difference in society—and yet also for practical reasons—as a first step into the job market. They pile up experience and references that enable them to advance quickly in the labor market. Why not provide something similar to teens in Missing Class neighborhoods? Nonprofit organizations are always in need of help. Young people and welfare recipients could obtain valuable training in white-collar job skills if there was a way to support the expense. An AmeriCorps "Junior" program could introduce younger people from near-poor households to nonprofit organizations as paid after-school interns. They would be able to live at home, thus cutting the cost of such a program, while collecting the kinds of credentials that would avail them at their next job interview. We need not delay access to opportunities of this kind to the age of eighteen. Catching kids while they are in high school and giving them stimulating summer internships and part-time jobs will encourage many to complete their education and position them for decent jobs after they get their diplomas.

For many young minority men, the employment picture is particularly bleak. Too often, the only track record they've acquired after eighteen years is the kind brimming with school absences, criminal charges, and failing skills assessments. Once upon a time, young men like these would have headed off to the factory when they left school and made respectable wages in the blue-collar world. Today's youth, however, can no longer follow their fathers or grandfathers onto the shop floor. The fact that manufacturing employment in America has tanked is partly to blame, but it's also true that in many parts of the country, we have utterly abandoned vocational education. Other countries have not been so rash. Germany still makes use of the apprenticeship system, which sandwiches the high school curriculum between stints at firms where young people learn market-worthy skills.

Adaptations of the German system could work here in the United States. Our junior colleges do a fairly decent job with vocational education, but they could make good use of additional funds for on-the-job training to complement what they do in class. Our high school curriculum needs rethinking to account for the approximately 25 percent of students who are not college bound. The mania for high-stakes tests, coupled with the legitimate recognition of the paucity of basic skills, has pushed us toward a one-size-fits-all educational system that is simply not working for many youth. Kids like Omar Guerra might have stuck it out in high school if they had had other options besides a regular academic track. Omar wanted to work. His teenage years would probably have turned out better if he could have married schooling with preparation for the workforce, including part-time jobs.

In America we rarely reward high school teachers for making links with employers on behalf of vocational students. When those connections develop, it is usually a result of the dedication of specific teachers who want the best for their charges. Vocational instructors in Japan, on

the other hand, are expected to maintain ongoing relationships with local employers, who turn to the teachers for recommendations in hiring.[31] Even though the Japanese economy is not blazing as brightly as
it once was, the average vocational student there is greatly advantaged
by the formal ties that bind schools and businesses. There is no reason
that our school systems could not follow suit by requiring shop teachers
to visit with local employers. Rewarding teachers with salary bonuses
for their success in job placements would be a worthy use of taxpayer
dollars.

EDUCATION

Rasheea Fletcher is a whiz in school, but she doesn't get much from her
classes because the kids around her aren't up to her level. Omar Guerra
has dropped out and is now lodged upstate at a juvenile detention center, a convicted sex offender in his teens. Safiya Wayne has started
kindergarten, but she's way behind other kids who already know their
numbers, letters, and the expectations of teachers for "circle time." All
three kids would have a better chance of remaining in the Missing Class
and even pushing beyond it if we could improve the schools they attend.
Unfortunately, most Missing Class parents are not in a position to make
up for what these schools lack. They cannot buy extra tutoring, enrichment courses, or the best teachers. They can no longer spare the time to
serve as an auxiliary teaching force. Meanwhile, high-stakes tests have
upped the ante and now threaten kids with the possibility of grade retention in their younger years, increasing the probability they'll ultimately drop out.

Social science and common sense alike tell us that every dime we
invest in improving education will redound to the nation's benefit many
times over. But how shall we spend that dime? First, we must replace
this patchwork child-care "system"—a term it barely merits—with a
comprehensive, public-supported network of day care (for kids aged six
months to three years) and kindergarten (starting at four). We know
that the majority of mothers of children under one are in the labor
force; no amount of wishful thinking is going to change that fact. Other
countries have long recognized the need to invest as heavily in the care
and education of preschool children as they do in their school-age

siblings. And their children are streaking ahead of us in academic performance. We are still "a nation at risk," as President Reagan's commission lamented back in 1983, and we cannot afford to let another quarter-century go by without doing something about this country's inequalities in early-childhood education.[32] Economist Robert Lynch has shown that the benefits of universal early-childhood education would outweigh the costs by $31 billion by 2030 if we factor in the expected returns on lifetime earnings and decreased criminal behavior alone.[33] So to those who ask, "Can we afford this?" we answer, "We cannot afford *not* to."

What can we do for older children like Rasheea? We should expand options for public school choice, including charter schools, and put more resources into our network of guidance counselors, so that these professionals have the knowledge and time to help students apply to the best exam-based schools. Many cities have invested in selective public schools to try to provide families of limited means with some of the educational opportunities that wealthier families enjoy through private schools. But a kid's chances of getting into these schools often depends on her parents' knowledge of exam preparation and awareness of the bureaucratic steps that must be religiously followed for a child to even be considered. A good number of Missing Class parents, such as Marisol Ramos, have figured other ways of getting their kids into better schools, such as using the address of a relative who lives in another neighborhood. But not everyone knows how to game the system. Rasheea's grandparents care very deeply about her academic success, but they are not well educated themselves. If her progress depends on their ability to maneuver through a large and intimidating bureaucracy, she won't get very far. The playing field could be leveled somewhat if public schools invested more in counseling resources so that a bright kid like Rasheea could be steered in the right direction.

And what of the hours after the school bell rings? For reasons we find hard to fathom, programs like "midnight basketball" have become targets of ridicule. This is absurd. School buildings should become community centers after hours and provide as much enrichment and safe recreation as possible. Missing Class parents have neither the time nor the resources to locate Little League games, soccer fields, and aca-

demic tutors spread throughout their neighborhoods. They are lucky
if they live in communities safe enough to let their kids play outside
unsupervised. Most end up plunking their children in front of a video
game or TV set just to be sure they stay out of trouble. This is neither
healthy nor wise. Kids, especially teens, need safe places to enjoy themselves. What's more, they need adults on hand who can answer questions
and guide them through their homework—a resource middle-class kids
can tap because their parents and extended family members are often in
a better position to help.

Addressing the fate of school dropouts is important as well. The rate
has declined in recent years, but it remains too high and consists disproportionately of minority kids. How do we give these failed students
a second chance? The largest "second chance" program in the country
is to be found in prisons, where pursuit of the General Education Diploma is common. But surely we want to do what we can to address the
problems of school dropouts before they get to that dismal point. Our
community colleges already make a difference by offering remedial education, albeit under great financial duress and the incessant drumbeat
of critics who argue that we should not be spending money in this way.

Establishing more second-chance schools that offer former dropouts one-on-one attention and a chance to earn a diploma at night or in
a community college would go far toward rescuing millions from a life
of poverty.[34] Other countries routinely send kids who are over sixteen to
"senior" schools that cater to both the university-bound and vocational
student. In Great Britain and Canada, "sixth-form colleges" offer instruction to a wide range of young people, from the brightest students
studying for advanced national exams to kids seeking vocational certificates. By separating out older teens and placing them in settings that
are not quite as infantilizing as high schools—with their bells, dress
codes, and strict regimes—we may be able to encourage more young
people to return to school and get a diploma. Dropouts need not be saddled for life by the bad decisions they made in the past.

Finally, for the Missing Class's most promising students, we come
to the question of access to college. Tuition is rising much faster than
inflation, which places college beyond the reach of an increasing portion of Americans in the middle and lower middle class. The sons and

daughters of all but the wealthiest families are ending their educational careers awash in extraordinary levels of debt, a burden that will weigh them down well into their adult years. Over the last decade, the amount that the average college senior owes on graduation day has soared to $19,200 in 2004, a 58 percent increase in inflation-adjusted dollars. In 1993 only 1.3 percent of seniors owed more than $40,000, but in 2004, 7.7 percent did.[35] The cost is driving many away from college altogether. The share of bachelor's degrees awarded to students from families making between $30,000 and $50,000—much more than the average Missing Class family sees in a year—fell from 15 percent in 1980 to 11 percent in 2004.[36] Many of these students are settling instead for two-year community colleges, which provide valuable training but will not shepherd them to the economy's highest-earning jobs.

Financial aid is one solution, but the federal government has been cutting the value of the main instrument—the Pell grant—for years now.[37] To make matters worse, the formula for awarding Pell grants discriminates sharply against high school students who are working to save money for college. Their earnings are added to their parents' income, and if the results exceed a very low threshold—about $35,000—they may be cut off from all federal student aid that does not come in the form of the very loans they are trying to avoid.[38]

One of the few places the federal government has not cut back on support for higher education is right in its own backyard, the District of Columbia. In 1999 Congress passed a bill that provides graduates of District high schools with as much as $10,000 a year to pay the difference between in-state and out-of-state college tuition at public colleges, and about $2,500 a year for private schools. Since 2000, the number of students from the nation's capital who attend college has grown by 35 percent. Republicans and Democrats alike agree the program has been a major success, bringing a college education within the reach of thousands of students from one of our nation's most impoverished cities.

Despite widespread publicity about the program, it has proven difficult to reach the poorest families with the news that their children are eligible.[39] Private firms—including the Washington Post Company, Verizon, America Online, Lockheed Martin, and ExxonMobil—have stepped up to this challenge by establishing the District of Columbia

College Access Program, which pays for college counselors to work in District high schools, assisting students with application and financial aid forms so that they can finally get the kind of advice that more affluent kids turn to parents for.[40]

How can we make college accessible and affordable for students outside the nation's capital? Senator John Edwards has established a pilot program in North Carolina, College for Everyone, whose objectives are similar.[41] The class of 2006 at Greene Central High School now qualifies for first-year college tuition and textbooks, courtesy of College for Everyone. In this rural, tobacco-growing county beset by economic hardship, students are now guaranteed the opportunity to pursue an education that many agree they would not be able to afford otherwise.

We need not stop at pilot programs. It is quite possible to scale initiatives of this kind up to the point where they reach a substantial population of Missing Class Americans. The state of Washington has taken a major step in that direction already.[42] In the fall of 2006, the state legislature declared the University of Washington free for all students whose families fall below the mandated income threshold ($46,500 for a family of four).[43]

The modern middle class was built on the back of the GI Bill, which promised a college education for millions of World War II veterans, many of whom were the first in their families to attend universities. The legislation also bestowed low-interest, zero-down-payment home loans upon these servicemen's families, another policy that helped transform an earlier Missing Class into the storied middle class of the postwar boom. If we hope to match the greatness of this Greatest Generation, we will do everything possible to enact and expand the ideas described above. The Missing Class will surely benefit, but so will we *all*—just as our nation reaped the bounty of the GI Bill long ago.

Is America prepared to recognize the struggles of the Missing Class? Are we ready to invest in the future of their children so that they start the race with a fighting chance? This is a critical goal in a country with abundant resources—natural, economic, and human—but a troubling pattern of inequality in their distribution. In the years since the attacks of September 11, we have been understandably preoccupied with terrorism and war. But international problems have obscured domestic concerns for too long. The long-term fate of the Missing Class—the fifty-seven million near-poor Americans who constitute a fifth of our population—should be high on the list of our priorities, starting yesterday.

We must attend to these millions of dedicated parents who struggle to keep their households above the poverty line through long hours on the job. We must ensure them decent housing that won't make their infants sick, and safe streets that won't corrupt and brutalize their teens. We must help them obtain quality child care and schooling that will keep their children out of harm's way and on the pathway to success. If we fail to provide the Missing Class with this equality of opportunity, then we will have reneged on a sacred promise: if you work hard, you prosper. If you sacrifice, you will see the rewards in this generation and the next. We have repeated this mantra countless times ever since we sent single mothers on welfare marching into the low-wage labor market. If it is a false promise for the near poor, a group nearly twice the size of the poor and clearly better off, then what confidence can anyone else have that this vaunted American Dream is anything more than a fable?

The near poor are not some distant tribe. They are the people middle-class Americans rub shoulders with every day. Missing Class men and women run our transit systems and care for our elderly and infirm. They stand guard at our workplaces and haul the trash from our homes. They count our change, cook our meals, and watch over our kids. Like us—like all Americans—they dream of a life of comfort and security, a chance to do what they love, a better tomorrow for their children. But the hurdles are higher for the Missing Class. Their hold on the well-being they have achieved is more tenuous.

The poor have always been with us. The missing are yet to be seen. We will all benefit if they can tighten their grip on prosperity and leave behind the suffocating confines of poverty for good. And we will all surely know the consequences—in reduced productivity, in wasted potential, in diminished ideals—if the children of today's near poor become the *truly* poor of tomorrow.

ACKNOWLEDGMENTS AND
A NOTE ON METHODS

This book began its life as an outgrowth of an earlier project sponsored by the MacArthur Foundation Research Network on Successful Mid-life Development. The oldest people studied for that project appeared in an earlier book by Katherine Newman, *A Different Shade of Gray: Midlife and Beyond in the Inner City* (New York: New Press, 2003). *The Missing Class* reports on some of the younger families who responded to a New York City survey (*n* = 900) of Puerto Ricans, Dominicans, and African Americans in 1994–95 and a more in-depth, multiyear follow-up of one hundred of them, consisting of two waves of interviews conducted in 1995–96 and 1997–98.

The nine families profiled here were part of a fieldwork-based project that permitted us a deeper understanding than those surveys and interviews alone permit. They were chosen from among the interview subjects who had, by then, been part of this project for four years. With their permission, Katherine Newman's research team spent countless hours in their homes, their workplaces, and their children's schools throughout 1999–2000 and 2002. In addition to these families, we interviewed service providers, local politicians, church leaders, day-care workers, teachers, guidance counselors, and anyone else who could shed some light on the challenges faced by the near poor.

The nine families profiled extensively in this book represent a small but important subset of the larger qualitative sample, whose demographics are reviewed in detail in the appendixes to *A Different Shade of Gray*. Their real names do not appear here, and identifying details have been altered to protect the privacy they were promised. But we thank them for opening their lives to us and making it possible for readers to appreciate the daily struggles of the near poor. Similarly, we appreciate the opportunity we had to spend time in their schools and workplaces. The names of the institutions and firms have also been changed to protect the privacy of our fieldwork families.

We are in debt to Newman's fieldwork team, who were responsible for gathering hundreds of pages of interviews, field observations, community newspapers, and local statistics on everything from food pantries to hospital admissions. During the first years of the study, Dan Zuberi, Marissa de la Vega, and Nancy Lopez composed the field team. In later years, Belkis Suazo deCastro, Rose Williams, Noemi Mendez, and Magdalena Rodriguez worked on the project. All of these colleagues did more than just collect data; they provided their own reflections on the meaning of what they saw and helped to inform us in the development of this book.

Absolutely essential to the completion of the project was the long labor of Margaret Chin, Associate Professor of Sociology at Hunter College, and Dr. Chauncy Lennon, then a postdoctoral fellow at Columbia University, now a senior program manager at SeedCo, a nonprofit organization in New York City. Chin and Lennon supervised the field teams for several years and managed the onrushing flow of transcripts, appointments, and bureaucratic hassles that inevitably accompany this kind of research. Jeanne Brooks-Gunn and her colleagues at Teachers College provided a congenial home for this project during its middle years, while Columbia University's Institute for Social and Economic Policy and Research, directed by Professor Peter Bearman and his associate, Kathryn Neckerman, hosted us during the latter years. We thank these colleagues for providing a home base and collegial atmosphere within which to work.

Without the contributions of the Ford Foundation, this book would certainly have taken a good deal longer to finish. Program officer

Nancy Sconyers and Helen Neuborne, senior program manager in the Community Development Division, were convinced of the value of this work, and along with Melvin Oliver, then a vice president of the foundation, helped to provide critical resources that made its completion possible. The same must be said of the National Science Foundation's Cultural Anthropology program, which awarded Katherine Newman research funds to support data collection from beginning to end in the form of Award No. 9802726. The Woodrow Wilson School at Princeton University provided Newman with generous research funds that helped to make the last year of writing possible. We thank Dean Anne-Marie Slaughter for her interest in this work and steadfast support of faculty research at Princeton. Lisa Adams, our literary agent, deserves our gratitude for helping this book find a home at Beacon Press, where it prospered under the watchful eye of our editor, Gayatri Patnaik.

Victor Chen would like to thank his academic mentor, Bill Wilson, and journalistic mentors, Bob Keeler and Tony Sipp; the Harvard Multidisciplinary Program in Inequality and Social Policy, the Joint PhD Programs in Social Policy, and the Harvard Sociology Department for supporting his work; Víctor Manuel Ramos for his cultural and linguistic insights; and his parents, Chu-Chen and Lawrence, his brother Vincent, and his wife, Emi, for their love and continual encouragement.

Katherine Newman owes ongoing thanks to her husband, sociologist Paul Attewell, and children Steven (twenty-four) and David (eighteen), who have (mainly) cheerfully put up with the demands that two writers place on family life.

ONE: The Missing Class

1. In 2006 dollars, Valerie's hourly wage of $13.68 (in 1999) would be $16.55.

2. This sketch is a composite of details from 1999–2000 and 2002.

3. Near-poor families come in many shapes and sizes. Twenty-nine percent of the nation's children who live with single mothers are near poor. A slightly smaller portion of children who live with single fathers are near poor as well. Households with more earners in them—and more adults to share the tasks of raising the kids—are greatly advantaged, but there are still a significant number of near poor among the nation's married families; 19 percent of children who live with both parents are in the Missing Class. Younger parents are at greater risk for joining the near poor than older parents, who have more job experience. Education is a powerful force that shapes the options for employment and therefore for family income. Thirty-two percent of children growing up in homes where parents have not graduated from high school are near poor, while only 16 percent of those whose parents have had at least some college are in the Missing Class. Hsien-Hen Lu and Heather Koball, *The Changing Demographics of Low-Income Families and Their Children* (New York: National Center for Children in Poverty, Columbia University, Mailman School of Public Health, Research Brief No. 2, 2003).

4. This is 100–200 percent of the official poverty line. The poverty line is adjusted for family size, and so are the income lines that demarcate the near poor. Therefore, a family of two would be among the near poor in 2006 if it had an annual income of $13,200–26,400, and a family of three would need

$16,600–33,200 to be ranked in the Missing Class. Actual expenses vary a great deal by locality, of course; a household income of $36,000 would sustain a decent standard of living in rural Arkansas but would not go very far in San Francisco. (The poverty line as described here is taken from the Health and Human Services Department's 2006 poverty guidelines, which can be found at http://aspe.hhs.gov/poverty/06poverty.shtml. The poverty thresholds released by the Census Bureau are more precise; for instance, the 2005 federal poverty line for a family of four was $19,971. See www.census.gov/hhes/www/poverty/threshld/thresho5.html.)

5. The table below summarizes the percentage change in family income divided by its poverty line in the base period (1996–98) and the average in 2000–2002. The data come from the Panel Study of Income Dynamics (PSID), a nationally representative longitudinal study of nearly eight thousand U.S. families and individuals who have been followed since 1968. The sample drawn for this table includes all PSID families with an average family income in 1996 and 1998 that is *above* the poverty line but below *twice* the poverty line and hence meets our definition of the near poor (or the Missing Class). The poverty line is adjusted for family size. These data were analyzed by Professor Peter Gottschalk, Department of Economics, Boston College (personal communication).

Percentage change	Frequency	Percentage	Cumulative
More than 30% decline	250	8.81	8.81
20–30% decline	118	4.16	12.97
10–20% decline	103	3.63	16.6
0–10% decline	159	5.6	22.21
0–10% rise	165	5.82	28.02
10–20% rise	159	5.6	33.63
20–30% rise	138	4.86	38.49
More than 30% rise	1,745	61.51	100
Total	2,837	100	100

6. Melvin Oliver and Thomas Shapiro, *Black Wealth / White Wealth: A New Perspective on Racial Inequality*, 2nd ed. (New York: Routledge, 2006), and Dalton Conley, *Being Black, Living in the Red: Race, Wealth, and Social Policy in America* (Berkeley: University of California Press, 1999).

7. Elizabeth Warren, "Show Me the Money," *New York Times*, October 24, 2005.

8. Mary Pattillo-McCoy, *Black Picket Fences: Privilege and Peril among the Black Middle Class* (Chicago: University of Chicago Press, 1999).

9. Katherine Swartz, *Reinsuring Health: Why More Middle-Class People Are Uninsured and What Government Can Do* (New York: Russell Sage, 2006).

10. Manny Fernandez, "A Study Links Trucks' Exhaust to Bronx School-children's Asthma," *New York Times*, October 29, 2006. For more on the relationship between asthma and pollution, see the citations in chapter 5.

11. Catherine Kenney argues that women in "fragile families"—low-income households with unmarried parents—are particularly disadvantaged when it comes to control over resources. Men exercise more power in allocation decisions and may choose to withhold income from their partners. Catherine T. Kenney, "The Power of the Purse: Allocative Systems and Inequality in Couple Households," *Gender and Society* 20 (2006): 354–81.

12. This term was coined by William Julius Wilson. See William Julius Wilson, *The Truly Disadvantaged: The Inner City, the Underclass, and Public Policy* (Chicago: University of Chicago Press, 1987).

13. See the appendixes to Katherine S. Newman's *A Different Shade of Gray: Midlife and Beyond in the Inner City* (New York: New Press, 2003) for a full treatment of the sample characteristics. As explained in the note on methods at the end of this volume, this book was the first to make use of the sample from which this fieldwork derived.

TWO: Whose Neighborhood Is This Anyway?

1. "Hit-and-run contractors" are a nuisance in neighborhoods across America. See, for example, Rachel Blackmon Bryars, "Contractor's Bid Too Low? Don't Bite," *Washington Post*, April 22, 2006.

2. The names of all firms used in this book have been changed. Home Builder is a pseudonym.

3. Nancy Beth Jackson, "Diversity, Culture and Brownstones, Too," *New York Times*, September 1, 2002; Gary Lee, "Brooklyn's Bridge to the Past," *Washington Post*, March 7, 2001.

4. Nelson George, "'I Feel Like a Native Son,'" *New York Times*, June 19, 2005; Michel Marriott, "Long Before He Was B.I.G.," *New York Times*, March 17, 1997; Todd S. Purdum, "Rapper Is Shot to Death in Echo of Killing 6 Months Ago," *New York Times*, March 10, 1997; Yanick Rice Lamb, "If You're Thinking of Living in Fort Greene," *New York Times*, October 15, 1989.

5. See Katherine S. Newman, *A Different Shade of Gray: Midlife and Beyond in the Inner City* (New York: New Press, 2003), and William Julius Wilson and Richard P. Taub, *There Goes the Neighborhood: Racial, Ethnic, and Class Tensions in Four Chicago Neighborhoods and Their Meaning for America* (New York: Knopf, 2006).

6. A 2005 study found that the Greenwich Village / Soho area had the highest median monthly rent in the city, at $1,640. In Bedford-Stuyvesant, the monthly median rent was $750; in Washington Heights / Inwood, it was $770; in Sunset Park, $892; in Fort Greene / Brooklyn Heights, $950. Vicki Been et al., *State of New York City's Housing and Neighborhoods, 2005* (New York: Furman

Center for Real Estate and Urban Policy, New York University School of Law, 2005).

7. See Jonathan Rieder's *Canarsie: The Jews and Italians of Brooklyn against Liberalism* (Cambridge, MA: Harvard University Press, 1985) for an excellent account of racial confrontation and white backlash in one Brooklyn neighborhood. See also Newman, *A Different Shade of Gray*, 10.

8. William Julius Wilson, *The Truly Disadvantaged: The Inner City, the Underclass, and Public Policy* (Chicago: University of Chicago Press, 1987), 55–58.

9. Ingrid Gould Ellen, *Sharing America's Neighborhoods: The Prospects for Stable Racial Integration* (Cambridge, MA: Harvard University Press, 2000).

10. Ruth Naomi López Turley, "Neighborhood Effects on Children: Mechanisms, Interactions, and Relative Deprivation" (PhD diss., Harvard University, 2001).

11. The *Newsweek* article is quoted in Francis Morrone, *An Architectural Guidebook to Brooklyn* (Salt Lake City: Gibbs Smith, 2001), 169.

12. Glenn Thrush, "The View," *City Limits Monthly* (January 1999); Fund for the Borough of Brooklyn, *Brooklyn Neighborhood Book* (Brooklyn, NY: Fund for the Borough of Brooklyn, 1985). In 1980, 45,868 of Brooklyn Community District 7's 98,564 residents were Hispanic, according to 1991 data from the Census Bureau; in 1990, 52,734 of the district's 102,553 residents were Hispanic. See also Philip Kasinitz, John H. Mollenkopf, and Mary C. Waters, eds., *Becoming New Yorkers: Ethnographies of the New Second Generation* (New York: Russell Sage, 2004).

13. In 1991 the 34th Precinct, which at the time covered Washington Heights and Inwood, reported 119 murders. Emily M. Bernstein, "Washington Heights; Homicide Rate Falls by 27 Percent," *New York Times*, October 31, 1993. In 1994 part of the 34th Precinct became the 33rd Precinct. The 33rd Precinct reported 6 murders in 1998, 8 in 2001, and 10 in 2005; the 34th reported 9 in 1998, 7 in 2001, and 10 in 2005. Reports of other crimes also fell. Statistics taken from reports by the New York City Police Department's CompStat Unit, viewable online at www.nyc.gov/html/nypd/pdf/chfdept/cso33pct .pdf and www.nyc.gov/html/nypd/pdf/chfdept/cso34pct.pdf. However, in recent years community residents have complained about a rise in crime. Jennifer Steinhauer, "Angry Crowd Scolds Mayor on Crime Rate in Washington Heights and Inwood," *New York Times*, October 20, 2004.

14. For more on the operations and organization of drug dealers, see Philippe Bourgois, *In Search of Respect: Selling Crack in El Barrio*, 2nd ed. (Cambridge: Cambridge University Press, 2003); Steven D. Levitt and Sudhir Alladi Venkatesh, "An Economic Analysis of a Drug-Selling Gang's Finances," *Quarterly Journal of Economics* 115 (2000): 755–89.

15. In a sense, parents like these look to the police as a source of social control to turn their children away from their neighborhood's bad influences—that

is, away from the "streetwise" skills that young people learn in poor neighborhoods, which help them to survive on the streets but also place them on a track toward academic and occupational failure. See Elijah Anderson, *Streetwise: Race, Class, and Change in an Urban Community* (Chicago: University of Chicago Press, 1992).

16. Elijah Anderson, *Code of the Street: Decency, Violence, and the Moral Life of the Inner City* (New York: Norton, 1999), 34.

17. Missing Class families live near poor families and are thus subject to the same influences. See Mary Pattillo-McCoy, *Black Picket Fences: Privilege and Peril among the Black Middle Class* (Chicago: University of Chicago Press, 1999).

18. This is the sort of neighborhood in transition that Elijah Anderson profiled in *Streetwise*.

19. For a discussion of the relationship between parental involvement and success in school, see Ronald F. Ferguson, "Toward Skilled Parenting and Transformed Schools Inside a National Movement for Excellence with Equity" (paper presented at the First Educational Equity Symposium of the Campaign for Educational Equity, Teachers College, Columbia University, New York, 2005).

20. See Jane Waldfogel's *What Children Need* (Cambridge, MA: Harvard University Press, 2006), which examines the evidence on parental employment and its effect on children of various ages.

21. This quotation and the description of the community garden below are from 1999–2000 data but are included in this 2002 section because they describe the ongoing state of the community.

22. Some nonprofit groups have even added community gardening to their arsenal of development strategies. One good example is Isles, Inc., a Trenton-based community development and environmental organization. According to the group's Web site, Isles' community gardens program "addresses the issues of hunger, open space, and recreation by building the capacity of residents to join together, grow their own food, and beautify their neighborhoods." See www.isles.org.

THREE: The American Dream, in Monthly Installments

1. See Katherine S. Newman's *Chutes and Ladders: Navigating the Low-Wage Labor Market* (New York: Russell Sage and Harvard University Press, 2006), which focuses on a sample of working poor individuals in Harlem, a fifth of whom found jobs paying more than $15.45 an hour (300 percent of the federal minimum wage) over the period of 1993–2002. Nevertheless, dramatic upward mobility in this country occurs less often than we might think, and intergenerational mobility is lower in the United States than it is in France, Germany, Canada, and a host of other high-income countries. Tom Hertz, *Understanding*

Mobility in America (Washington, DC: Center for American Progress, 2006), www.americanprogress.org/issues/2006/04/b1579981.html. See also Lawrence Mishel, Jared Bernstein, and Sylvia Allegretto, *The State of Working America, 2004/2005* (Washington, DC: Economic Policy Institute / Cornell University Press, 2005), and its fact sheet titled "Inequality" at www.epinet.org/books/ swa2004/news/swafacts_inequality.pdf.

2. Julia's earnings were substantially above the poverty line for a family of four, which was $16,895 in 1999.

3. Data on household credit card use suggest that this is less of a problem for the have-nots than for the have-very-littles—workers with insufficient incomes who, having graduated from the ranks of the desperately poor, become impatient for a level of middle-class luxury that has been denied them for so long. Surveys of British credit card holders, for example, find that unemployed individuals tend to use their cards "sparingly, usually keeping them for emergencies or to buy necessities," whereas low-wage workers tend to "use their cards regularly for both discretionary expenditure and more general spending on food and other necessities." Karen Rowlingson and Elaine Kempson, *Paying with Plastic: A Study of Credit Card Debt* (London: Policy Studies Institute, 1994), 8.

4. Elizabeth Warren and Amelia Warren Tyagi, *The Two-Income Trap: Why Middle-Class Mothers and Fathers Are Going Broke* (New York: Basic Books, 2003), 19. See also Teresa A. Sullivan, Elizabeth Warren, and Jay Lawrence Westbrook, *The Fragile Middle Class: Americans in Debt* (New Haven, CT: Yale University Press, 2000).

5. Juliet B. Schor, *The Overspent American: Upscaling, Downshifting, and the New Consumer* (New York: Basic Books, 1998), 232; David S. Evans and Richard Schmalensee, *Paying with Plastic: The Digital Revolution in Buying and Borrowing*, 2nd ed. (Cambridge, MA: MIT Press, 2005), 88; Robert D. Manning, *Credit Card Nation: The Consequences of America's Addiction to Credit* (New York: Basic Books, 2000), 11.

6. Warren and Warren Tyagi, *The Two-Income Trap*, 139.

7. According to 2005 census data, the lower limit of the second quintile was an annual household income of $19,178; the lower limit of the middle quintile was $36,000. See Census Bureau, "Table HINC-05: Percent Distribution of Households, by Selected Characteristics within Income Quintile and Top 5 Percent in 2005," *Current Population Survey: 2006 Annual Social and Economic Supplement* (2006), http://pubdb3.census.gov/macro/032006/hhinc/new05_000 .htm. As a result, the second quintile roughly equates with the Missing Class, given our definition of households with annual incomes between 100 and 200 percent of the poverty line, or $20,000 to $40,000 for a family of four.

8. Evans and Schmalensee, *Paying with Plastic*, 89 (figure 4.1). See also Rowlingson and Kempson, *Paying with Plastic*. According to this British study

of credit-card use and debt, the higher your household income, the greater the likelihood of having a credit card. However, card holders in lower-income households tend to be more active users of credit and tend *not* to pay their balances in full every month.

9. Lack of knowledge of the way that credit works is not confined to the Missing Class, of course. See Evans and Schmalensee, *Paying with Plastic*, 98–100, for a discussion of "irrational" behavior in credit card borrowing.

10. For more on rotating credit associations, see Shirley Ardener, "The Comparative Study of Rotating Credit Associations," *Journal of the Royal Anthropological Institute of Great Britain and Ireland* 94 (July–December 1964): 201–29; Carlos G. Vélez-Ibáñez, *Bonds of Mutual Trust: The Cultural Systems of Rotating Credit Associations among Urban Mexicans and Chicanos* (New Brunswick, NJ: Rutgers University Press, 1983); Pyong Gap Min, *Ethnic Business Enterprise: Korean Small Business in Atlanta* (New York: Center for Migration Studies, 1988); and Jennifer Lee, *Civility in the City: Blacks, Jews, and Koreans in Urban America* (Cambridge, MA: Harvard University Press, 2002). For a discussion of *sociedades* among Puerto Rican families, see Irma M. Olmedo, "Voices of Our Past: Using Oral History to Explore Funds of Knowledge within a Puerto Rican Family," *Anthropology and Education Quarterly* 28 (1997): 550–73.

11. See Katherine S. Newman, *Declining Fortunes: The Withering of the American Dream* (New York: Basic Books, 1993); Katherine S. Newman, *Falling from Grace: Downward Mobility in the Age of Affluence* (Berkeley: University of California Press, 1999); and Lillian B. Rubin, *Worlds of Pain: Life in the Working-Class Family* (New York: Basic Books, 1992).

12. In 2002 the poverty threshold for a family of six with three related children under eighteen was $24,797 (see www.census.gov/hhes/www/poverty/threshld/thresh02.html). Two hundred percent of that threshold would be $49,594. In other words, with her undeclared income, Julia and Juan are on the borderline between Missing Class and middle class. Without Juan's income, Julia would be depending on her $30,000 salary and would still be squarely within the Missing Class.

13. Figures come from a 2000 interview with Mark Levine, the cofounder of Credit Where Credit Is Due. The situation may have improved slightly in recent years—one real estate agency now lists fifteen bank branches in Washington Heights—but the neighborhood remains greatly underserved when compared with other parts of the city. The Midtown East neighborhood, for example, has more than three hundred branches; Harlem has twenty-seven branches. See Brown Harris Stevens, "A Real Estate Guide," www.brownharris stevens.com/guide4.aspx.

14. New York has strict regulations for how much check-cashing services can charge. By law, the fees may not exceed 1.58 percent of the face value of the

check or $1, whichever is higher. Nineteen states have no such limits. Matt Fellowes, *From Poverty, Opportunity: Putting the Market to Work for Lower Income Families* (Washington, DC: Brookings Institution, 2006). See also Mark Flannery and Katherine Samolyk, *Payday Lending: Do the Costs Justify the Price?* (Washington, DC: Center for Financial Research, Federal Deposit Insurance Corporation, Working Paper 2005-09, 2005), and Jean Ann Fox and Patrick Woodall, *Cashed Out: Consumers Pay Steep Premium to "Bank" at Check Cashing Outlets* (Washington, DC: Consumer Federation of America, 2006).

15. "Into the fold," *The Economist*, May 6, 2006; Maria Bruno-Britz, "Targeting the Unbanked/Underbanked with the Right Solutions," *Bank Systems and Technology*, July 28, 2006, www.banktech.com/features/showArticle.jhtml?articleID=191203058.

16. A 1999 study by the Credit Union National Association and the Consumer Federation of America found that about 70 percent of credit unions offer free checking accounts, while only 13 percent of banks do so. Vernon Silver, "Invest Time to Duck Bank Fees," *Chicago Sun-Times*, January 16, 2000. Details from an earlier report are online: Consumer Federation of America press release, "Banks Charge More Fees and Higher Fees Than Credit Unions" (February 3, 1998), www.consumerfed.org/pdfs/bankchgpr.pdf.

17. Joint Center for Housing Studies of Harvard University, *State of the Nation's Housing, 2005* (Cambridge, MA: Joint Center for Housing Studies, 2005), 1.

18. In 2005, 68.5 percent of all American households lived in homes they owned. These home owners included 46.1 percent of households in the first income quintile (with an annual income of under $19,178), 58.2 percent of households in the second income quintile (an income of under $36,000), and 68.8 percent of households in the third income quintile (under $57,658). Authors' analysis of data from Census Bureau, "Table HINC-05."

FOUR: The Sacrificed Generation

1. See Katherine S. Newman's *Chutes and Ladders: Navigating the Low-Wage Labor Market* (New York: Russell Sage and Harvard University Press), 57–83, for an analysis of the effect of this booming economy on labor-market mobility.

2. See Katherine S. Newman's *A Different Shade of Gray: Midlife and Beyond in the Inner City* (New York: New Press, 2003), 201–4, for a discussion of the obligations and tensions that exist between generations living in these New York neighborhoods.

3. Evaluations of various day-care arrangements find that children enrolled in center-based care programs tend to score higher on cognitive assessments than children attending other forms of nonparental child care. Jane Waldfogel, *What Children Need* (Cambridge, MA: Harvard University Press, 2006), 95.

4. Jane Jacobs, *The Death and Life of Great American Cities* (New York: Vintage Books, 1992), 74–80; Mitchell Duneier, *Sidewalk* (New York: Farrar, Straus and Giroux, 1999), 115–20.

5. Research shows that psychiatric disorders (including depression), domestic violence, and other barriers to employment are common among both those who receive welfare and those who leave it. Sheldon Danziger, "Comment: Will TANF Work for the Most Disadvantaged Families?" in *The New World of Welfare*, ed. Rebecca Blank and Ron Haskins (Washington, DC: Brookings Institution, 2001), 328–34.

6. Most New York City schools can accommodate only half of the students in the lunchroom, and some even fewer, so lunch must be eaten in shifts, with the youngest children fed first.

7. For an analysis of the relationship between available school resources and student behavior, see Michael Eskenazi, Gillian Eddins, and John M. Beam, *Equity or Exclusion: The Dynamics of Resources, Demographics, and the New York City Public Schools* (New York: National Center for Schools and Communities, Fordham University, 2003), which also includes a discussion of school violence and government responses.

8. Being held back a grade is the single strongest predictor of dropping out, and retained students fall behind their never-retained counterparts on a variety of academic measures. Pete Goldschmidt and Jia Wang, "When Can Schools Affect Dropout Behavior? A Longitudinal Multilevel Analysis," *American Educational Research Journal* 36 (1999): 715–38; Melissa Roderick, "Grade Retention and School Dropout: Investigating the Association," *American Educational Research Journal* 31 (1994): 729–59; Ann R. McCoy and Arthur J. Reynolds, "Grade Retention and School Performance: An Extended Investigation," *Journal of School Psychology* 37 (1999): 273–98. Boys are more likely than girls to be retained, and the gender gap grows with age. Robert M. Hauser, *Shall We End Social Promotion? Truth and Consequences* (Madison: Center for Demography and Ecology, University of Wisconsin-Madison, Working Paper 99-06, 1999), www.ssc.wisc.edu/cde/cdewp/99–06.pdf. See also Katherine S. Newman and Margaret M. Chin, "High Stakes, Hard Choices: Time Poverty, Testing, and the Children of the Working Poor," *Journal of Qualitative Sociology* 26 (2003): 3–34.

9. Karl L. Alexander, Doris R. Entwisle, and Susan L. Dauber, *On the Success of Failure: A Reassessment of the Effects of Retention in the Primary Grades*, 2nd ed. (Cambridge: Cambridge University Press, 2003). Alexander et al. note that students retained in the first grade "fall farther and farther behind never-retained youngsters for as long as we can monitor their progress."

10. In 2001 seventy-two thousand New York City elementary school students were placed in this at-risk category, and 40 percent of them failed the tests given at the end of the summer. Edward Wyatt, "Wide Disparity on Promoting

Failing Pupils," *New York Times*, August 23, 2001, and Yilu Zhao, "One-Third of Public School Students Enroll for Summer School," *New York Times*, July 3, 2001.

11. There is disagreement about what problems, if any, children experience when their mothers move from welfare to work. See Waldfogel's *What Children Need*, 133–34, which summarizes research showing that mothers' transitions to work have either positive or no effects on the school achievement of young children but negative effects on the school achievement of older children; see also Hirokazu Yoshikawa, Thomas S. Weisner, and Edward D. Lowe, eds., *Making It Work: Low-Wage Employment, Family Life, and Child Development* (New York: Russell Sage, 2006), for a discussion of how low-quality or unstable child care produces negative outcomes for children. For another view, see P. Lindsay Chase-Lansdale et al.'s "Mothers' Transitions from Welfare to Work and the Well-Being of Preschoolers and Adolescents," *Science* 299 (2003): 1548–52, which does not find any association between negative outcomes for children and their mothers' transitions from welfare to employment.

12. See Annette Lareau's *Unequal Childhoods: Class, Race, and Family Life*, 2nd ed. (Lanham, MD: Rowman & Littlefield, 2000), 5, which observes that there is more talking in middle-class homes than in their working-class or poor counterparts, leading to greater "verbal agility" and other benefits for children.

13. See Aurora P. Jackson's "Well-Being among Single, Black, Employed Mothers," *Social Service Review* 66 (1992): 399–409, which finds that single black working mothers are more satisfied with their lives than their nonworking counterparts—but no less depressed.

14. George J. Sefa Dei, Josephine Mazzuca, and Elizabeth McIsaac, *Reconstructing "Dropout": A Critical Ethnography of the Dynamics of Black Students' Disengagement from School* (Toronto: University of Toronto Press, 1997); Jonathan Kozol, *Savage Inequalities: Children in America's Schools* (New York: Harper Perennial, 1992)

15. See Edwin Martin, "Learning Disabilities and Public Policy: Myths and Outcomes," in *Better Understanding Learning Disabilities: New Views from Research and Their Implications for Education and Public Policies*, ed. David B. Gray, James F. Kavanagh, G. Reid Lyon, and Norman Krasnegor (Baltimore: Paul H. Brookes, 1993), 325–42, which finds that 26.7 percent of high school students classified as having learning disabilities drop out of school before graduation. Referenced in "Learning Disabilities," by G. Reid Lyon, *The Future of Children* 6 (1996): 54–76.

16. "Low-income" is defined as families with incomes below 150 percent of the poverty line, which means that this designation includes some of the Missing Class. The category of "working" includes part-time and full-time work. Sharon K. Long and Sandra J. Clark, *The New Child Care Block Grant: State Funding Choices and Their Implications* (Washington, DC: Urban Institute, As-

sessing the New Federalism, Series A, no. A-12, 1997), 6; Annie E. Casey Foundation, "Care for School-Age Children," www.aecf.org/publications/child/care.htm.

FIVE: In Sickness and in Health

1. According to 2005 census data, 24.4 percent of people with household incomes below $25,000 were uninsured, compared with 20.6 percent of those with incomes between $25,000 and $49,999, 14.1 percent of those with incomes between $50,000 and $74,999, and 8.5 percent of those with incomes above $75,000. Carmen DeNavas-Walt, Bernadette D. Proctor, and Cheryl Hill Lee, *Income, Poverty, and Health Insurance Coverage in the United States, 2005* (Washington, DC: U.S. Census Bureau, Current Population Reports: Consumer Income, P60–231, 2006), www.census.gov/prod/2006pubs/p60-231.pdf. The growth of the uninsured population in recent years is the result of declining rates of employer-sponsored health coverage; see Center on Budget and Policy Priorities, *The Number of Uninsured Americans Is at an All-Time High* (Washington, DC: Center on Budget and Policy Priorities, 2006), www.cbpp.org/8-29-06health.htm.

2. See, for example, Jody Heymann, *The Widening Gap: Why America's Working Families Are in Jeopardy—and What Can Be Done About It* (New York: Basic Books, 2000).

3. R. H. Miller and H. S. Luft, "Does Managed Care Lead to Better or Worse Quality of Care?" *Health Affairs* 16 (1997): 7–25. In their metanalysis of peer-reviewed studies published as of early 1997, Miller and Luft find that "quality-of-care evidence from fifteen studies showed an equal number of significantly better and worse HMO results, compared with non-HMO plans.... However, in several instances, Medicare HMO enrollees with chronic conditions showed worse quality of care."

4. See Cathy Schoen, Michelle M. Doty, Sara R. Collins, and Alyssa L. Holmgren's "Insured but Not Protected: How Many Adults Are Underinsured?" *Health Affairs* 24 (2005): 289–302, which estimates that nearly sixteen million people between the ages of nineteen and sixty-four were "underinsured" in 2003, meaning one of the following: medical expenses amounted to 10 percent of their income or more; among low-income adults (below 200 percent of the federal poverty level), medical expenses amounted to at least 5 percent of income; or health-plan deductibles equaled or exceeded 5 percent of income. "Underinsured adults were more likely to forgo needed care than those with more adequate coverage and had rates of financial stress similar to those of the uninsured" (289). See also David U. Himmelstein, Steffie Woolhandler, Ida Hellander, and Sidney M .Wolfe, "Quality of Care in Investor-Owned vs. Not-for-Profit HMOs," *JAMA* 281 (1999): 159–63. Himmelstein et al. conclude that investor-owned HMOs, which, they note, now dominate the managed-

care market, "are associated with reduced quality of care" and spend less on patient care (162).

5. A variety of studies document the extent to which both race and socioeconomic status are correlated with mortality/morbidity. For more on the socioeconomic linkage, see Norman Daniels, Bruce Kennedy, and Ichiro Kawachi, *Is Inequality Bad for Our Health?* (Boston: Beacon Press, 2000); Stephen S. Feinstein, "The Relationship between Socioeconomic Status and Health: A Review of the Literature," *Milbank Quarterly* 71 (1993); Michael G. Marmot, "Social Differentials in Health within and between Populations," *Daedalus* (Fall 1994); Gregory Pappas et al., "The Increasing Disparity in Mortality Rates between Socioeconomic Groups in the United States, 1960 and 1986," *New England Journal of Medicine* 329, no. 2 (1993). For more on the racial linkage, see Daisy S. Ng-Mak et al., "A Further Analysis of Race Differences in the National Longitudinal Mortality Study," *American Journal of Public Health* 8, no. 11 (1999); Paul Sorlie et al., "Black-White Mortality by Family Income," *Lancet*, August 8, 1992.

6. The risks of respiratory illness tend to be higher in lower-income, nonwhite communities. R. Charon Gwynn and George D. Thurston, "The Burden of Air Pollution: Impacts among Racial Minorities," *Environmental Health Perspectives* 109, no. 4 (2001). The causes of asthma are debated, but it is clear that those living in poorer neighborhoods have a greater risk of developing the condition; the prevalence is 10.6 percent among poor children, compared with 5.6 percent among children in the highest income bracket. Black poor children were 15 percent more likely to have asthma than nonblack poor children; black children from higher-income families were 87 percent more likely to have asthma than their nonblack counterparts. Jane E. Miller, "The Effects of Race/Ethnicity and Income on Early Childhood Asthma Prevalence and Health Care Use," *American Journal of Public Health* 90, no. 3 (2000).

Lead poisoning is not just a problem affecting poor neighborhoods; in New York, for example, the tony Upper West Side had a lead poisoning rate of 14 children per 1,000 tested, whereas Washington Heights' rate was 9 per 1,000. New York City Department of Health and Mental Hygiene, *Community Health Profiles* (New York: New York City Department of Health and Mental Hygiene, 2006). That said, national survey data show that children who are racial minorities, come from poor households, or live in older housing tend to have higher blood lead levels than other children. James L. Pirkle et al., "Exposure of the U.S. Population to Lead, 1991–1994," *Environmental Health Perspectives* 106, no. 11 (1998). Furthermore, it is unclear whether poor or Missing Class households receive adequate testing, treatment, or follow-through on the prescribed regimen of care for lead-poisoned children. General Accounting Office, *Lead Poisoning: Federal Health Care Programs Are Not Effectively Reaching At-Risk Children* (Washington, DC: GAO, GAO/HEHS-99-18, 1999). The fact that Missing Class households do not have access to Medicaid for treatment services may create additional barriers to proper care.

African Americans, especially poor African Americans, tend to live closer to toxic sites than whites do. Susan A. Perlin et al., "Residential Proximity to Industrial Sources of Air Pollution: Interrelationships among Race, Poverty, and Age," *Journal of the Air and Waste Management Association* 51 (March 2001).

7. See, for example, David B. Peden, "Pollutants and Asthma: Role of Air Toxics," *Environmental Health Perspectives* 110 (2002): 565–68.

8. In Washington Heights and the adjoining neighborhood of Inwood, 1 in 3 children—14,000 in total—has asthma. The national average is 6.2 percent. Columbia University Mailman School of Public Health press release, "Merck Awards $2 Million Grant to Improve Asthma Care for Children in Northern Manhattan" (December 20, 2005), www.mailman.hs.columbia.edu/news/merck-win-asthma.html. The area also has a significant risk of lead poisoning. Ninety-two percent of its housing stock was built prior to 1960; it has the fifth-oldest housing stock and tenth-highest rate of lead poisoning of the city's thirty health districts. Columbia Center for Active Life of Minority Elders, www.cumc .columbia.edu/dept/calme/Wash1.htm.

9. Six of the city's nineteen bus depots are located in Harlem and Washington Heights. Tri-State Transportation Campaign, "Just Transportation?" *Mobilizing the Region*, no. 195 (November 6, 1998), www.tstc.org/bulletin/pdf/mtr195.pdf.

10. Matthew Schuerman, "The Talking Cure," *City Limits Monthly* (June 2004); Molly McNees, "Addressing Cultural and Linguistic Diversity in the Community Health Center Environment: The Sunset Park Family Health Center Network," in *Bridging Cultures and Enhancing Care: Approaches to Cultural and Linguistic Competency in Managed Care* (Rockville, MD: Health Resources and Services Administration, Department of Health and Human Services, 2002), www.hrsa.gov/reimbursement/bridging-cultures/default.htm.

11. See, for example, Dorothy D. Dunlop et al.'s "Racial/Ethnic Differences in Rates of Depression among Preretirement Adults," *American Journal of Public Health* 93 (2003): 1945–52, which finds that "major depression and factors associated with depression were more frequent among members of minority groups than among Whites" (1945); the national survey data analyzed in this study also show that African Americans are more likely than whites to report chronic conditions such as arthritis, diabetes, hypertension, stroke, and obesity, whereas Hispanics suffer disproportionately from diabetes when compared with whites.

12. Women in particular draw heavily upon such social supports during times of stress or trauma. See Shelley E. Taylor et al., "Biobehavioral Responses to Stress in Females: Tend-and-Befriend, Not Fight-or-Flight," *Psychological Review* 107 (2000): 411–29.

13. Gary Taubes, "As Obesity Rates Rise, Experts Struggle to Explain Why," *Science* 280 (1998): 1367–68; Douglas J. Besharov, "We're Feeding the Poor as If They're Starving," *Washington Post*, December 8, 2002.

SIX: Romance without Finance Is a Nuisance

1. William Julius Wilson, *The Truly Disadvantaged: The Inner City, the Underclass, and Public Policy* (Chicago: University of Chicago Press, 1987), 90–92; see also William Julius Wilson, *When Work Disappears: The World of the New Urban Poor* (New York: Vintage, 1997), 95–97.

2. In 1999 Tomás's annual income was about $19,000, while the poverty threshold for a household of just one individual under the age of sixty-five was $8,667. In 2002 his annual income was about $25,000, and the relevant poverty threshold was $9,359.

3. Matthew D. Bramlett and William D. Mosher, "Cohabitation, Marriage, Divorce, and Remarriage in the United States," *Vital Health Statistics* 23 (July 2002). "First marriages are more likely to disrupt [end in separation or divorce] in communities with higher unemployment, lower median family income, and a higher percent[age] of families below poverty level or receiving public assistance.... First marriages are also more likely to disrupt in central cities, and in communities with a lower percent[age] of college-educated, a higher crime rate, and a higher percent[age] of women never-married" (19). The probability that a first cohabitation breaks up is also substantially higher in lower-income communities.

4. Kathryn Edin and Maria Kefalas, *Promises I Can Keep: Why Poor Women Put Motherhood before Marriage* (Berkeley: University of California Press, 2005), 134.

5. This interview was conducted on July 26, 2000, when Janchill was the center's director of clinical services.

6. See Margaret M. Chin, *Sewing Women: Immigrants and the New York City Garment Industry* (New York: Columbia University Press, 2005).

7. See Federal Interagency Forum on Aging-Related Statistics, *Older Americans Update, 2006: Key Indicators of Well-Being* (Hyattsville, MD: Federal Interagency Forum on Aging-Related Statistics, 2006), www.agingstats.gov/update 2006/Population.pdf. In 2004, 39.7 percent of women sixty-five and over lived alone, 41.6 percent lived with a spouse, and 16.8 percent lived with other relatives. Among Hispanic women sixty-five and over, however, only 24.8 percent lived alone, 37.1 percent lived with a spouse, and 36.0 percent lived with other relatives.

8. A 1999 study found that among households where at least one adult was between the ages of 51 and 62 and lived with a spouse or domestic partner, 29 percent transferred resources of money, time, or space to elderly parents. Rachel F. Boaz, Jason Hu, and Yongjia Ye, "The Transference of Resources from

Middle-Aged Children to Functionally Limited Elderly Parents: Providing Time, Giving Money, Sharing Space," *Gerontologist* 39 (1999): 648–57. Nationally, 17 percent of American households contain at least one caregiver who assists someone aged 50 or older. Among caregivers, 32 percent are ages 35 to 49, and 30 percent are ages 50 to 64. Twenty-four percent say that the recipients of their care live in the same house, and 42 percent say they live within a twenty minutes' drive. National Alliance for Caregiving and AARP, *Caregiving in the U.S.* (Bethesda, MD: National Alliance for Caregiving, 2004), www.caregiving .org/data/04finalreport.pdf.

9. Stack writes: "While cooperating kinsmen continually attempt to draw new people into their personal networks, they fear the loss of a central, resourceful member in the network." While Stack is speaking of women being pressured not to marry, the same appears to apply to men as well. Carol Stack, *All Our Kin* (New York: Basic Books, 1974), 114.

SEVEN: On the Edge: Plunging Out of the Missing Class

1. For more on the upward mobility of the poor in the late 1990s, see Katherine S. Newman's *Chutes and Ladders: Navigating the Low-Wage Labor Market* (New York: Russell Sage and Harvard University Press, 2006).

2. Gesemia Nelson, "Buffers against Uncertainty: Material Hardship and Poverty" (PhD diss., Harvard University, 2004).

3. Daniel Sandoval, Thomas Hirschl, and Mark Rank, "The Increase of Poverty Risk and Income Insecurity in the U.S. since the 1970s" (paper presented at the American Sociological Association Annual Meeting, section on the demography of poverty, 2004); Erik Eckholm, "America's 'Near Poor' Are Increasingly at Economic Risk, Experts Say," *New York Times*, May 8, 2006.

4. Tom Hertz, *Understanding Mobility in America* (Washington, DC: Center for American Progress, 2006), 26–27, www.americanprogress.org/issues/ 2006/04/b1579981.html. Two-thirds of households in the bottom quintile— those with incomes of less than $18,880—gained income during 1990–91, 1997–98, and 2003–4. The second quintile—those with incomes between $18,880 and $34,510, or roughly the Missing Class—fared less well: 53.8 percent gained income in 1990–91, 60.4 percent in 1997–98, and 55 percent in 2003–4. As noted in chapter 1, more than 16 percent of Missing Class households sustained substantial income losses, amounting to 10 percent or more, in the period from 1996 to 2002.

5. The unemployment rate for workers over twenty-five with just a high school degree, which was 4.3 percent in 2006, was about twice that for those with at least a bachelor's degree; this ratio has largely remained constant for more than a decade. Likewise, the unemployment rate of African Americans, which was 8.9 percent in 2006, was about twice that of whites; this ratio has also remained constant over more than three decades. Figures are from an analysis

of 1972–2006 Current Population Survey data from the Bureau of Labor Statistics Web site, www.bls.gov. It should be noted that the government's employment statistics count only those who are officially searching for work but have come up empty-handed; those who have given up on the legal labor market are not counted. See also Christian E. Weller, *Weakening Labor Market Exposes Vulnerabilities of Minorities* (Washington, DC: Center for American Progress, 2006), www.americanprogress.org/issues/2006/08/b2001883.html.

6. See, for example, Katherine S. Newman, *No Shame in My Game: The Working Poor in the Inner City* (New York: Knopf and Russell Sage, 1999).

7. The Jiggets program is rent assistance for welfare recipients with children. Named after a court case, it is provided to people who are being sued in court for back rent. See the Legal Aid Society Community Website, "What Is Jiggets?" www.legal-aid.org/community/benefits/jiggets.html.

8. See Kathryn Edin and Laura Lein's *Making Ends Meet: How Single Mothers Survive Welfare and Low-Wage Work* (New York: Russell Sage, 1997), 42–45, which discusses how welfare recipients are forced to seek out other sources of (prohibited) income because their families can't survive on the amount of public assistance provided.

9. Increases in the Earned Income Tax Credit (EITC) and the minimum wage since 1989 have dramatically improved the returns to work among low-wage workers: a single mother with one child working full-time at the minimum wage made $9,856 a year in 1989 but $12,510 in 1997—a 26.9 percent increase. Rebecca M. Blank, "Enhancing the Opportunities, Skills, and Security of American Workers," in *A Working Nation: Workers, Work, and Government in the New Economy*, by David T. Ellwood et al. (New York: Russell Sage, 2000). See also Norma B. Coe, Gregory Acs, Robert I. Lerman, and Keith Watson, *Does Work Pay? A Summary of the Work Incentives under TANF* (Washington, DC: Urban Institute, Assessing the New Federalism, Series A, No. A-28, 1998). In 2004 the maximum credit for families with one eligible child was $2,604; for families with two or more qualifying children, the maximum credit was $4,300. In comparison, the monthly TANF benefit for a family of three with no income in New York State was $577 in June 2002, which amounts to $6,924 a year. Congressional Budget Office, "Response to a Request by Senator Grassley about the Effects of Increasing the Federal Minimum Wage versus Expanding the Earned Income Tax Credit" (January 9, 2007), www.cbo.gov/ftpdocs/77xx/doc7721/01-09-MinimumWageEITC.pdf; Office of Family Assistance, Administration for Children and Families, Department of Health and Human Services, *Temporary Assistance for Needy Families (TANF): Sixth Annual Report to Congress* (Washington, DC: Administration for Children and Families, 2004), www.acf.hhs.gov/programs/ofa/annualreport6/ar6index.htm.

10. See, for example, Sarah J. Mahler, *American Dreaming: Immigrant Life on the Margins* (Princeton, NJ: Princeton University Press, 1995), and Cynthia J.

Cranford, "Networks of Exploitation: Immigrant Labor and the Restructuring of the Los Angeles Janitorial Industry," *Social Problems* 52 (2005): 379–97, for a discussion of the even worse position of illegal immigrants who cannot complain for fear of discovery and are at the mercy of unscrupulous low-wage employers and even their own countrymen.

11. "A 7A administrator may be appointed after the petition of 1/3 of the tenants in the building or if the City's Department of Housing Preservation & Development asks the courts to appoint an administrator. The administrator basically takes control of the building from the owner and uses the rents to remedy dangerous conditions in the building." New York City Rent Guidelines Board, "Repairs and Maintenance FAQ," www.housingnyc.com/html/resources/faq/repairs.html#7a.

12. Stephen Ohlemacher, "Numbers Up at U.S. Soup Kitchens, Second Harvest Says," Associated Press, February 23, 2006.

13. Wade Henderson, "Immigration Band-Aids," *TomPaine.com* (June 7, 2006), www.tompaine.com/print/immigration_bandaids.php.

14. Most recently, see Sudhir Venkatesh, *Off the Books: The Underground Economy of the Urban Poor* (Cambridge, MA: Harvard University Press, 2006).

EIGHT: Missing Class Mobility

1. Indeed, even those young men who have *never* been in trouble with the law are suspect in the eyes of employers because the completely innocent are tarred by the felonious behavior of the large number who have served time. Devah Pager, "The Mark of a Criminal Record," *American Journal of Sociology* 108 (2003): 937–75; Devah Pager, *Marked: Race, Crime, and Finding Work in an Era of Mass Incarceration* (Chicago: University of Chicago Press, forthcoming); and David Harding, "Jean Valjean's Dilemma: The Management of Ex-Convict Identity in the Search for Employment," *Deviant Behavior* 25 (1993): 571–95.

2. Carmen DeNavas-Walt, Bernadette D. Proctor, and Cheryl Hill Lee, *Income, Poverty, and Health Insurance Coverage in the United States, 2005* (Washington, DC: U.S. Census Bureau, Current Population Reports: Consumer Income, P60–231, 2006), 22, www.census.gov/prod/2006pubs/p60-231.pdf; Cathy Schoen, Michelle M. Doty, Sara R. Collins, and Alyssa L. Holmgren, "Insured but Not Protected: How Many Adults Are Underinsured?" *Health Affairs* 24 (2005): 289–302. A brief by the Kaiser Family Foundation notes that nearly a quarter of *insured* families spent $2,000 or more out of pocket to cover health-care expenses in a year; nearly one-fifth postponed seeking medical care; and premiums for employer-sponsored coverage have been rising. Kaiser Commission on the Medicaid and the Uninsured, *Underinsured in America: Is Health Coverage Adequate?* (Washington, DC: Kaiser Family Foundation, 2002), www.kaisernetwork.org/health_cast/uploaded_files/4060.pdf.

3. This benefit is available only to taxpayers with incomes high enough

to itemize deductions; 63 percent of those deductions goes to Americans in
the top fifth of the income distribution, and only 18 percent goes to those in
the bottom fifth, since they are not affluent enough to make itemization a
good deal. Winton Pitcoff, "Has Homeownership Been Oversold?" *Shelterforce
Online*, no. 127 (January/February 2003), www.nhi.org/online/issues/127/
homeownership.html.

4. See the notes in chapter 3 for statistics on home ownership among poor
and Missing Class households. When the poor do own their own homes, it is
often because they are retired workers who were once middle class but have
fallen below the poverty line in their old age, though they still hold on to this
important asset. Prime-age workers who are low income are much less likely to
own their own homes. At any given income level, whites are more likely to own
homes and remain home owners for a longer period of time than African Americans. Nancy A. Denton, "Housing as a Means of Asset Accumulation: A Good
Strategy for the Poor?" in *Assets for the Poor: The Benefits of Spreading Asset Ownership*, ed. Thomas M. Shapiro and Edward N. Wolff (New York: Russell Sage,
2001), 232–66; Carolina Katz Reid, "Achieving the American Dream? A Longitudinal Analysis of the Homeownership Experiences of Low-Income Households" (St. Louis, MO: Center for Social Development, George Warren Brown
School of Social Work, Washington University, Working Paper 05-20, 2005),
http://gwbweb.wustl.edu/csd/Publications/2005/WP05-20.pdf.

5. Furthermore, minorities purchase their first homes at a later age in life,
have less time (in their life course) to pile up equity, and owe more to banks
when compared with whites with similar earnings. Census Bureau press release,
"Census Bureau Reports on Residential Vacancies and Homeownership," October 27, 2006, www.census.gov/hhes/www/housing/hvs/qtr306/q306prss.pdf.
Blacks and Hispanics in Boston were 56 percent more likely to be turned down
for a conventional mortgage loan than whites, after controlling for credit qual-
ifications and types of loans. The minority denial rate was 17 percent compared
with 11 percent for whites. Alicia H. Munnell, Geoffrey M. B. Tootell, Lynn E.
Browne, and James McEneaney, "Mortgage Lending in Boston: Interpret-
ing HMDA Data," *American Economic Review* 86 (1996): 25–53, referenced in
"Homeownership across the American Life Course: Estimating the Racial
Divide," by Thomas A. Hirschl and Mark R. Rank (St. Louis, MO: Center for
Social Development, George Warren Brown School of Social Work, Washing-
ton University, Working Paper 06-12, 2006), http://gwbweb.wustl.edu/csd/
Publications/2006/WP06-12.pdf.

According to 2006 census data, 76 percent of non-Hispanic whites own
their homes, while only 48.6 percent of African Americans and 49.7 percent of
Hispanics do so. Census Bureau, "Census Bureau Reports on Residential Vacancies," 8. For more on nonwhite home ownership, see Kerwin Kofi Charles
and Erik Hurst, "The Transition to Home Ownership and the Black-White

Wealth Gap," *The Review of Economics and Statistics* 84 (2002): 281–97, and Hirschl and Rank, "Homeownership across the American Life Course."

6. See especially Melvin Oliver and Thomas Shapiro, *Black Wealth / White Wealth: A New Perspective on Racial Inequality*, 2nd ed. (New York: Routledge, 2006), and Dalton Conley, *Being Black, Living in the Red: Race, Wealth, and Social Policy in America* (Berkeley: University of California Press, 1999).

7. Reid Cramer, Leslie Parrish, and Ray Boshara, *The Assets Report, 2006: A Review, Assessment, and Forecast of Federal Assets Policy* (Washington, DC: New America Foundation Asset Building Program, 2006), 6.

8. Barbara Sard, *The Family Self-Sufficiency Program: HUD's Best Kept Secret for Promoting Employment and Asset Growth* (Washington, DC: Center on Budget and Policy Priorities, 2001), www.cbpp.org/4-12-01hous.htm.

9. Pitcoff, "Has Homeownership Been Oversold?"

10. Metropolitan Policy Program, Brookings Institution, *An Agenda and Models for Better Meeting the Market Needs of Lower Income Consumers* (Washington, DC: Brookings Institution, 2006), www.brookings.edu/metro/pubs/20060718_policies.pdf, 58.

11. The National Housing Institute is a nonprofit organization that "examines the issues causing the crisis in housing and community in America." Pitcoff, "Has Homeownership Been Oversold?" Regarding the effect of the economic downturn, Pitcoff observes: "Foreclosures on FHA-backed loans to low-income households have risen the fastest, to a rate of nearly 3 percent, with an additional 12 percent behind in their payments in the second quarter of 2002."

12. See Elizabeth Warren, "Show Me the Money," *New York Times*, October 24, 2005.

13. Daniel Schneider and Peter Tufano, "New Savings from Old Innovations: Asset Building for the Less Affluent" (paper prepared for the Community Development Finance Research Conference hosted by the Federal Reserve Bank of New York, 2004).

14. Ibid., 20.

15. Ibid., 28, 29.

16. Ibid., 33.

17. See Robert Greenstein and Joel Friedman, *Saver's Credit for Moderate-Income Families Would Fade Away over Time if Not Indexed for Inflation* (Washington, DC: Center on Budget and Policy Priorities, 2006), www.cbpp.org/3-3-06tax.htm.

18. Caroline Glackin and Eliza Mahoney, "Savings and Credit for U.S. Micro-Enterprises: Integrating Individual Development Accounts and Loans for Micro-Enterprise," *Journal of Microfinance* 4 (2002): 99, referenced in "New Savings from Old Innovations," by Schneider and Tufano.

19. Schneider and Tufano, "New Savings from Old Innovations," 35. See

also Esther Duflo et al., "Saving Incentives for Low- and Middle-Income Families: Evidence from a Field Experiment with H&R Block" (London: Centre for Economic Policy Research, Discussion Paper No. 5332, 2005).

20. Schneider and Tufano, "New Savings from Old Innovations," 38; U.S. Census Bureau press release, "Income Climbs, Poverty Stabilizes, Uninsured Rate Increases," August 29, 2006, www.census.gov/Press-Release/www/releases/archives/income_wealth/007419.html.

21. Theda Skocpol, "Targeting within Universalism: Politically Viable Policies to Combat Poverty in the United States," in *The Urban Underclass*, ed. Christopher Jencks and Paul E. Peterson (Washington, DC: Brookings Institution, 1991), 411–36.

22. See Metropolitan Policy Program, Brookings Institution, *An Agenda and Models for Better Meeting the Market Needs of Lower Income Consumers* (Washington, DC: Brookings Institution, 2006), www.brookings.edu/metro/pubs/20060718_policies.pdf, 53–55.

23. Credit Where Credit Is Due, "Neighborhood Trust Federal Credit Union," www.cwcid.org/ntfcu/default.htm. Other figures are taken from a March 23, 2000, interview with Mark Levine.

24. See Metropolitan Policy Program, *An Agenda and Models*, 57.

25. See California Department of Insurance press release, "Insurance Commissioner John Garamendi Announces Expansion of State's Low Cost Auto Insurance Program," September 15, 2006, www.insurance.ca.gov/0400-news/0100-press-releases/0070–2006/release114-06.cfm.

26. See Metropolitan Policy Program, *An Agenda and Models*, 59; The Reinvestment Fund (TRF), "Pennsylvania Fresh Food Financing Initiative," www.trfund.com/financing/realestate/supermarkets.html.

27. Joan Fitzgerald, *Moving Up in the New Economy: Career Ladders for U.S. Workers* (Ithaca, NY: Cornell University Press, 2006).

28. Ibid., 34.

29. Ibid., 36.

30. Ibid., 42.

31. James E. Rosenbaum, *Beyond College for All: Career Paths for the Forgotten Half* (New York: Russell Sage, 2001).

32. In 1983 a commission formed by Secretary of Education Terrel H. Bell produced a report titled *A Nation at Risk*, whose grim assessment of America's public school system prompted a wave of reforms. National Commission on Excellence in Education, *A Nation at Risk: The Imperative for Educational Reform* (Washington, DC: U.S. Department of Education, 1983), www.ed.gov/pubs/NatAtRisk/index.html.

33. Robert Lynch, *Exceptional Returns: Economic, Fiscal, and Social Benefits of Investment in Early Childhood Development* (Washington, DC: Economic Policy Institute, 2004).

34. Senator John Edwards has made second-chance schooling for dropouts a cornerstone of his presidential platform. John Edwards, "National Press Club Policy Address" (June 22, 2006), http://johnedwards.com/news/speeches/20060622.

35. The $40,000 benchmark is in 2004 dollars. Project on Student Debt, *Quick Facts about Student Debt* (Berkeley, CA: Project on Student Debt, 2006), http://projectonstudentdebt.org/pub_view.php?idx=125; Project on Student Debt, *High Hopes, Big Debts* (Berkeley, CA: Project on Student Debt, 2006), http://projectonstudentdebt.org/pub_view.php?idx=157. See also Heather Boushey, *Student Debt: Bigger and Bigger* (Washington, DC: Center for Economic and Policy Research, 2005), www.cepr.net/publications/student_debt_2005_09.pdf.

36. Meanwhile, the portion of degrees going to students from more affluent households has grown from 72 percent to 79 percent over this period. Stephen Burd, "Working-Class Students Feel the Pinch," *Chronicle of Higher Education* (June 9, 2006). Within private schools, an internal redistribution system that takes from those who have higher earnings and gives to those at the very bottom threatens to make the cost of a college education impossibly high for those in the middle. Furthermore, educational advocates allege that the wealthiest families are still being coddled by the system; for a discussion of how financial aid goes disproportionately to families with incomes over $100,000 at the nation's fifty "flagship" universities, see Danette Gerald and Kati Haycock, *Engines of Inequality: Diminishing Equity in the Nation's Premier Public Universities* (Washington, DC: Education Trust, 2006).

37. In 2005–6, the average Pell grant per recipient was $2,354. The maximum Pell grant remains at $4,050; this grant level was last increased in 2003–4, when it rose by $50. Twenty years ago, the maximum Pell grant covered nearly 60 percent of the average tuition, fees, room, and board at a public four-year college; in 2005–6, it covered only 33 percent. College Board, *Total Pell Grant Funding Declines for First Time in Six Years* (New York: College Board, 2006), www.collegeboard.com/prod_downloads/press/cost06/pell_grants_06.pdf.

38. About 90 percent of families receiving Pell grants make less than $35,000 a year, though under the government's formula a family of four may qualify if it earns less than $50,000. Dan Morgan, "Change Means Fewer Students Will Be Eligible for Pell Grants," *Washington Post*, December 24, 2004; Jonathan D. Glater, "M.I.T. to Match Federal Grant Money for Lower-Income Students," *New York Times*, March 7, 2006. Also, the federal formula for aid distinguishes between student savings and parental savings: students are supposed to spend 35 percent of their assets on college each year, compared with 5.6 percent or less for their parents. Kathleen Pender, "How to Pay for College," *San Francisco Chronicle*, November 23, 2003.

39. The same problem confronts advocates of school voucher programs.

Extensive outreach is necessary to alert low-income parents to the options for their kids and even more effort to get them to apply when the paperwork burden is significant. Jay P. Greene, William G. Howell, and Paul E. Peterson, "Lessons from the Cleveland Scholarship Program" (paper prepared for presentation before the Association of Public Policy and Management, 1997), www.spa.ucla.edu/ps/pdf/Soo/PS294/green-howell-peterson(1997).pdf; Sewell Chan, "Many D.C. School Vouchers Go Unused," *Washington Post*, September 1, 2004.

40. The College Opportunity and Career Help (COACH) program at Harvard University tries to do something similar for low-income students in Boston's public high schools. Harvard undergraduate and graduate volunteers are trained to help high school students with the intricacies of applications and assist them in gaining access to scholarship funds that are actually available but often go unused. See Christopher Avery and Thomas J. Kane, "Student Perceptions of College Opportunities: The Boston COACH Program," in *College Choices: The Economics of Where to Go, When to Go, and How to Pay for It*, ed. Caroline M. Hoxby (Chicago: University of Chicago Press, 2004), 355–91.

41. Karen McConkey, "GCHS Seniors to Pilot National Program," *Kinston (NC) Free Press*, September 29, 2005, www.kinston.com/SiteProcessor.cfm?Template=/GlobalTemplates/Details.cfm&StoryID=30861.

42. Christine Frey, "5,000 to Get Free UW Tuition," *Seattle Post-Intelligencer*, October 12, 2006.

43. This easily includes all Missing Class families in the state. Wealthy private universities—including Princeton, Harvard, and Columbia—offer even more generous financial-aid packages for students from low- and middle-income households. For instance, in 2006 Harvard announced that families with annual incomes of under $60,000 would no longer be expected to contribute to the cost of undergraduate education. Harvard University press release, "Harvard Expands Financial Aid for Low- and Middle-Income Families" *Harvard University Gazette*, March 30, 2006, www.news.harvard.edu/gazette/daily/2006/03/30-finaid.html. For a list of universities that have eliminated most or all loans from aid packages for low-income students, see FinAid, "No Loans for Low Income Students," www.finaid.org/questions/noloansfor lowincome.phtml.

AFSCME 1199C, 217
All Our Kin (Stack), 170
American Dream Downpayment
  Initiative, 207
America's Second Harvest, 193
Annie E. Casey Foundation, 116
Apple Health Care, 217
assets. *See* home ownership; savings
asthma, 130, 133–34, 242n6, 243n8
Atlanta Journal-Constitution, 47
automobile purchase and insurance,
  214–15

banking services: at check-cashing
  stores, 74–75, 237n14; and impediments for low-income savers,
  74–76, 210–11; and incentives
  and initiatives, 210, 211–12, 213;
  and mistrust of traditional banks,
  73–74; and underservice in low-
  income neighborhoods, 74, 210,
  237n13. *See also* loans
bankruptcy, 47, 209
broken families. *See* relationships
Brookings Institution, 213

Burgher, Renee, 14–15
Bush, George W., 206, 211

Cape Cod Hospital, 216
Car Buyer's Bill of Rights, 214
career-ladder programs, 216–18
car purchase and insurance, 214–15
Center for Family Life, 162–64
check-cashing stores, 74–75, 237n14
Chicago Sun-Times, 158
child care. *See* day care
Child Health Plus, 133
children. *See specific issues*
church-based support systems, 140,
  146, 162–64, 192–93
City Limits Monthly, 21
Clinton, Bill, 207, 211
cognitive development, 89, 91, 100,
  131–32, 143, 240n11
college education, 4, 222–24,
  251nn36–39, 252n40, 252n43
College for Everyone, 224
College Opportunity and Career
  Help (COACH), 252n40
community gardens, 45–46, 235n22

consumer issues. *See* debt; shops
Cooperative Home Care Associates
    (CHCA), 217
credit. *See* debt; loans
credit card issuers, 6, 66–68, 209
credit card ownership and usage,
    59, 63, 67–68, 236n3, 236n8
Credit Where Credit Is Due, 74,
    213–14
crime: "broken window" theory of
    policing, 36–37; gangs and, 33–
    34, 38–40, 163; and model-block
    policing strategy, 33; and police
    presence in neighborhoods, 24,
    30, 34–37, 39; prevalence of, 16–
    17, 20, 23, 28–29; reduced, with
    gentrification, 30–31, 44–45,
    234n13
criminal justice system, 113–14, 177,
    203

day care: basic education in, 78,
    220–21; center-based, 84, 238n3;
    dependence upon relatives for,
    88–90; need for investment in,
    220–21; substandard, 91, 100, 117;
    unavailability and unaffordability
    of, 84, 166; for working mothers,
    83–84, 220
debt: accumulation of, 63; and bank-
    ruptcy, 47, 209; and credit card
    ownership, 59, 63, 67–68, 236n8;
    impatience for middle-class luxu-
    ries and, 48, 50, 57–61; lack of
    financial acumen and, 6, 68; and
    payday advances, 75; student
    loans, 223; and unscrupulous
    lenders, 12, 13, 207, 209. *See also*
    loans
developmental problems, 89, 91, 100,
    131–32, 143, 240n11
District of Columbia College Access
    Program, 223–24

Do the Right Thing (film), 13–14
dropping out of school: child as
    wage-earner, 112–13; grade reten-
    tion as predictor of, 95, 97, 220,
    239n8; as gradual process, 112;
    learning-disabled children and,
    116, 240n15; remedial education
    and second-chance schools, 222
drug abuse: D.A.R.E. education pro-
    gram, 39; and neglect of children,
    1, 38, 90, 173; prevalence of, 14,
    16–17, 23

Earned Income Tax Credit, 187–88,
    216, 246n9
Edin, Kathryn, 160–61
education and training of adults, 186,
    216–18, 231n3
education of children and youth:
    after-school programs, 221–22;
    college, 4, 222–24, 251nn36–39,
    252n40, 252n43; in day care and
    kindergarten, 78, 220–21; and
    failure on standardized tests, 7, 97;
    and grade retention, 95, 96–97,
    220, 239nn8–10; mothers as auxil-
    iary teaching force, 7, 115; and
    No Child Left Behind Act, 6–7;
    parents' work obligations and, 7,
    43, 111, 115–17; and reading pro-
    ficiency, 115; selective public
    schools, 221; special education,
    105; vigilance and attention of
    parents, 43–44, 97–98, 100; voca-
    tional training and placement,
    219–20; white-collar job training,
    218–19. *See also* dropping out of
    school; schools
Edwards, John, 224
employment: career ladders in,
    216–18; and Earned Income Tax
    Credit, 187–88, 216, 246n9; edu-
    cation attainment and, 231n3; and

effects of mass incarceration practices, 203, 247n1; and improvement in self-esteem, 58, 94; and
inflexible work schedules, 111,
133, 189; language skills and, 187;
low-wage jobs and, 4–5, 108–10;
and neglect of children, 7, 43, 100,
111, 115–17, 177; prospects for
unskilled workers, 179; of teenagers, 112–13; and unemployment
rate, 179, 245n5; vocational training and placement, 219–20; and
welfare work requirement, 84–86,
186; white-collar job training,
218–19; of youth within own
neighborhoods, 45, 208–9
entitlements and rights, ignorance of:
in contract law, 207–8; in dealings
with government agencies, 196;
educational access, 4, 221, 223–24,
251n39, 252n40; in health care,
133; in housing issues, 189–90,
198–200; in immigration law,
183–84; and legal system, 131; and
workmen's compensation, 51, 189
environmental hazards, 128, 130–
31, 133–34, 189–90, 242n6,
243nn8–9
Espaillat, Adriano, 73–74

families: absent or neglectful fathers,
92, 120, 136–37, 139; counseling
and support for, 35–36, 163–64;
recombinant, complications of, 8,
166, 233n11; responsibilities and
dependence within, 59, 69–70,
88–90, 168–70, 173–75, 244n8;
and responsibilities borne by
children, 95, 100; responsible
ex-spouses, 155–56; single- and
two-adult, near-poor children in,
231n3; as social networks, 165,
243n12; two-income, 59, 72, 79,

130, 151, 237n12. *See also* relationships
Family Health Plus, 133
Family Self-Sufficiency Program, 207
financial issues. *See* banking services;
debt; loans
Fitzgerald, Joan, 217–18
fixers, 196, 198–200
food pantry program, 192–93
Fresh Food Financing Initiative, 215

gangs, 33–34, 38–40, 163
gentrification: benefits to neighborhood of, 14, 25–26, 37, 44–45,
135; effect on children, 42; negative effects of, 12–13, 17–18, 32,
46; reasons for, 15, 17; and victim-
ization of low-income residents,
12–13
grade retention, 95, 96–97, 220,
239nn8–10
Greater Philadelphia Urban Affairs
Coalition, 208

health care: cash payment for, 132;
HMOs, 123–24, 127, 241nn3–4;
and hospital emergency rooms,
132, 134, 135; and ignorance of
entitlements and rights, 133; and
impediments for near-poor households, 130; for Medicaid patients,
124, 132–33; for middle-class
versus poor, 124–25, 134
health conditions, racial disparities
in, 7–8, 127, 134, 243n11
health insurance: initiatives for
Medicaid-ineligible persons, 133;
Medicaid, 124, 129–30, 132–33;
and underinsured population, 2,
123–24, 241n4, 247n2; and uninsured population, 122, 129–30,
132, 134–35, 241n1; as union
benefit, 123

Hertz, Tom, 178
Heymann, Jody, 122
higher education, 4, 222–24,
    251nn36–39, 252n40, 252n43
home ownership: benefits of, 79,
    178, 205–6, 247n3; denial of
    mortgages, 126, 248n5; and fore-
    closure, 12, 209, 249n11; inac-
    cessibility of, 5–6; initiatives to
    foster, 206–8, 212; rates of, 5, 79,
    206, 238n18, 248nn4–5; repair
    and rehabilitation assistance,
    208–9; subprime mortgages, 208;
    as symbol of success, 76, 79, 81;
    and victimization by unscrupulous
    contractors, 12, 207; and vulnera-
    bility to foreclosure, 207, 209
Homeownership Voucher Program,
    207
households. See families
housing: city administration of,
    190–92, 247n11; discrimination
    in, 16, 191; and lead poisoning
    risk, 131, 189–90, 242n6, 243n8;
    public, conditions in, 19, 93; and
    renovations, with gentrification,
    25; and rent assistance, 186,
    246n7; and rent increases, with
    gentrification, 12, 17, 25. See also
    home ownership
Hughes, James, 134–35

illness: asthma, 130, 133–34, 242n6,
    243n8; of caregiver, 121, 122, 145–
    47; lead poisoning, 131, 189–90,
    242n6, 243n8; and racial dispari-
    ties, 7–8, 127, 134, 243n11. See also
    health care
immigrants: and adjustment to
    American life, 165; bigotry
    toward, 168; denial of public assis-
    tance for, 184; deportation threat,

180, 182–83, 197; ignorance of
    legal options, 183–84; reluctance
    to pursue legal options, 195–96;
    swindling of, 193
income: education attainment and,
    231n3; and entitlement to middle-
    class luxuries, 48, 50, 57–61, 143,
    236n3; poverty line and income
    levels, 231n4, 236n2, 236n7;
    secrecy concerning, 8, 233n11.
    See also employment
individual development accounts
    (IDAs), 211–12
inheritance, 169, 205
insurance, automobile, 214–15
insurance, health. See health insur-
    ance
Isles, Inc., 207–8, 235n22

Janchill, Mary Paul, 162–66
jobs. See employment

Kaiser Family Foundation, 247n2
Kefalas, Maria, 160–61
Kids Investment and Development
    Savings (KIDS), 212

lead poisoning, 131–32, 189–90,
    242n6, 243n8
Lee, Spike, 13–14
legal issues: contracts, 12, 207–8;
    disillusionment with legal system,
    195–96; immigration rights,
    183–84; injury cases, 131, 189–
    90; lay legal advisors, 196, 198–
    200; reluctance to pursue legal
    recourse, 195, 201; swindlers, 193;
    workmen's compensation, 51, 189
Levine, Mark, 74–76, 213–14
loans: initiatives for low-income bor-
    rowers, 74, 213–14; loan sharks,
    76; mortgages, 126, 208, 209,

248n5, 249n11; to service credit
card debt, 48, 71; unprofitability
of small loans, 75–76. *See also* debt
Lynch, Robert, 221

marriage. *See* relationships
Medicaid, 124, 129–30, 132–33, 134
medical care. *See* health care
medical insurance. *See* health insurance
Minneapolis Star-Tribune, 145
Missing Class. *See* near poor
mortgages, 126, 208, 209, 248n5,
249n11
Moving Up in the New Economy
(Fitzgerald), 217

National Housing Institute, 209,
249n11
National Review, 83
near poor: definition and characteristics of, 3–9, 231–32nn3–4; vulnerability to downward mobility, 4,
5, 178, 245n4
Neighborhood Trust Federal Credit
Union, 213–14
Newman, Katherine, 207, 216
New York Daily News, 27
New York Times, 11, 128, 149
No Child Left Behind Act, 6–7, 115
Northern Manhattan Improvement
Corporation, 190
No Shame in My Game (Newman),
216
Notorious B.I.G., 13

on-the-job training, 216–18

Paraprofessional Healthcare Institute, 217
parents: absent or neglectful fathers,
92, 120, 136–37, 139; as auxiliary

school teaching force, 7, 115; drug
addicts as, 1, 38, 90, 173; involvement of in child's education, 7,
43–44, 97–98, 100, 111, 115–17;
responsible ex-spouses, 155–56; as
school volunteers, 99; and supervision of child's behavior, 7, 95,
115–17, 177
Pell grants, 223, 251nn37–38
police, 24, 33, 34–37, 44–45, 234n15
poverty line, 3–4, 9, 178; and income
levels, 231n4, 236n2, 236n7
predatory lending practices, 12, 13,
75, 76, 208, 237n12
preschool. *See* day care
property. *See* home ownership
public assistance: congressional
reform of, 85, 134, 184; and
"encouragement" of absentee
husbands, 92; enrollment rates,
85, 179–80; intrusive application
process, 185–86; Medicaid, 124,
129–30, 132–33, 134; oversight
of recipients, 55; rent assistance,
186, 246n7; Social Security, 105,
108, 194–95, 199–200; stability
afforded by, 54, 55; subsidized
housing, 19, 93; work requirement, 84–86, 186

relationships: disappointment and
cynicism, 155, 159, 161; divorce,
likelihood of, 155, 244n3; financial
considerations, 8, 151–53, 158–61;
government initiatives to foster,
149; for immigration purposes,
183; irresponsible behavior, 154–
55; multiple remarriages, 166;
responsibility to original family,
153, 170–71; role model for children, 162; secrecy concerning
financial matters, 8, 233n11; short-

age of available men, 158. *See also* families
relatives. *See* families
retirement savings, 211–12
Robert Wood Johnson Foundation, 218

Saver's Credit, 211
savings: banking impediments, 74–76, 210–11; bank underservice, 74, 210, 237n13; as buffer against downturn, 5, 178; difficulty in amassing, 5; incentives and initiatives for, 210, 211–12, 213; mistrust of traditional banks, 73–74; *sociedades*, 68
Savo Island Cooperative Homes, 207, 209
Schneider, Daniel, 210–11
schools: administrative instability of, 95, 96, 102–3, 107; disruptive students in, 95, 96, 104; in gentrified neighborhoods, 45; parental involvement in, 45, 95, 98–99, 103; reliance upon volunteers of, 99; unchallenging, for gifted children, 38. *See also* dropping out of school; education of children and youth
self-esteem, 58, 85
Serrano, Hector, 32–36
Shelterforce, 209
Shepard, Peggy, 133–34
shops: and absence of big chains, 192; closure of, with gentrification, 17–18, 20; higher prices in, 6, 213, 215
single-parent families: near-poor children in, 231n3; and neglectful

fathers, 120, 136–37, 139; and rate of school grade retention, 97; and responsible ex-spouses, 155–56
Social Security, 105, 108, 194–95, 199–200
sociedades, 68
spending. *See* debt
SSI, 105, 108, 194–95, 199–200
Stack, Carol, 170
Stiles, Jim, 134
stores. *See* shops
St. Petersburg Times, 193

Tobia, Geraldine, 162
training, vocational and white-collar, 216–20
Tufano, Peter, 210–11
two-income households, 59, 72, 79, 130, 151, 237n12

underinsured health care, 2, 123–24, 241n4, 247n2
unemployment rate, 179, 245n5
uninsured health care, 122, 129–30, 132, 134–35, 241n1
union benefits, 1, 123
Universal Savings Account, 211

Vehicles for Change, 214
vocational training, 216–18, 219–20

Wall Street Journal, 180
Warren, Elizabeth, 67
Warren Tyagi, Amelia, 67
Washington Post, 76, 166
welfare. *See* public assistance
Whitney, Curtis L., 192
work. *See* employment
Wright, Richard, 13